Golf Courses of the
PGA European Tour

AURUM PRESS

in association with
PGA European Tour Enterprises Ltd

Golf Courses of the PGA European Tour

Peter Dobereiner

With Gordon Richardson · Photography by Brian Morgan

First published 1992 by Aurum Press Ltd,
10 Museum Street, London WC1A 1JS
in association with PGA European
Tour Enterprises Ltd
Copyright © 1992 by PGA European Tour Enterprises Ltd
Main text copyright © 1992 by Peter Dobereiner
Additional course text copyright © 1992 by Gordon Richardson
Photographs copyright © 1992 by Brian Morgan
Map illustrations copyright © 1992 by Aurum Press Ltd

Maps of the courses at Falsterbo, Kennemer, Chantilly,
Las Brisas based on maps from *The World Atlas of Golf*,
© Mitchell Beazley Publishers, London.
Photograph of Bokskogens on pp. 194–5 by Mikael Lindström
Aerial photograph of Barsebäcks on p. 196 by Ronny Karlsson

A catalogue record for this book is available from the British
Library

ISBN 1 85410 089 0

1   3   5   7   9   10   8   6   4   2
1993   1995   1996   1994   1992

Map illustrations by Pete Ferris

Typeset by Tradespools Limited, Frome, Somerset
Printed in Singapore

Previous pages: *The seventh hole at La Grande Motte*

CONTENTS

FOREWORD

The golf courses of the PGA European Tour hold happy memories for me. From Sweden in the north to Tenerife in the south, and from Killarney in the west to Salzburg in the east, many great European courses have hosted our best players competing at the top of their abilities. Excellent additional venues in North Africa and the United Arab Emirates have also hosted recent Tour competitions.

Many of these courses – old and new – now feature in this superb publication, and my hope is that readers will quickly identify with their favourite courses and locations. European golf at all levels has thrived on a variation of courses and weather conditions. A number of our great traditional links courses are featured in this book, together with the equally venerable inland heathland heather and pine courses. Here at Wentworth we have had many great moments on the famous West Course, while nearby Sunningdale and Walton Heath are similarly steeped in international traditions.

Exciting venues in Continental Europe are happily being widely introduced to followers of golf, and the age of satellite television will ensure that this continues apace.

I hope you enjoy our first venture in this very special and extremely visual area of our great game. On your behalf may I express appreciation to Brian Morgan for his artistry with the camera, to Pete Ferris for his skilful illustrations, and to Peter Dobereiner and Gordon Richardson for their detailed narrations.

Ken Schofield
Executive Director
PGA European Tour

LONDON AREA

The capital city is not generally associated with golf, certainly not to the extent of, say, Edinburgh or Melbourne. London suffers severely from golf starvation, with most clubs having long waiting-lists. And a fair proportion of the golf courses in and around London are of indifferent quality. And yet, thanks to a geological accident, there lie within a thirty-mile radius of Trafalgar Square some of the most celebrated inland courses in the world. Alluvial deposits of sand created what golfers loosely term Surrey heathland and this area, supporting the characteristic heather, gorse, bracken, silver birch and pine, forms the perfect raw material for golf of the inland variety.

Some purists argue that golfing perfection demands the close proximity of the sea, with capricious winds shifting direction at the turning of the tide and the exhilarating tang of salt in the air. Inland golf tends to be milder, as a broad generalization, the wind more constant although not necessarily less violent, as that Surrey heathland discovered to its heavy cost during the hurricane of 1987. But if variety is the spice of life, then golf offers no more beguiling condiment than a round with agreeable companions on a fine day on one of the masterpieces of heathland courses. For the seaside fanatics, the rigours of the Kent coast are less than an hour away down the motorway and there, at Deal and Sandwich, they can indulge their Calvinistic notions that golf should be an ordeal of body and spirit. The effete, and rather more popular, view that golf should be a pursuit of many diverse pleasures finds its finest expression on the Surrey heathland, which assembles all the most desirable characteristics of great courses.

The greatest of these characteristics, beyond question, is its sand. It is called silver but, prosaically, the colour is grey and, since it is not rich in nutrients, the grass which it sustains is slow-growing and delicate in texture. It would take a cow a week to crop a decent

Heather abounds on the eleventh at Wentworth

meal on these impoverished grasses, but they afford the golfer the blessing of a perfect lie, the equal of the finest seaside turf. There is a sensuous pleasure in hitting a crisp shot off close, sand-based turf and the more practical advantage that backspin can be imparted consistently with every shot and never a qualm about catching a flyer. It might be as well to catalogue here some of the other qualities required for a great course: beautiful natural surroundings, a certain flow or movement in the ground to add interest and variety, different forms of natural hazard, such as ponds and streams, to relieve the challenge of trees or heather, and a feeling of serenity created by the absence of houses, offices and factories. Escapism, after all, is one of the major appeals of golf.

The function of the golf course architect is to add the strictly golfing qualities of balance, graduated punishment to fit the crime, playability for every class of golfer, the requirement to think before hitting, a fair presentation of the problem confronting the golfer, flexibility to accommodate changing weather conditions, and an examination for every club in the bag. Not one of the London courses fulfils this specification in every last detail, but several come close enough to qualify as greens of outstanding quality.

Sunningdale must take precedence, if only for its unique place in British golf. Exactly what that place might be is difficult to define, since by its constitution it is no more and no less than a gentlemen's golf club, just one among some 1,500 clubs throughout the land. Yet Sunningdale exercises an influence on golf which might reasonably be compared to that of the 1922 Committee on a Tory Government. It has been called the Royal and Ancient golf club of the South but, like all labels, this is not entirely satisfactory. Many of its members are also members of the R and A, but the same could be said of any of Britain's leading clubs. To a large extent Sunningdale's influence is an inheritance from Gerald Micklem, for many years the high priest and ultimate

The seventeenth hole at Sunningdale

arbiter of golf, and through him Sunningdale maintained standards for the way in which a club and its golfers should deport themselves. The influence goes a good deal deeper, however, than simply setting an example. Perhaps it is best to leave it with a recognition of that influence, without seeking too hard to analyse the intangibles of power-broking.

The original course was built by Willie Park in 1900, in the days when the scope for earth-moving was severely restricted by the capacity of teams of horses drawing scraping boards. Thus what is now called the Old Course has some old-fashioned features, being on the short side with some outdated bunkering and a number of blind shots. It remains, however, a good test of golf and represented a stern challenge in the days of hickory shafts. These days a score of sixty-six is unexceptional among the leading professionals and nobody would apply the word 'perfect' to such figures. But when Bobby Jones returned such a score in a qualifying round for the Open championship in 1926, there was a certain justification for such a description of his round of thirty-three putts and thirty-three other shots with hardly a blemish worth mentioning. A word or two may be in order at this point on the subject of blind shots, such as the approach to the second and the tee shots on the seventh and eleventh. A blind shot by definition means that the problem is not fairly presented to the player and, while the members who play regularly are not inconvenienced and naturally resist any revisions of their historic course, it must diminish the quality of the course for the golfer facing it for the first time.

In Sunningdale's case there is no pressing reason to alter the historic Old Course because they have a second course, the New, of equal – if not superior – quality. The New was designed by the club's secretary, Harry Colt, in 1922. It is undoubtedly a fairer course by the lights of the above strictures and, in the opinion of many good judges, a sterner challenge, while sharing the same charm of the ancient forest where the Kings of England once hunted wild boar and more recent Kings (George VI and Edward VIII) hunted birdies and eagles.

Walton Heath is another club which enjoys the blessing of two courses of more or less equal quality. In this case the heathland is more exposed and, while woodland does come into play at a number of holes, its most valuable function is to screen the courses from roads, houses and the adjacent motorway. Heather comes into its own as the front line of defence, and very effective it is too. Overseas visitors confronted by heather for the first time are in for a shock, because the dainty, bell-shaped purple flowers and the dark green fronds convey no hint of menace. A mis-hit drive can surely be recovered without any great effort or threat to the score. How many sprained wrists must have punished such complacency, for heather shares with the willow scrub of Royal Birkdale the reputation of the toughest shrub in golf. Some immensely strong golfers, such as the late Harry Weetman, can bludgeon approach shots, but ordinary mortals soon learn to limit their ambitions to chopping the ball back on to the fairway via the nearest route and, from long experience, are happy to forfeit just the one stroke.

If Sunningdale's heritage is royal, Walton Heath's is political. Winston Churchill and the Allied Supreme Commander, General Dwight D. Eisenhower, were regular visitors during the Second World War and important conferences were held in the clubhouse. There were different but no less stern challenges to be faced on the golf course, because General Eisenhower took his golf very seriously.

For many years before and after the war Walton Heath was the home of the PGA match-play championship, and so the club has a lengthy and honourable association with professional golf, reinforced by the long tenure of the great champion, James Braid, as club professional. In recent times, for important events such as the Ryder Cup match and the European Open, it has become customary to play a composite course, partly to accommodate the tented village and parking and partly, or so it seems, in response to the common attitude among club members that the pros must not be allowed to make a fool of their course. The resulting composite course has been a monster, enormously long and demanding.

Woburn, regular home of the British Masters, was the most exciting site to come up for golf development for many years, because preliminary work on the course had been in progress for several centuries in the maturing of mighty oaks and other hardwoods under the husbandry of foresters to successive Dukes of Bedford. The design was entrusted to the experienced Charles Lawrie, a man who well understood that a golf course should be structured like a symphony, opening with a slow movement and building through shifts of mood to the grand climax of the finishing holes. This exercise of giving the course an emotional rhythm, gradually tightening the screws of nervous tension, was probably the best element of a highly competent design. And then, for reasons which no doubt seemed paramount at the time, the site for the clubhouse was moved and expediency destroyed the artistry, if not the craft, which Lawrie had created. So now the course ends on a note of anti-climax, on the holes which Lawrie had intended as the lull before the storm of the heroic allegro.

It may be asked what possible difference this makes to the course, since all the holes have to be played some

The fourteenth hole at Walton Heath

time or other. For answer let us take the example of the famous Road Hole at St Andrews where so many players have come to grief. In its position at number seventeen this hole looms like an Everest in the mind of the golfer, nagging away with its threat of undoing the good work of the previous sixteen holes. It therefore exercises its baleful influence all the way round, urging the player to press for birdies to cushion him against potential disaster and generally insinuating itself into his tactical thinking, much as the dread of landing must affect an airline pilot who knows that his undercarriage is faulty. It therefore demands a higher degree of self-control and discipline to play the Old Course, which is one of the reasons why the great players are usually successful at St Andrews. At the Old Course the seventeenth has not done with its mischief even after it has been played, because the inexperienced golfer enjoys such a surge of relief that he may drop his guard and play the innocuous-looking eighteenth with less than due caution, only to fall foul of its subtle dangers.

If the Duke's Course at Woburn is somewhat less than the sum of its parts, it is nevertheless a popular tournament course, particularly for television, because of its magnificent backdrops of forest and fern. Moor Park is also part of a noble estate, a category of club which is uniquely British. American architects often favour the neo-classical idiom for clubhouses, but in Britain many a clubhouse is a genuine stately home, with pillared portico, saved from decay by golf. For many people there is a sadness in seeing these great houses fallen on hard times, like a Rolls-Royce converted into a delivery van. Stately homes are best preserved by their ancestral families as lived-in homes supported by their estates, but the two inescapable fates, death and taxes, increasingly make this impractical and preservation through golf is greatly preferable to some of the alternatives. Even so, the incongruity of an orangery used as a snack bar, or the facility for changing your shoes in a wine cellar, strike many as an affront to the nation's heritage. Oddly

The eighteenth hole and clubhouse at St Andrews

Jack Nicklaus plays his second shot to the first hole at Wentworth during the World Match Play Championship

enough, the same regrets do not arise in the case of other historic buildings, such as the fortified farmhouse converted into the clubhouse for the Escorpion Club in Spain, which prompt feelings of admiration. Be that as it may, the two courses, High and Low, at Moor Park are built in the ancient park, with the holes changing mood as the golfer progresses from dense woodland on to the open pastures.

The best-known of the London area courses is undoubtedly the West Course at Wentworth, home to the PGA Championship and, for more than a quarter of a century, to the World Match Play Championship. Wentworth was built in conjuction with an estate of houses for well-to-do suburbanites. It came to prominence in 1956 when it hosted the Canada Cup, forerunner of the World Cup. The United States was represented by Ben Hogan and Sam Snead. Hogan was, if anything, even more meticulous than Jack Nicklaus in studying every nuance of a course before a tournament, to the extent that his regular Ryder Cup partner wrote of him, 'Ben wants to know the place so well that he could give a biologist a thorough life history of the four rabbits who hole up off the fourteenth fairway.' Knowing that Snead had previously played Wentworth, Hogan asked him what it was like. Snead gave the question considerable thought and then drawled, 'It's a sonofabitch.' As to the truth of that, like any course Wentworth can be a trial in adverse conditions, but Snead did the course less than justice. It is long but its reputation as a monster, perpetuated by its ludicrous

nickname of the Burma Road, is undeserved. Most of the holes fall well within the scope of the average golfer, and the image of relentless slogging really arises from three big par-fours which should be discounted by handicap allowances. It has done no harm to Wentworth, however, to have had the monster label attached to it, because there is no more potent bait to golfers than a challenge to their muscular prowess.

It is one of the most heavily wooded of the Surrey heath courses, with most of the holes threaded through avenues of pine and hardwood, so that accuracy with the driver is paramount. It also has rather more severe contouring of the greens than is normal for British golf – too severe for comfort in the case of the third green, which was eventually reshaped after a series of embarrassing incidents when players chipped up, only to have the ball make a U-turn on reaching the ridge of the two-tier green and roll back past them. Both Jack Nicklaus and Tom Kite suffered this expensive fate before the club decided to eliminate this humiliation factor. More than most courses, Wentworth changes character with the seasons. In high summer when the fairways are running it can yield some astonishingly low scores, but in a wet autumn, when the match-play championship is held, it becomes a different proposition. Even so, the big hitters, such as Sandy Lyle and Severiano Ballesteros, have regularly thrilled the huge galleries with sequences of birdies and eagles, a testimony both to their exceptional skills and to the superb condition in which the course is invariably presented.

Moor Park

Many tournaments were staged over the High Course at Moor Park, with its magnificent mansion clubhouse, before a composite championship test, combining the High and West Courses, came into play for the Four Stars National Pro Celebrity event.

The High culminates in a downhill par-three across the main drive to the club, where South African Harold Henning once won £10,000 for a hole-in-one, but the new Tour layout ends with a testing par-four below the galleried gardens to the rear of the mansion in which Henry VIII stayed on hunting trips.

It is uphill all the way at the opening hole, with two bunkers left to catch the errant drive and a well-bunkered green, then a sharp turn left down the second, with woods all the way on the left and more trees right.

The third (the ninth on the High) is a 480-yard par-five with an uphill tee shot to a fairway, whose right half is obscured by a spinney of trees and a two-tier green, and the fourth is a par-four plunging blindly downhill towards a line of bunkers, then rising steeply to a plateau green, where accuracy is everything.

Expect the 198-yard fifth, across a deep valley crossed twice by streams and bristling with undergrowth, to play longer than it looks. The two-level green rises five feet and is guarded on both sides by big bunkers.

The 471-yard sixth is played from an elevated tee back across the valley to a fairway sloping steeply down to

The magnificent clubhouse at Moor Park

the right, and the land falls away sharply right from the green towards the adjoining municipal course.

There is out of bounds all the way down the right at the seventh, and a hidden stream crossing the fairway some eighty yards short of the big sloping green, while you play out of the trees to the downhill eighth, with a road and trees beyond down the right.

You drive over a large pond at the 517-yard ninth, then, often using a wood, aim to miss a bunker sixty yards short of the green in the left half of the fairway, while at the tenth you must not stray right into the trees from the tee.

The 165-yard eleventh has a well-bunkered target, the 457-yard twelfth a blind tee shot over a hill. The line is down the right to a long two-tier green sloping right to left. You then drive blind over the hill down the thirteenth, and hit to another green sloping right to left, before tackling a 184-yard par-three in front of the clubhouse. The road, right, is out of bounds and there is a big bunker below the green right.

The 320-yard fifteenth, played from an elevated tee, offers a good birdie chance, but the sixteenth, back down the hill and then up to a plateau green across the road, is much more testing. The par-five seventeenth, climbing up and around a wooded hill, is tougher still, with a wickedly undulating green, and the eighteenth is a fine finishing hole between tall trees, demanding an accurate approach over sand to the green.

Sunningdale

Willie Park, son of the first Open Champion in 1860 and himself twice Open Champion, laid out the Old Course at Sunningdale in 1900 and three years later the PGA Match Play Championship was played there, with James Braid emerging the winner.

That was the first of many big events, including the European Open, to be played over this great heathland course, with its pine, birch and heather, and fine turf, which lies just down the road from Wentworth and had the New Course built alongside it by Colt in 1922.

Unusually, the opening hole is a par-five, with out of bounds beyond the trees to the right. That is the side to aim, however, to afford a clear approach to a green with scrub and bunkers to the left. You play out of the trees towards a road crossing the fairway at the 471-yard second, which narrows beyond two bunkers downhill towards a green, which is out of sight for the approach.

At 296 yards the third is virtually reachable, but you must fly your ball over heather and bunkers. The 161-yard fourth is played steeply uphill, and you must carry heather and scrub and three big bunkers. Then it is back downhill from a high tee at the panoramic fifth. Keep left of two deep fairway bunkers, then aim over the edge of a pond to a green guarded by four sand-traps.

The target from the sixth tee is an island fairway, and the uphill second is testing with trees beyond and to the right, towards which the green falls. The drive up the seventh is blind, with the fairway running right to left, and you bear right to fire to a raised green, then play to a well-bunkered target at the 182-yard eighth, with the left-to-right fall certain to accentuate a push or slice.

Overleaf: *Players approaching the eighteenth green during the European Open*

The seventeenth hole

At 280 yards the ninth is an almost automatic birdie hole for the pros. It is followed by another panoramic drive from high on the hill to the tenth fairway, but the green is long and sloping.

There is another blind tee shot over a heathery hill and trees at the right-hand dog-leg eleventh (325 yards), with the trees right the place not to be, while at the twelfth the drive must bisect two big bunkers and the approach, uphill, be flown over a nest of traps to a green at eleven o'clock.

You face a deceptive shot from another lofty tee down over heather and bunkers at the 185-yard thirteenth to a green with a ditch left, and at the par-five fourteenth an angled string of cross-bunkers is a hazard as you toil uphill.

The Old Course presents a stern test over the closing holes, with the 226-yard fifteenth heavily bunkered and a ring of cross-bunkers to be negotiated short of the uphill sixteenth.

At the seventeenth you must keep to the left of two huge traps on the right edge of the fairway but stay short of a clump of trees, and at the uphill eighteenth beware trouble right from the tee, before firing over deceptive cross-bunkers to a big, flat green, with its famous oak beyond and out of bounds left.

Walton Heath

Walton Heath's Old Course was the first to be designed by Herbert Fowler, who was related by marriage to Sir Cosmo Bonsor and his son Malcolm, the founder of the club. And James Braid, club professional for forty-five years, teamed with the other two members of golf's 'Great Triumvirate', J.H. Taylor and Harry Vardon, to open the course with an exhibition match in 1904. In 1907 Fowler began work on the adjacent New Course.

Of the great events played over the heath, the News of the World Match Play Championship is probably the best-known. First winner of the title over the course, in 1905, was appropriately Braid, who was five times Open Champion.

Lloyd George and Winston Churchill were once club members and the Duke of Windsor was Captain at Walton Heath in 1935.

The Championship course, which is a composite of both Old and New Courses, was first used in the European Open in 1978, and in 1981 it staged the Ryder Cup matches.

The fifth hole, which during the tournament plays as the third

First hole on the championship course is a 410-yard par-four, and players must beware the trees left as they try to hit down into the valley bottom. The second is an intimidating dog-leg right, of 516 yards, with out of bounds left and a large bunker right facing the drive, and bunkers left and right to be bisected with the approach, while the third is a dog-leg left demanding the most perfectly struck second between punishing bunkers to a tricky raised green.

Having skirted the sand-trap left off the fourth tee, the second across the road must fly a ridge short of the green, which tends to deflect balls into the left-hand bunker. A left-to-right-shaped tee shot around the big bunker at five o'clock is demanded at the short fifth, while drive and second shot at the narrow sixth, shortest par-five on the course at 489 yards, must be straight and true.

Aim to the right of the fairway from the tee and be bold with the approach at the 390-yard, right-to-left seventh to avoid a front of green bunker. The eighth bends the other way, and the tee shot should land between bushes and a bunker left and trees right to set up the second across a valley.

The ninth is a 189-yard par-three with an uphill sloping green, while the tenth is a 341-yard right-hand dog-leg where you might be tempted to emulate Henry Cotton's corner-cutting drive in a 1930s challenge match.

The fourteenth hole

The short second on Walton Heath's New Course

The eleventh, a dog-leg par-five, and the par-four twelfth demand accuracy with drive and second to greens sloping away from you. A bunker right must be avoided off the long par-four thirteenth tee.

New forward tees have turned the fourteenth, the longest hole of the course, into a 465-yard par-four, which has bunkers all along its length and a heather bank at driving distance. Bunkers right lie in wait at the fifteenth, with its severely sloping green, and the sixteenth is an even more challenging par-four at 475 yards, with a big bunker fronting the green right.

It is all carry over a 'moat' bunker at the 165-yard seventeenth, while the last, with its two-tier green and out of bounds just beyond, is a fine finishing hole.

The Wentworth Club

Wentworth's 'Burma Road' West Course has been the stage on which countless golfing dramas have been played out over the years, including the Ryder Cup matches in 1953. Tony Jacklin, Peter Oosterhuis, Bernhard Langer, Ian Woosnam, Nick Faldo and Severiano Ballesteros are among those who have won the Volvo PGA Championship over the course, which has been the setting for the World Match Play Championship since 1964. Arnold Palmer won that year. Gary Player has won five times, Severiano Ballesteros five, Greg Norman three and Ian Woosnam twice.

A third championship course, the 'Edinburgh', has been added to the West and East Courses on the elegant Wentworth Estate near Virginia Water, twenty minutes' drive from London's Heathrow Airport.

You drive at the 471-yard first from an elevated tee across the road, then face another long hit across a valley to an elevated green, with a steep fall-away left and bunkers left and right. The 155-yard second is played from a high tee across a valley to an elevated green, with a huge tree on the right and bunkers left – a spectacular hole, of which you must not be short.

You must keep left of a big bunker off the tee at the uphill third with its difficult three-tier green, then you face a blind tee shot down over the hill at the 501-yard fourth, a dog-leg to the left with the approach played across a ditch to an offset, well-bunkered green.

Four large bunkers and tricky undulating green present problems at the 191-yard fifth, but the sixth, at 344 yards, offers a real birdie chance if you land your tee

The thirteenth hole

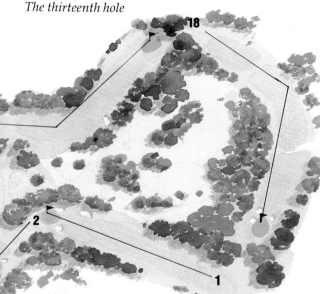

shot in position 'A' just left of centre fairway and negotiate approach bunkers left and right.

The drive at the seventh is steeply downhill to a landing area short of a deep ditch, from where you fire up to a hilltop green with trouble aplenty to the right. The eighth is a classic par-four with the second played over a lake to a green tucked into the trees.

At 450 yards and mostly uphill, with the out of bounds railway left, the ninth is among the toughest of par-fours, and the all carry tenth, at 186 yards, with trees left and right and an awkwardly angled green, is no easy par-three.

There is a good birdie opportunity at the down-and-up 376-yard eleventh and at the 483-yard twelfth, where you drive over big trees towards the right half of the fairway to gain entry to a green in the trees.

The thirteenth is also a dog-leg left around high trees and across a ditch, and the steeply uphill 179-yard fourteenth a most demanding par-three.

Aim for the left half of the fairway at the testing 466-yard fifteenth to get a clear view of the target, then hope to pick up a birdie at the 380-yard sixteenth, avoiding the strategically placed bunker from the tee and its bunkers right of the green.

The West's two finishing par-fives – 571 and 502 yards – have decided many an epic title tussle. Out of bounds gardens left and a blind second are features of the left-hand dog-leg seventeenth. The eighteenth bends equally severely right around the trees, and the second shot is a real nerve-tingler with trees closing in to the right.

Overleaf: *The eighth hole*

Below: *The eighteenth green*

The fourth hole – the tournament third

The second hole – the tournament first

Woburn Golf and Country Club

The Duke's and Duchess's Courses are set in the wooded heart of the Woburn Abbey Estate amid towering pines, silver birch and chestnut trees and masses of rhododendrons, heather, bracken and gorse.

Woburn Abbey, home of the Marquis and Marchioness of Tavistock and one of the first stately homes to be opened to the public in 1955, is only two and a half miles away from the Duke's Course, designed by the late Charles Lawrie and opened in 1976. It has since played host to many events, including the English Strokeplay Championship and the Dunhill British Masters, whose first five winners were Lee Trevino, Severiano Ballesteros, Mark McNulty, Sandy Lyle and Nick Faldo.

Trying to cut the corner at the dog-leg par-four first is not recommended, and beware the optical illusion that the green slopes steeply towards you as you play down the hill. A treetop-level tee and a green way down below you in the valley bottom make judgment of distance tricky at the panoramic 134-yard second, with its vast natural spectator gallery.

You must keep your drive right at the left-hand dog-leg third up the valley, and the same applies at the par-

five fourth, where you have to fly a deep gulley with your next shot, while at the 207-yard fifth there are trees all along the right and a bunker left of the green.

The sixth is another dog-leg left, where aiming well right pays dividends, with the fairway in front of the green sloping sharply left and steep banks surrounding the putting surface. The 409-yard seventh is not too inhibiting as long as you avoid the birch trees in the fairway.

A prevailing right-to-left wind can land your tee shot in the left-hand trap at the 177-yard eighth, while at the ninth tall trees left and right and two hollows in the fairway are hazards to contend with. Keeping the ball in the right half of the fairway is best at the 502-yard tenth, and aiming for the back of the uphill green of the 193-yard eleventh is recommended.

Drive too far left at the twelfth and your ball could kick into the pine trees; come up short with your second and you are likely to find yourself in sand. At the monster 565-yard thirteenth, however, you must be left off the tee to avoid a big bunker and deep gulley beyond, and then aim right of a fairway trap eighty yards from the green.

The third hole – the tournament second

The main problem at the fourteenth is out of bounds beyond a bunker left of the green. Two sand-traps on the left are very much in range off the fifteenth tee. At the sixteenth a hooked drive will be severely punished – aim at the tall pine right and hope for a bounce left to centre fairway, and don't be short with your second.

The par-four seventeenth is a gentle dog-leg right. Overhit drives can tear on into the trees, but it is a real birdie opportunity. So is the 514-yard eighteenth, provided you avoid the out of bounds left and the fall-away into trouble right with your drive.

The first hole – the tournament eighteenth

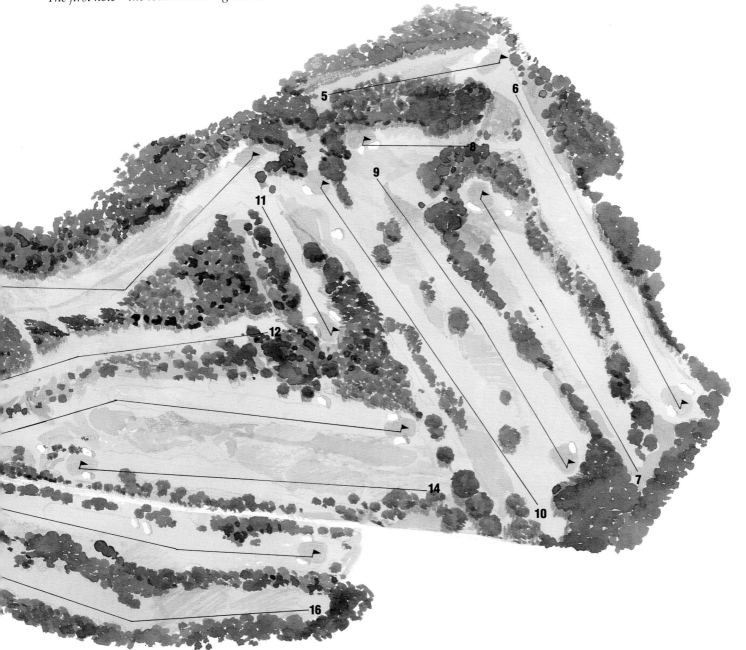

IRELAND

No eyebrows were raised in surprise when in 1987 the players of the PGA European Tour voted the Carrolls Irish Open their favourite tournament of the year. Many years of effort and financial commitment by the sponsor had been devoted to polishing every facet of the tournament with the aim of making the Irish Open the most agreeable tournament of the year for the players, officials, spectators and, not least, the press.

The Irish Open was inaugurated in 1927 and spluttered to its demise in 1954 for lack of financial backing. A decade later the P. J. Carroll company started its international tournament which was played mainly at Woodbrook, an undistinguished meadow course on the clifftops south of Dublin. As Ireland's premier professional tournament, the Carrolls International was the *de facto* national championship and in 1975 it became such in name as well – the Carrolls Irish Open. Purists might argue, and did so in those long-lost days of purity, that a tobacco company promotion could not call itself a national championship. The same objection was raised in England over another tobacco company promoting the world match-play championship, on the grounds that even the egotism of tobacco barons must surely draw the line at claiming sovereignty over the whole universe of golf. In both cases the sheer excellence of the promotions eventually won over the diehards, or at least stilled their objections.

The inaugural playing of the revived Irish Open was at Woodbrook, and by a stroke of good luck gained an immediate injection of credibility and popularity through the victory of Christy O'Connor Jr. Known as Junior, he endured the mixed blessing of being the nephew of the great Christy O'Connor, whose worldwide exploits had elevated him to the status of a secular saint in Ireland. This was no more than he deserved, for he must be ranked among the outstanding players of the twentieth century. His achieve-

ments were all the more remarkable because everywhere he went he was lavishly fêted by the local Irish community. Every national golfing hero is subjected to tremendous pressure when playing in front of his own countrymen, but in most cases this means when playing in his own country. In O'Connor's case he was figuratively swaddled in the tricolour every week, for no nation has colonized the world more thoroughly, or to more beneficial effect, than the Irish. So, apart from being a golfer, he was also a roving ambassador, with social obligations as well as a responsibility to put on a good show for the expatriate Irish colony. It is a debatable point whether he would have retired at ten o'clock every night with an improving book and a glass of mineral water if he had been free of these obligations. What is quite certain, however, is that he would have preferred as a dedicated professional golfer to have been fêted rather less lavishly at times. But there is an insistent quality about Irish hospitality, a challenge in the cry of 'A bird can't fly on one wing' as the glass is refilled, and only a churl would abandon a party prematurely when, as the guest of honour, he was giving so much pleasure to his hosts. It might be that O'Connor would have achieved even more if he had been born, say, a Hungarian, but his acceptance of his role as an Irishman first, a golfer second, increased his popularity wherever he went. So Junior had to live in the shadow of this national institution and attempt to make his way in golf against a background chorus of voices whispering, 'He is a good player but . . .'

Victory in that first Carrolls Irish Open established Junior as a star in his own right and not just a satellite palely orbiting the great luminary, and the championship was off to a good start. The first priority was to switch to a course worthy of a great championship and the obvious candidate was Portmarnock, the internationally acclaimed links on Dublin Bay. There could be no doubts about Portmarnock's qualifications as an examination for the world's great players. Ireland

The par-three fifteenth hole at Portmarnock

The scene at the final green during the 1988 Irish Open

abounds in glorious courses, many of them all the more inspiring for the grandeur of their scenery, for their remoteness from the hurly-burly of urban life, and for the roistering welcome of their clubhouses. For sheer enjoyment there is nowhere on earth to compare with the necklace of courses starting in the south-west extremity of Ireland and progressing in a leisurely pilgrimage up the coast into Donegal and then along the northern sweep and down the east coast to Royal County Down. As therapy for a jaded soul or embattled spirit such a peregrination is a hundred times more effective than a course of psychoanalysis, and much cheaper. But professional golf is not about enjoyment, still less spiritual regeneration. It is pragmatic, a fiendishly contrived ordeal to test a person's skills and temperamental resources to the limit, and Portmarnock is just that, an exposed links where the wind blows in from the Irish Sea to spice the challenge of the strategic, as opposed to penal, design. Since the club also has ample space for parking, practice and a tented village, it is an ideal venue for a major golf promotion, and the sports-mad Irish ensure that it is just that, with galleries to match those of the Ryder Cup and the Open.

The popularity of the championship creates one serious problem, because access to Portmarnock is con-

fined to one narrow road on to the promontory. The Irish have a saying, however, that a problem may be critical but never serious, and so the difficulty of getting players and golf writers to the airport after the championship, when that one road is clogged with the cars of the departing thousands, has been overcome by an exercise which has become legendary in professional golf. Those who urgently need to catch the last flight assemble in the car park in a convoy of courtesy cars and, in a meticulously co-ordinated operation, the police momentarily stem the flow of traffic on to the access road. Motor-cycle outriders of the President's squad lead the convoy with sirens howling, sheep-dogging pedestrians and cars out of the way, and the convoy departs at speed. In time some of the spectators latched on to this strategy and the more alert among them try to tag on to the end of the convoy, or cut into the middle of it, so drivers are exhorted by radio to keep in tight formation and maintain the exhilarating pace. Once on the main road, with the outriders racing ahead to halt traffic at intersections, the convoy really picks up speed, with passers-by pressing themselves into doorways as the cars roar past. What must they imagine is the cause of this extraordinary cavalcade? But no one has ever missed the last flight and, as the players relax gratefully in the departure lounge and reflect on a farewell as considerate as their Irish welcome, it is hardly surprising that they determine to vote the Irish Open their favourite event of the year.

In 1983 Carrolls and Portmarnock could not agree on a fair charge for the course, so the Open was taken to Royal Dublin for three years. By no stretch of the imagination could this switch have been considered suitable. Access to Royal Dublin, along the causeway built by Captain Bligh (of HMS *Bounty* fame), is, if anything, even more restricted than the road into Portmarnock. The space for car parking proved to be inadequate even when the entire practice area was commandeered for the purpose. The players had to practise before the place filled up with cars, being forced to reverse the usual routine and finish with little wedge shots. The tented village was cramped and when the vast crowds arrived – a goodly number having got in for a cut-rate fee through an illegal gate which a budding entrepreneur had cut in the perimeter fence – there was barely room to move. It is a fine course, however, and no push-over; famous for the madcap antics of the hares which proliferate on the island. Every morning the ground staff had a hare sweep, chivvying the creatures on to the neighbouring links of St Anne's but, of course, they returned to their favourite haunts. You would swear they understood the game and how to disrupt it to maximum effect, by the way they timed their scampering runs across the greens or leapt from the rough just as the start of the downswing.

If Royal Dublin was tight across the shoulders of the championship it nevertheless produced the most memorable tournaments, involving dramatic clashes between Severiano Ballesteros and Bernhard Langer. This raises an interesting and important point. Everyone accepts that in order to have a great tournament you must go to a great golf course. But the Opens at Royal Dublin were wildly successful. The course unerringly singled out the greatest players year after year and the finishes were as thrilling as any tournament golf seen in Europe since the Tour began. So can there be no place in competitive golf for courses which are less than entirely suitable for today's massive promotions? It would be

the greatest of pities to think that the rich potential for drama in Royal Dublin would not be exploited again by the great stars of professional golf for our entertainment.

On this theme, Waterville, on the enchanted coast of the Ring of Kerry, has disappeared from the annual golfing itinerary simply because of its remoteness, and professional golf is the poorer for its absence since the demise of the Kerrygold tournament.

An astonishingly high proportion of golfers list angling among their favourite hobbies and at Waterville the best of both worlds coincide: a great links course and, in Butler's Pool, one of the most famous salmon swims in Europe. Maybe one day an enterprising sponsor will put two and two together and come up with a combination tournament for club and rod, and then we shall all have an excuse to return and enjoy the luxury of the hotel and the finest view to be seen from any dining-room in the whole of Ireland. Robert Louis Stevenson described Pebble Beach as the most noble meeting of land and sea in the world. Obviously he had never visited Waterville.

Exceptionally, because Portmarnock was being made ready for the Walker Cup match, the Carrolls Irish Open was played at Killarney in 1991 and was such a great success that the Open returned in 1992. The sheer beauty of the site, no less than the quality of the course, makes Killarney popular with golf promoters, and there is no doubt that the PGA European Tour will seize any future chance to return. The club has an interesting history. For the first half of the twentieth century the golfers of Killarney played on the deer park of the Earl of Kenmare's estate for a rent of a shilling a year. When the land agent proposed a rent of £1,500 a year, the members were outraged – like golfers everywhere when asked to pay realistic fees – and they petitioned the Earl for permission to use a tract of overgrown scrubland bordering Lough Leane. The Earl's heir, Lord Castlerosse, a London man-about-town, bon viveur and keen golfer, invited the golf writer Henry Longhurst to inspect the property and give his opinion. Henry's verdict was, 'You could build the most beautiful golf course in the world here.' And that is what they did.

Portmarnock

The Portmarnock Club, close to Dublin, was founded in 1894 and now has thirty-six holes. The championship course evolved over the years, with no single designer, as such, able to take the credit. Harry Vardon won the first professional tournament at Portmarnock with scores of seventy-two and seventy-nine in 1899, the year he won his third Open Championship.

Originally the club was reached by boat from the Sutton peninsula, with a horse-drawn carriage bringing members across the inlet at low tide.

The Carrolls Irish Open has been played at Portmarnock twelve times since 1976. Americans Ben Crenshaw and Hubert Green won the first two championships, while Britain's Ian Woosnam won in 1988 and 1989, and Spain's José Maria Olazabal in 1990. The Irish Open itself was first staged there in 1927, with George Duncan emerging champion in a force-nine gale, his closing seventy-two being the only score under eighty. Sam Snead and Arnold Palmer won the Canada Cup (now the World Cup) over the links in 1960.

The sixth hole

The first, with out of bounds short of the water all the way down the right, is a 377-yard par-four; the second, of similar length, bends slightly left and its two-tier green is heavily guarded by bunkers short, left and right.

Holes three and four, also par-fours, both also bend from right to left and the fourth fairway is liberally sprinkled with pairs of bunkers on the right side and has mounds and depressions on the left short of the green.

There are two bunkers on the right within driving range after a long carry at the fifth, and fairway traps and a ridge to clear to reach the green, while the narrow fairway at the 601-yard sixth rolls over a series of ridges, passing a pond on the left in the second-shot landing area.

Bunkers left and right guard the short seventh. The par-four eighth is a left-hand dog-leg to a raised green, while you drive over a ridge at the right-hand dog-leg ninth back to the clubhouse, with plenty of trouble short right of the target. The tenth is also a dog-leg right towards a green, which falls away steeply left and right. Two bunkers lie in wait for tee shots too far right at the eleventh, while two bunkers at the front and another left guard the short twelfth back to the sea. There are bunkers left and right in the landing area from the tee at the par-five thirteenth, and eight more traps are lined up to swallow underhit approach shots.

Steer right of a bunker at the fourteenth before aiming at a target at eleven o'clock over a ridge and two more fairway traps, then tackle a scenic par-three from a high tee along the out of bounds seashore to the right.

A bunker right is very much in play from the tee at the par-five sixteenth, which has more traps short of the green, but not half as many as lie in wait for the drive and approach at the seventeenth; and the eighteenth, bearing right around three bunkers, demands a precise second over more sand.

The fourteenth hole

The 144-yard par-three twelfth hole

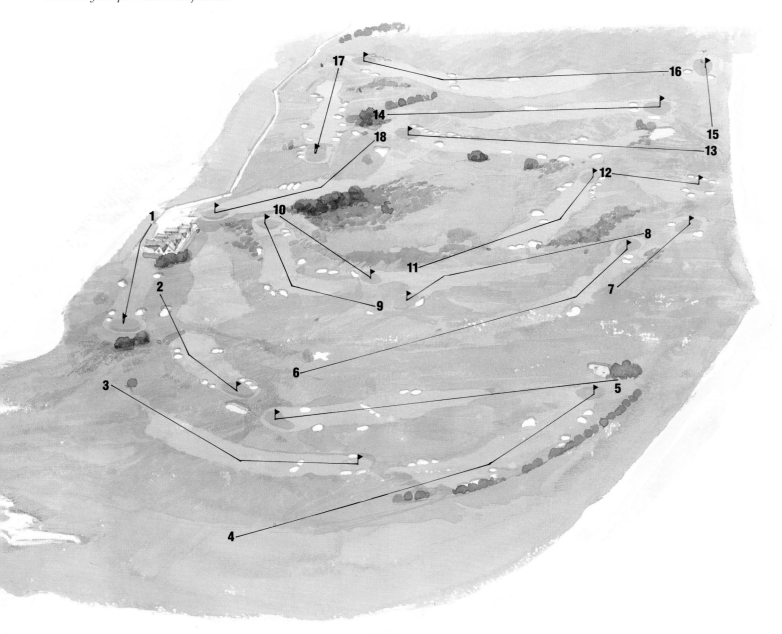

Royal Dublin

Severiano Ballesteros, twice, and Bernhard Langer were the winners of the Irish Open when it was played three years running on the links of Royal Dublin in the early 1980s, which bears testimony to the quality of this course, a short drive from the centre of Dublin.

Langer, who also won the French, Dutch and Spanish Opens that year (1984) to finish top of the European order of merit, fired a truly impressive twenty-one below par 267. Lesser mortals can never hope to get close to scoring like that on an island layout where the wind invariably plays a vital role.

Crosswinds from left to right generally make the 397-yard first a tricky hole, with a mound with bunkers set in it to the left an obstacle to be avoided, but the par-five second is a real birdie chance. It is a right-hand dog-leg and there is a big bunker to the left of a long, narrow green.

The par-four third is also a right-hand dog-leg, played from an elevated tee with a blind drive, while the 180-yard fourth can play from a seven- to a three-iron depending on the wind, and the low-lying green is well trapped left and right.

Long-time Royal Dublin professional Christy O'Connor describes the 460-yard fifth as 'probably as good a par-four as you will find in golf'. You drive into a narrow tunnel, with trouble to the right, then flirt with bunkers and out of bounds right as you play your next.

A big bank crossing the fairway will not trouble the big hitters at the 370-yard sixth, with its plateau green, while a narrow rising pear-shaped green, bunkered left and right, faces you at the 145-yard seventh.

The 509-yard eighth is a key hole, a right-hand dog-leg to a high green with two sand-traps right and a deep fall-off on the left, but the 179-yard ninth, well protected by front bunkers, offers some relief. You start home with a challenging par-four, avoiding bunkers and out of bounds on the right and a cross-fairway ditch, then face a 538-yard par-five, with out of bounds threatening and a green running away from you.

The 207-yard twelfth can play a wood into the wind, with a drain thirty yards short of the green and a menacing mound to the left, while the thirteenth is a very long par-four at 468 yards – O'Connor's 'toughest hole on the course', with out of bounds right and a notoriously narrow green beyond a bottleneck of mounds.

Enjoy the wonderful view of Dublin Bay from the high fourteenth tee, then beware the bunkers within driving range and the ditch eighty yards short of the green. The fifteenth, a dog-leg inclining right to left, is another testing par-four, but the 270-yard sixteenth is driveable as long as you miss the cross bunkers 220 yards out.

You must skirt the out of bounds and huge bunkers on the right at the 380-yard seventeenth to set up the correct approach to a narrow-necked green, then it is on to the most celebrated hole on the course.

Sandy Lyle once ran up double figures at this 463-yard par-four, which bends almost at right-angles around the out of bounds, while 'Professor' O'Connor, whose association with Royal Dublin began in 1959, once completed an eagle-birdie-eagle finish here when this hole was a par-five.

'The Pot', the par-three sixth hole

SCOTLAND

Whether or not the Scots invented golf, adapted an existing game or imported it will probably never be established beyond doubt, so there is no point in labouring the issue. What is absolutely certain is that the Scots nourished and developed the game, kept it alive when it was withering, discovered the cheap gutta-percha ball that restored it to health and then exported it all over the world. In the process golf became Scotland's national game, which is why Scotland is rightly regarded as the home of golf. It is therefore a place of pilgrimage for golfers from all over the world, and one of the shrines high on the list of visitors' priorities is Gleneagles. The hotel's symbol of an eagle on a bag tag or luggage label is a potent badge of status from Tokyo to Tallahassee, and this is probably not the place to revive the controversy about whether the name Gleneagles derives from the French 'glen '*d'églises*', or glen of churches. Sufficient that there is a glen of unsurpassing beauty, complete with eagles, distant churches and four courses, the King's, Queen's, Prince's and Glendevon. The Prince's and the Glendevon have now disappeared, reappearing with Jack Nicklaus's guiding hand as the Monarch Course – surely a tribute in this superb setting to the 'Monarch' of golf himself.

The interest for present purposes is the King's, laid out by James Braid on moorland of knolls and ridges and valleys. The first hole rises quite steeply on to the moor, no great hardship at the beginning of the round but a boon beyond price after seventeen holes, when the golfer plays the long hole home down the slope towards an aperitif and the finest golf club lunch to be found anywhere in the world. In an ideal world all golf courses would end with a downhill hole, especially one like this which offers a good opportunity for a birdie to put the golfer in celebratory mood.

The other great virtue of Gleneagles is that this is a course which it is impossible not to enjoy, even when

A view over the fifteenth hole at Gleneagles towards the glen

you play badly. There is nothing like the sight of a deer dashing elegantly across the fairway to ease the disappointment of having driven into the heather. The novelist John Updike insists that golfers do not appreciate beautiful surroundings because they are too bound up in their selfish problems, morosely rehearsing possible remedies for a sudden attack of the slice, as they trudge the fairways looking at their boots. But even golfers such as these, and we all know the type, occasionally raise their heads to growl agonized pleas to the heavens, and their glazed eyes must take in the scenery. Nobody has ever actually died of asphyxia from observing a spectacular sunset but the writers of holiday brochures insist on describing such experiences as breathtaking. That adjective comes as close to being suitable at this spot as on any golf course in Britain. At the far end of the course is a hilltop from which you can look around through every point of the compass without seeing, or hearing, anything made by man, observing an unbroken panorama of distant mountains and the bracken, gorse and heather of the moor. The motor car might never have been invented, nor offices or hamburger joints or television soap operas or property developers. Out of sight, out of mind, and that is one of the chief pleasures, not to say benefits, of golf.

Tournament golfers enjoy these pleasures and benefits, but they are not the purpose of their game. Their concern is the simple arithmetic of their score cards, and so in their case different criteria must be applied to the King's Course. In the form which Braid created, the course had become outdated by the time the Scottish Open was inaugurated in 1986. Modern equipment had emasculated the course's defences, because the fairway bunkers did not come into play and the course was too short to provide a comprehensive examination of the fairway woods and long irons. A programme of modernization was introduced, a sensitive task if the stroke values of Braid's concept were to be observed. By general consensus the stretching and revising were

Ian Woosnam putting at Gleneagles during the 1987 Scottish Open, which he won

successful, perhaps not up to the accepted standards for a championship course but certainly high enough to provide a worthy test for the best players. The week before the Open championship is a difficult tournament slot because everyone is becoming preoccupied with the big one. Those who have to qualify for the Open are neurotic; even more so the ones doing well enough in the Scottish Open to entertain hopes of Open championship exemption through a high finish. At the best of times professional golfers are inveterate complainers, quick to find fault with the course or the organization, or the prize money or the accommodation, and this week is not the best of times. The highest compliment which can be paid to those common sources of complaint at Gleneagles is that they do not form a cause for complaint. It is possibly the best-humoured week of the golfing calendar, thanks in due measure to the King's Course.

Turnberry on the Ayrshire coast, exposed to the full ferocity of Atlantic gales in season, has its moments of enchantment, but intrinsically it is a stern dominie of a course, standing no nonsense and quick with the tawse to chastise those who stray from the straight and narrow. It too has a magnificent hotel, high on a ridge above the course, a highly specialized intensive-care unit where golfers ravaged by the elements and bludgeoned by the Ailsa Course are expertly restored to good health and sanity. It is, in short, just the kind of course which the championship committee of the Royal and Ancient Golf Club of St Andrews – a secular reincarnation of the Spanish Inquisition, as it seems at times – likes for the Open championship, given a good measure of turbulent weather. In 1977 the course proved its quality by exposing the weaknesses and breaking the hearts of all but two players, Jack Nicklaus and Tom Watson, both at or near their prime and unquestionably the two greatest golfers in the world at the time. Having been identified by the Ailsa Course, without the benefit of foul weather it should be recorded, and separated from the pack, the two titans were left to compete in their own private tournament, virtually at match-play while the rest engaged in their own minor competition for the lesser prize money. This, in the opinion of many who watched the fascinating duel, was the greatest Open of all time. Watson, keeping in touch with prodigious recoveries and telling thrusts, was never in the lead until the seventy-first hole, where Nicklaus unaccountably failed to make the birdie which his power and skill deserved as of right. He then drove into bushes at the last but still contrived to make a birdie, only for Watson to clinch the title with a scarcely less improbable birdie of his own.

In 1986 the gales raged and only a player of exceptional power; control and inner strength could hope to prevail against the combination of the Ailsa Course and the elements. Greg Norman rose to the challenge magnificently to confirm his reputation as a player worthy of golf's highest distinction.

During the Second World War Turnberry was turned into an RAF airfield. The task of restoring it, virtually starting from scratch and creating a new course, was entrusted to Mackenzie Ross. The course starts with a disappointingly mundane hole alongside the main road, followed by two more relatively humdrum holes of no particular distinction. The real Turnberry begins with the teasing short fourth; it then starts to reveal its true nature with a tightly guarded green on the fifth, a short par-five and reasonable enough as such, except that the pros play it as a two-shotter and both shots have to be of high quality. Now the screw begins to turn, with a run of increasingly daunting holes through the valleys of the dunes out to the rocky headland at the end of the course to the famous ninth. It was here that one illustrious professional had to be blindfolded and led on to the platform tee built on the rocks because he suffered from vertigo. The drive past the ruins of Bruce's castle to a hogsback fairway is one of the most testing shots on the course, and the tenth, a long par-four around the sweep of the foreshore, is reckoned by many to be the best of Turnberry. The holes returning on the inland stretch are less scenic but damnably difficult in their treacherous subtlety, although the eighteenth is something of a let-down despite recent attempts to give it the zest of a true finishing hole.

Muirfield, home of the Honourable Company of Edinburgh Golfers, is a true links, although a mile or so inland from the Firth of Forth. The site is flattish, apart from one steep ridge, and the dunes are of modest proportions compared with the monsters of Royal Birkdale or Ballybunion. It was therefore more important than usual for the hand and imagination of man, rather than nature, to create the golfing qualities of Muirfield. This is the third course of the Honourable Company, and when the club moved to its latest home and staged the 1892 Open, the first championship to be played over seventy-two holes, it seemed that the hand and imagination of man had not done much of a job. Andrew Kirkaldy, the Scottish pro noted for his waspish tongue, called Muirfield 'nothing but an auld water meddie'.

Then began a long and continuing process of revision, improvement and the acquisition of extra land. Gradually the course evolved to the point where it was acclaimed as the fairest and surest test of golf among the rota of championship courses. That judgement is not, of course, universal since golfers are notoriously argumentative about such subjective issues, but it is probably true to say that those who advance claims for the superiority of Royal Lytham, Royal Birkdale or

Greg Norman, the eventual winner, putting on the eighth green during the 1986 Open Championship at Turnberry

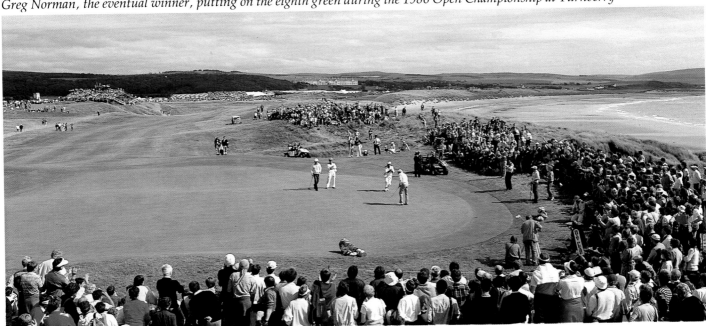

Carnoustie invariably concede second place to Muir-field. So whether a vote were taken on proportional representation or on the basis of first past the post, Muirfield would surely come top of the poll.

It would probably win with an even higher majority in a vote by American players because Muirfield is, above all, an honest course. The problems, although severe, are presented in plain view, except for the drive at the eleventh where the line is obvious enough. Another considerable virtue is that the bunkers are genuine hazards with none of those effete saucers from which professionals unhesitatingly hit three-wood shots to the green without being inconvenienced in the slightest degree. Muirfield's numerous fairway bunkers are of the pot variety, deep caverns with elegant walls of layered turf which limit ambitions to splashing the ball back on to the fairway, sideways if need be. Worse, or better according to your philosophy, the bunkers gather the ball, so it is impossible to flirt with them, or run through them. The bunkering in combination with truly penal rough makes Muirfield a placement golf course in the American idiom, where you cannot get away with an indifferent shot.

The first hole is misleading, lacking in definition and cruelly difficult for an opener. Thereafter the course assumes its true persona as an exhilarating challenge, long enough to require the driver and tight enough to make you wish you could use an iron from the tees. And for the big hitters it poses some exquisite dilemmas, such as the ninth, a short par-five along the boundary wall, where they can get home in two if they have the nerve and the skill to drive into the narrow neck of the hour-glass fairway.

Like all championship courses, Muirfield provides the bonus of walking in the footsteps of the legends of golf. Here Harry Vardon won the first of his record six Opens. James Braid won twice. Ted Ray, Walter Hagen, Gary Player and Jack Nicklaus all contributed their lustre to Muirfield's championship history. Here Henry Cotton had his finest hour, with a King in his gallery cheering him to victory. And here too Lee Trevino crushed Tony Jacklin's spirit with one of the most outrageous flukes of any championship, during a week when he seemingly could do no wrong. On the seventy-first hole in the 1972 Open he drove into one of those pot bunkers, splashed out, hooked his third into the rough and then sent his fourth over the green on to a bank. Jacklin had played the hole with two perfect shots followed by an indifferent pitch, although it looked adequate enough in view of his rival's misadventures. Trevino thought so too and admitted afterwards that he had mentally conceded the championship to Jacklin. He

Deep bunkers on the short thirteenth at Muirfield

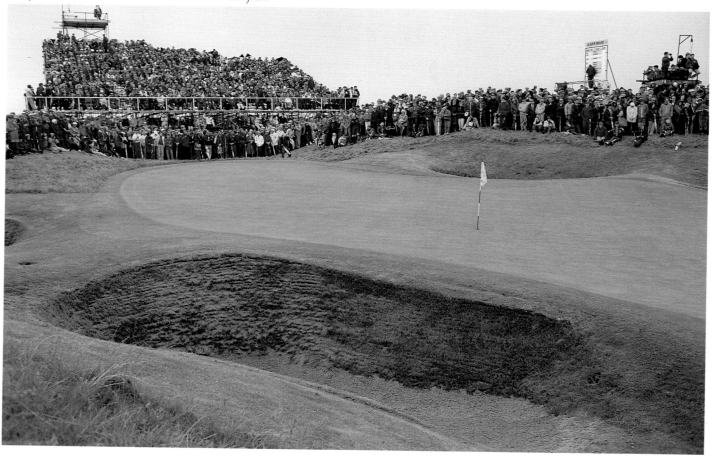

The first group tees off for the 1984 Open at St Andrews

had to complete the formalities of finishing his round, however, and in this frame of mind he made a carefree swing of his wedge at the ball, which hopped on to the green and proceeded to roll straight into the hole. The dumbfounded Jacklin three-putted, and before he could collect his senses the astute Trevino had run to the last tee and hit his drive. Jacklin finished third.

But surely there can have been no championship at Muirfield quite like the melodrama of 1987, when ferocious gales and icy rain put the golf at the limits of playability. The tented village was reduced to a quagmire of ankle-deep, malodorous black slime. But out they had to go and the scoreboard read like a horror story. As always on these occasions some players had to endure the worst of the tempest, among them Sandy Lyle who played the round of his life on the third day. The contest came down to the steady Nick Faldo and the unlikely figure of the young American, Paul Azinger – unlikely because of his inexperience of links golf or such appalling conditions. On the final day Azinger made a spirited bid, playing beautifully in the buffeting wind and nullifying his errors with birdies. Faldo, confident with the revised swing which he had spent two years perfecting under the guidance of David Leadbetter, ground out par after par. On the last hole Azinger faltered, finding one of those bunkers from which no man escapes unscathed. Faldo coolly completed his eighteenth par of the day to win. Eighteen straight pars

may sound like a dull round; some people in their ignorance even described it as such. To real golfers it was anything but: one of the most outstanding accomplishments they had ever been privileged to witness.

And so to St Andrews, the ultimate golf course and the daddy of them all. Because of the history and mythology of the Old Course, many people have an impression that it has been there ever since golf began and remains as a living museum of golf's distant origins. The fact is that no course has undergone more changes. The original strip of foreshore has been vastly extended over the years, with at least three sea walls now buried beneath the dunes. The course has been revised over and over again in a long process of evolution, although the basic structure of shared fairways and double greens has happily survived as a reminder of the informality of early golf. Some courses had only four holes, or six, or twelve as at Prestwick. St Andrews once had twenty-two holes and it was with the intention of improving some holes with extra length, by means of amalgamating them, that St Andrews, as the premier club, set the convention that eighteen holes constitute a round of golf.

The history of the Old Course goes back at least to the year 1552, when a licence granted the citizens of St Andrews the right to catch rabbits, and to 'play at golf, futeball and schuting' on the links. The breadth of that licence gives us an insight into the nature of early golf

Severiano Ballesteros, Open Champion at St Andrews

at St Andrews. Anything resembling a formal course would have been out of the question while bowmen were practising their archery skills, boys were kicking inflated pigs' bladders about, housewives were draping their washing on the whin bushes to dry and men were trying to catch rabbits. The golfers, using rudimentary clubs and balls of turned hardwood, would have been forced to direct their play in areas temporarily unoccupied by other citizens, playing to improvised holes as they went along, and no doubt in time the golfers formed opinions about which stretches of the links made for the best holes. The convention, as we must assume from the earliest written codes of the game, was to tee your ball alongside the hole just played, and it is easy to imagine the state of the ground after a few groups had played a hole. So putting, in the sense we know it, must have been more of a chipping art.

In 1754 'twenty-two Noblemen and Gentlemen, being admirers of the ancient and healthful exercise of the Golf', subscribed for a silver club as a prize for annual competition, following the example of the golfers of Edinburgh ten years previously. So was born the Society of St Andrews Golfers, later to become the Royal and Ancient Golf Club of St Andrews. By that time the course had become formalized into pretty much its present state, although the revision to eighteen holes was still to come. The narrowness of the links imposed the necessity for shared fairways and double greens, an arrangement which permitted the course to be played anti-clockwise, the conventional arrangement today, or backwards in a clockwise route with the first hole played to the seventeenth green. The course is still played in reverse order on occasions.

No architect ever had a hand in the Old Course, which remains the result of pure evolution. Yet the Old Course constitutes the model for architects, by far the greatest influence on golf course design the world over. Every principle and trick of design is to be found at St Andrews, from the strategy of luring the golfer to play towards the safety of the middle of the course, when most often the premium golfing line is close to the boundaries, to the shape and siting of the bunkers. Originally sand bunkers were accidents of nature, formed during droughts when the grass on the top of the knolls withered and the wind blew away the sandy subsoil, leaving a depression as sheep huddled in them to shelter from the elements. Only the hardiest, salt-resistant plants can survive on the poverty of pure sand: at St Andrews there are seaside grasses and shrubs such as gorse, or whins, as they are generally known in Scotland.

So at first sight the flat links of the Old Course seem unprepossessing, leading the visitor to ask what all the fuss is about. On his first visit Sam Snead looked out of the window of the train and remarked that it appeared there had been a golf course on the links at some time. On first playing the Old Course some visitors come to the conclusion that there still is not a golf course there.

One such was the youthful Bobby Jones when he played the Open of 1921. He could make nothing of the course, and when he took six at the short eleventh after a series of misadventures he tore up his card in a fit of temper. When he was made a freeman of St Andrews thirty years later, having completed the Grand Slam and enslaved the world of golf by his brilliance and sporting demeanour, he was moved to declaim, 'The more I studied the Old Course, the more I loved it and the more I loved it, the more I studied it, so that I came to feel that it was for me the most favourable meeting ground possible for an important contest. I felt that my knowledge of the course enabled me to play it with patience and restraint until she might exact her toll from my adversary, who might treat her with less respect and understanding.' Does this mean that the Old Course suffers from the weakness that it takes long experience before its subtleties can be appreciated and overcome? Tony Lema won the 1964 Open on his first acquaintance, having played only nine holes in practice. But then Lema did have the advantage of a caddie who knew every mood and detail of the Old Course.

Most of us think of golf in terms of lines, hitting from the tee to a point on the fairway and from there to the green. We are reinforced in this concept of linear golf by looking at diagrams of golf holes, in tournament programmes and suchlike, which commonly show lines depicting the ideal way to play the hole. But golf course architects do not work in lines; they work in angles. The beginner does not hit the ball very far and he tends to be wild. Therefore the architect must provide a forward tee and a fairway wide enough in the landing area to receive a drive which may deviate five degrees either side of the centre line. The fairway can now continue at this width because the better players off the middle tees should be able to drive longer and straighter, deviating no more than three degrees either way. Likewise the standard of accuracy from the championship tees must be limited by an even more acute angle of deviation. The same process is repeated for the second and third shots and these angles determine the size of the green.

By such means the proportions of every hole are calculated and the punishments are graduated to fit the length and lateral deviation by which each category of player strays outside his allotted playing corridor. For example, a tiny green on a long par-four is by this reckoning a bad design.

Royal Troon is a well-proportioned links, but those angles are slightly compressed, leaving less than the usual margin for error. Ask Hermann Tissies, whose tee shot to the short eighth, known as the Postage Stamp and the shortest hole in championship golf at 126 yards, deviated less than two degrees from the perfect line. His ball lay in a pot bunker and by the time he eventually finished popping it from one bunker to another, admittedly taking five attempts in one of them, and holed out on the minuscule green, he had run up a score of fifteen. On the other hand, Gene Sarazen, making a sentimental appearance in the Open fifty years after winning the championship at Sandwich, holed in one.

The eleventh is another good example of the severity of these ancient links. The tee is perched among the dunes near the railway line and you drive over a wilderness of hummocks and rough to a narrow fairway which is angled to the line of the shot. Both length and direction, not to mention judgment of your own capabilities, have to be pretty well perfect to set up the long second shot for a birdie on this short par-five. A minimal error in length or line puts you into the perdition of gorse bushes or the scarcely less inconvenient rough. That second shot also has to be absolutely straight and true, with something like a one-iron, because the railway is hard behind the green. Tom Watson's play of this hole laid the foundation for his Open championship victory in 1982, just as it dashed Jack Nicklaus's chances twenty years earlier when he ran up a ten. Tom Weiskopf, a classic stylist but a perfectionist whose impatience with himself often betrayed his gigantic talent, kept everything under control for the 1973 Open, playing one of the great final rounds of the modern era to win with a score of 276 and gain a well-deserved place among the roll of champions.

Gleneagles Hotel Golf Courses

By 1924, when the lavish Gleneagles Hotel was opened, the King's and Queen's Courses had already been in use for several years. In 1921, in fact, the first professional match between Britain and the United States was played over the King's, with the home side winning by a handsome nine points to three. It sowed the seeds for the first Ryder Cup matches in 1927.

James Braid, five times Open Champion and a member of that 1921 side, was commissioned to design the two courses. The King's is the regular venue for the Bell's Scottish Open and the hotel, which can accommodate 450 guests, boasts four all-weather tennis courts, a grass court, jogging circuits, pitch and putt, a bowling green and croquet lawns, as well as the Jackie Stewart Shooting School and Mark Phillips Equestrian Centre. It also incorporates a Country Club with squash courts, gymnasium, billiard and pool tables and a swimming pool.

The fifteenth hole

Jack Nicklaus has built a new championship course alongside the King's, which opens with a 362-yard par-four with a generous fairway and a big bunker to clear in front of the up-sloping green.

Aim as close as possible to the bunker at the second, which dog-legs gently left downhill, then try to position your tee shot on the right at the uphill third hole, with its blind second over a ridge towards a two-tier green.

The fourth is a long and difficult uphill par-four into the prevailing wind and, at 466 yards, plays a par-five for most, and there is little room for error at the 178-yard fifth with its plateau green protected front right by four bunkers.

Avoid being too far left off the tee at the par-five sixth, then try to keep your second on the right. At the seventh hole, named 'Kittle Kink', which means 'a tricky bend', you face a challenging tee shot over a ridge to an angled fairway. Then it is necessary to veer left to

The first hole

hit a second that must clear bunkers situated short of the target.

The tee at the short eighth is some twenty feet higher than a green ringed by four bunkers, while there is a two-tier green at the ninth, where you must drive on the left to find the best line in. A bunker on the left severely narrows the driving area at the tenth, a long and difficult par-five with a narrow two-tier green, replaced in 1990 to Braid's original design. Also long and difficult is the 230-yard 'short' eleventh, heavily bunkered left and right.

The tee shot at the 442-yard twelfth is blind over a bunkered ridge and must be kept left to open up the approach to a target narrowed by bunkers left and right.

Beware the 'Old Nick' bunker on the left when you drive up the 464-yard thirteenth, 'Braid's Brawest', then hope to snap up a birdie – maybe even an eagle two – at the driveable fourteenth.

You face another blind tee shot at the downhill 459-yard fifteenth and the line is on or left of the marker. An array of bunkers guards the green, with its steep slope beyond, at the tricky par-three sixteenth, and it is uphill all the way at the slight left-hand dog-leg seventeenth, where you must avoid trouble short right of the green.

Finally it is back downhill to the last, with the big hitters able to clear the large ridge crossing the fairway to get within range of a sizeable green, whose approach is heavily sand-trapped.

The par-three sixteenth hole   Overleaf: *The seventeenth green, with the hotel and the eighteenth hole behind*

Left: *the par-three thirteenth hole*

Above: *the fourth green*

Muirfield – The Honourable Company of Edinburgh Golfers

When the Open Championship was first staged in 1892 on the great links of Muirfield, on the Firth of Forth east of Edinburgh, celebrated amateur Harold Hilton won with a score of 305.

Harry Vardon won with a 316 tally there in 1896 and James Braid with 309 in 1901. Britain's Nick Faldo took the title with a 280 aggregate in 1987, but the Muirfield record is the 271 of Tom Watson in 1980, after a third-round sixty-four gave him a four strokes lead. Lee Trevino, Jack Nicklaus, Gary Player and Henry Cotton have been the other Open winners since the Second World War at the home of The Honourable Company of Edinburgh Golfers.

Nicklaus, who first played Muirfield as a teenage member of the 1959 US Walker Cup side, named the course he built in his home state of Ohio 'Muirfield Village', as a token of the esteem in which he held the East Lothian links.

The landing area at the par-four first hole narrows to around eleven yards, and many are the Open contenders who have come to grief there, but the 351-yard second, despite the out of bounds over the wall left and a nest of bunkers right of the green, offers a real birdie chance.

You lay up short of bunkers at the foot of two sand-hills guarding the narrow green at the 379-yard third, before firing to the elevated green, with four bunkers in front, at the par-three fourth. Then you face a 559-yard par-five, with a string of bunkers in driving range on the right and a ring of sand round the green.

To have a realistic chance of attacking the pin you must land your tee shot in the right half of the fairway at the long par-four sixth, a gentle dog-leg left, while the 185-yard seventh, again with an elevated, well-bunkered green, is played into the prevailing wind.

Nicklaus has described Muirfield's bunkers as 'the most fastidiously built I've ever seen', and there are seven of them on the right as you drive at the par-four eighth, a dog-leg right, partly blind over cross-bunkers.

An out of bounds wall left, leading up to the Greywalls Hotel, is a daunting feature of the 504-yard ninth, generally played into the wind. Nicklaus rates the 475-yard tenth, with its two big cross-bunkers, 'one of my all-time favourites', and the undulating eleventh, with its blind tee shot and ring of greenside bunkers, another fine hole.

The 381-yard twelfth demands deadly accuracy with drive and approach, while the uphill thirteenth measures only 152 yards, but its long narrow green is guarded by bunkers from which it is near-impossible to escape. Another testing par-four is the 449-yard fourteenth, with five bunkers along the left, and you must negotiate no fewer than thirteen bunkers at the 417-yard fifteenth before teeing up at the 188-yard sixteenth, with its right-to-left sloping target.

The 550-yard seventeenth, whose fairway is sprinkled with bunkers, is where Trevino spectacularly chipped in to wrest the lead from Tony Jacklin in the 1972 Open, and the 448-yard final hole has two large greenside bunkers, one with a grassy island in the middle.

The Royal and Ancient clubhouse and the eighteenth green

The Royal and Ancient Golf Club of St Andrews

The Old Course at St Andrews can count J.H. Taylor, James Braid, Jack Nicklaus, Bobby Jones, Severiano Ballesteros, Nick Faldo, Sam Snead, Peter Thomson and Bobby Locke among its Open Champions.

It is the very home of golf. The Royal and Ancient Golf Club of St Andrews, the game's ruling body, has its headquarters there, and golfers from all corners of the world make pilgrimages to play the centuries-old links which Old Tom Morris and his son once strode.

At nearly 7,000 yards, with its blind shots, vast double greens and cavernous bunkers, it presents a mighty test, yet, in 1970 before a storm brought play in the Open to a halt, defending champion Tony Jacklin went to the turn in twenty-nine strokes, and in the 1987 Dunhill Nations Cup matches Curtis Strange of the United States accumulated ten birdies in a sixty-two.

The opening hole on the Old Course possesses the widest fairway in the world. The premium is on the second shot across the famous – or infamous – Swilcan Burn, frequently to a flag close to the bank just beyond. Play too safe and three putts threaten.

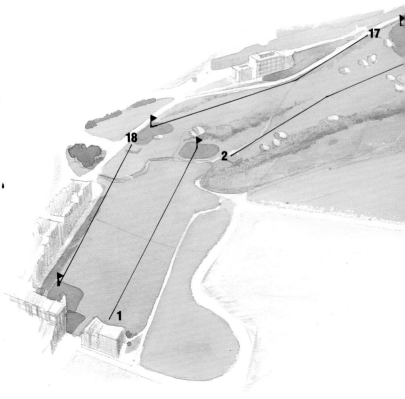

There is masses of room to the left over the first few holes. The one thing not to do is slice your tee shot. However, as at the second, the best line from which to attack the flag is from the right. Beware a wickedly undulating green.

Favour the right side again off the tee at the third, but avoid a string of pot bunkers, while you could choose to aim way left from the tee at the 463-yard fourth, then fire over a veritable ocean of sand-traps. Seven bunkers await the drive on the right at the 564-yard fifth, so keep left, then either lay up short of a hill set with two bunkers or go for the huge green beyond.

The fairway is invisible from the sixth tee, but you must bisect two clusters of bunkers before playing over a plateau to the green. Then it is into the famous six-hole 'Loop' with a blind drive over the hill at the seventh (372 yards), then the first of only two short holes (178 yards) and the almost driveable 356-yard ninth, with its two big fairway bunkers.

The tenth is similar at 342 yards, again with heather and gorse left, while at the 172-yard eleventh the severely sloping green is wider than it is deep and pro-tected by the Strath and Hill bunkers. The 316-yard twelfth can be driven – through a 'minefield' of hidden hazards – to a narrow, undulating green.

It is trouble all the way at the par-four thirteenth, where you aim left or right of large bunkers, risking evil kicks, while the 567-yard fourteenth is a classic par-five with out of bounds right, the Beardie bunkers left, and Hell Bunker to negotiate with your approach.

The 413-yard fifteenth offers some relief, but at the next you must choose between driving 'twixt the out of bounds and the Principal's Nose bunkers, or aiming much further left.

You must drive over 'the sheds' at the corner of the dog-leg seventeenth, with the Old Course Hotel grounds out of bounds, to set up your approach to the celebrated 'Road Hole', so called because of the road beyond. Often the Road Bunker on the other side of the green causes more grief. The 354-yard eighteenth, with its Valley of Sin in front, has often been driven, but its big green is testing.

'Hell Bunker' on the fourteenth hole

'Road Hole Bunker' on the seventeenth

A view across the Old Course back towards the Old Town of St Andrews

Swilcan Bridge on the eighteenth hole, with the clubhouse in the background

Overleaf: *Early morning on the Old Course, with players putting on the first green*

Royal Troon

Royal Troon on Scotland's Ayrshire coast was the scene of the 1989 Open Championship, when America's Mark Calcavecchia defeated Australians Greg Norman and Wayne Grady in the Championship's first four-hole play-off.

Conditions were dry and fast-running as the trio tied on 275, thirteen below par, but it was a different story in 1982 when Tom Watson won with a 284 total, and the course's testing finishing stretch became a trial of strength and stamina.

Britain's Arthur Havers won with a score of 295 when in 1923 the Open was first played at Troon, over which the Jumbo jets now take off from the adjacent Prestwick International Airport.

The 364-yard first, with the beach to the right, offers a quick birdie, but the second, with three cross-bunkers in range from the tee, is much tougher. Players have to lay up in front of Gyaws Burn, which crosses the third fairway 275 yards out, before tackling the 557-yard fourth, where you must steer left of a big fairway bunker and finally overcome a split-level green.

Many players in the 1989 Open fell into the trap fronting the right half of the green at the 210-yard fifth high above the beach, but there are three more bunkers to the left and you must take enough club. The sixth, at 577 yards, is the longest hole in championship golf in Britain, with bunkers all along its length and a deceptive two-tier green to contend with.

The 'Postage Stamp' eighth hole

They call the 402-yard seventh 'Tel-el-Kebir' and it is a real tester, with a big carry from the tee to a target surrounded by cross-bunkers, and then a second to an upward-sloping target set in the hill. The 'Postage Stamp' 126-yard eighth is one of the most famous holes in golf. In 1950 German amateur Hermann Tissies took fifteen here. In 1973 the 71-year-old Gene Sarazen holed it in one. It is a tiny target in a sea of sand.

You must lay up short of the bunkers left from the tee at the picturesque ninth, with its small contoured green and trees beyond. There are dunes left and heather and gorse right at the tricky tenth, and the railway running down the right at the eleventh passes within a few feet of the green.

The 431-yard twelfth is not too demanding, but the 465-yard thirteenth certainly is as you aim out to a distant angled fairway. Three bunkers protect the entrance to the green at the 179-yard fourteenth, and you must drive long and straight at the fifteenth to avoid three fairway traps, before playing to a narrow green.

Into the wind a ditch crossing the fairway must often be played short of, at the 542-yard sixteenth. The one shot to be played at the par-three seventeenth is of 223 yards and, with the green falling away steeply on both sides, it is most demanding. The carry to the fairway is some 225 yards from the Open tees at the eighteenth, with its intimidating out of bounds path in front of the clubhouse just beyond the green.

The 'Railway Hole' eleventh

The seventh hole

The sixth hole

The eighteenth hole, with the hotel behind on the hill at Turnberry

Turnberry Hotel and Golf Courses

Turnberry is surely among the world's most spectacularly beautiful settings for a golf course – in this case two courses, the Ailsa Championship layout and the gentler Arran.

The links, on the Ayrshire coast, is spread in front of the grand Turnberry Hotel atop the hill, and affords magnificient views across the sea to the mountainous Isle of Arran, the Mull of Kintyre and the Ailsa Craig.

Eight of its first eleven holes are beside the sea, the ninth with the lighthouse on the left. The wind is a vital factor. When it is calm scores like the sixty-three of Greg Norman *en route* to victory in the 1986 Volvo Seniors British Open, and the 268 total by which Tom Watson pipped Jack Nicklaus in their epic Open duel of 1977, are possible. When it blows anything below eighty can be impressive.

You must pick your way between fairway bunkers off the tee at the 350-yard first. The second, back towards the first tee, and the third, in the opposite direction, are more testing par-fours.

The 167-yard fourth, frequently called 'Woe-be-Tide', is the first of the seaside holes, a tricky par-three fronted by a deep bunker, while the fifth hole is a 440-yard par-four, where you must drive to the right of two big sand-traps.

At 222 yards the sixth is a long short hole, and when the wind is against you, you can be hitting all you've got. You play out to the right across an unnerving expanse of rough ground, then veer left at the uphill par-five seventh. The eighth fairway slopes left to right towards a big bunker in the driving area, and the target is a plateau green.

It is the thrill of most golfers' lives to drive at the ninth from a tee perched high above the rocks and lapping waves. You aim at a cairn on the horizon and must avoid a hook at all costs.

You then drive down along the rocky shoreline at the left-hand dog-leg tenth hole, and climb to another pulpit tee situated high above the rocks to play the 177-yard eleventh.

A monument high on the right at the 441-yard twelfth commemorates those who died in the First World War. The thirteenth, with its tricky plateau green, requires a drive between two big bunkers, and the fourteenth demands that you keep right of another big trap and is often played into a stiff breeze.

The 209-yard fifteenth usually plays a long iron. The big trouble is to the right, but if you go too far left you risk bunker trouble.

If you are short in two at the sixteenth your ball can spin back down the bank into the 'moat', and there is a long carry to the uphill-all-the-way 500-yard seventeenth.

At 431 yards the last hole is not over-demanding, but you must avoid bunkers left and clinging scrub to the right from the tee, before pitching to the broad green where Watson hit to within inches of the flag to close out Nicklaus in 1977.

The fifth hole

Left: *The seventh hole, with the lighthouse in the distance*

The long par-three sixth

REST OF BRITAIN

The history of competitive golf in Britain is enriched at regular intervals by mention of Royal Lytham and St Anne's – rather surprisingly, some may think, in view of its location. Golf is essentially a rural pursuit, a cross-country game, and was so in the early days of this club. But today the course is an oasis in the middle of a town, the forerunner of purpose-built new town developments. In this case the town was not inspired by any public authority but was the brainchild of enterprising Victorian builders, who recognized the demand for pleasant villas in an agreeable seaside area to house the wealthy merchants and businessmen of Liverpool and Blackpool. Since this district was conveniently located on the railway line between these two major centres it was the ideal site. Lytham is thus a unique town because, unlike the vast majority of towns, which develop over the centuries, it was created in a short space of time and remains a monument to almost pure Victorian architecture and values. This means, however, that the golf course is penned in by the railway line along one border and by residential streets along the others. Access is accordingly severely restricted, and such amenities as car parking must be provided far from the course with shuttle buses to convey spectators to the club.

Every time a major event is held at Lytham there is speculation that this, surely, must be its last tournament, because it cannot possibly accommodate ever-bigger promotions. Such speculation started as long ago as the 1963 Open championship, but on each occasion rumours of Lytham's demise as a major venue have proved to be premature. There are two reasons why the Royal and Ancient Golf Club of St Andrews and the PGA European Tour remain faithful to Lytham despite the inconvenience: it has a well-earned reputation for enthusiastic co-operation with promoting bodies and for unstinting efforts to make the system

The eighteenth hole and hotel at the Belfry

work; and the course is of such quality that any notion of dropping it from championship golf is all but unthinkable. Every championship course has its adherents, but it is more than likely that a survey of the best and most experienced golfers would put Lytham top of the poll as the most comprehensive examination of golfing skill and character. Having said that, it must be admitted that Lytham does not look the part. Although it is a links, it is a mile inland and the dunes, if such they can be called, are puny hummocks, mere corrugations on an otherwise flat expanse of featureless land relieved only by the occasional tree or shrub. There is nothing heroic about the landscape and this economy of scale is one of the elements which makes Lytham such a good test. After all, a small rise will deflect an ill-directed golf ball as surely as a mountain and we might define the secret of Lytham as the subtlety of minimalism. There is nothing minimal about the bunkering, for the playing surface is pockmarked by a profusion of deep pots, sometimes arranged in ribbons as if an enemy squadron in line ahead had unloaded its bombs across the fairway.

One such hole is the seventeenth, site of the most famous shot in golf. In the 1926 Open championship Bobby Jones pulled his drive into the angle of the dog-leg and his ball finished in sand. The mashie shot of 175 yards which Jones played to the heart of the unseen green is commemorated by a plaque, and the club with which he performed this championship-winning stroke is displayed in the clubhouse. It was at Lytham in 1969 that Tony Jacklin consolidated his place among the modern greats of golf by winning the Open championship, to which he added the American Open eleven months later; and it was at Lytham that Severiano Ballesteros won his first championship in 1979. Much play was made at the time of Ballesteros's luck in finding a playable lie when his ball finished in a car park. The incident was greatly exaggerated because, as at all Opens, a drive which just trails off the fairway is

Denis Thatcher congratulates Tony Jacklin on retaining the Ryder Cup at the Belfry

severely punished by the rough, whereas a really wide drive, as Ballesteros well appreciated, finishes on clear ground where the grass has been trampled flat by the gallery. Ballesteros made a point of provoking his rivals, and their taunts about luck, every time he won a major championship for years afterwards. And when he repeated his triumph at Lytham in the storm-lashed 1988 championship he played one of the great rounds of modern golf. Going into the last round Nick Price led by two strokes and he scored sixty-nine – effectively sixty-eight, because he deliberately charged his approach putt on the home green in a do-or-die attempt to force a play-off. Even a final sixty-nine on top of a two-stroke lead would have been good enough to win almost any championship, but Price finished second to the amazing Spaniard.

Other historic feats at Lytham in recent years include Brian Huggett crafting a winning seventy-four in a full gale which sent scores rocketing into the mid-eighties in the 1970 Dunlop Masters, and the coming of age of Nick Faldo in the Ryder Cup match of 1977. Once again Huggett was involved, this time as captain of what was then still the British and Irish team. Faldo was then a callow nineteen-year-old and had not yet won a major tournament. Huggett thus faced a common dilemma

for captains of that era: whether to pair his strong players together and risk throwing away a few points by pairing the novices with each other, or to mix youth with experience and give the veteran the traditional instruction of a father taking his son to a cat-house: 'I give you the boy; give me back the man.'

Huggett gave Faldo to Peter Oosterhuis, a man who had topped the order of merit table four years in a row. Oosterhuis had an outstanding record in the Ryder Cup as a singles player, but his erratic brilliance made him a difficult man to fit into a partnership. The pairing was a gamble and, if the truth were known, Huggett probably reasoned that this pairing was an exercise in damage limitation. But, as was to happen ten years later when Severiano Ballesteros nursed the young José Maria Olazabal safely through his nervous baptism of Ryder Cup warfare, the experience of Oosterhuis and the talent of Faldo proved an irresistible combination on that occasion. They beat Raymond Floyd and Lou Graham in the foursomes and Jack Nicklaus and Floyd in the fourballs, and when it came to the time for Faldo to go solo, he knocked off Tom Watson in the singles while his mentor beat Jerry McGee. So that motley partnership accounted for four of the home team's seven and a half points.

Lindrick has a special place in the annals of professional golf because it was on this lovely heath course, unfortunately split by a busy road, that in 1957 Britain and Ireland had their solitary success in the Ryder Cup match, interrupting a bleak succession of failures. On the face of it, this triumph was a slightly freakish result, one of those things which come along occasionally in sport. After all, the same players had been trounced before and would be trounced again.

But anyone who was privileged to know that year's captain will also know that Dai Rees was a man who was incapable of contemplating the possibility of defeat. Rees was indefatigable. Like those mechanical toys in television advertisements, he was the one with the long-life battery. He knew that he could beat any golfer who ever lived and, by a mixture of bombast, Welsh oratory and enthusiasm, he persuaded his team that they could too: a considerable feat of evangelism in the light of experience. Rees also led by example, gaining the only point in the foursomes in partnership with Ken Bousfield, and then inspiring his troops to rally in the singles by overwhelming Ed Furgol seven and six in the singles.

Yorkshire has to yield the palm to its sporting rival and neighbour, Lancashire, in great links courses such as Royal Birkdale, Hillside, Southport and Ainsdale, Formby and Royal Lytham, but the county of the white rose comes into its own for heath courses. Ganton, near Scarborough, is a gem, although some of the bunkering sets it in the era when Harry Vardon was the club professional. Even when the wind comes whistling across the moors, some of the hazards do not come into play for professionals armed with the latest high-tech equipment, making it somewhat of a second shot course in tournament trim. But the tight and cunning design still preserves Ganton as a fine test for the best players, and an outstanding one for the fortunate members.

Moor Allerton is one of a distinguished run of courses just north of Leeds, including the renowned Moortown and the less well-known but arguably superior

Nick Faldo on his way to winning the Open championship

Sandy Lyle, Open Champion at Royal St Georges in 1985, holes a birdie putt on the fifteenth hole

Alwoodley. Moor Allerton is built on land as turbulent as a rumpled eiderdown. Some of the climbs are fearsome, particularly when climbing up to the clubhouse plateau wearied by exertion, but this is the price which must be paid for the exhilaration of the most stimulating shot in golf, hitting from a high tee into a beckoning valley. Once down in the valley the golf changes mood with a succession of holes which put more strain on the brain than the calf muscles. In these sheltered nether regions the course is more heavily wooded than is usual for heath courses, and there is a high premium on shaping your shots to find the greens. For tournament golf a brisk wind is a positive asset to lend spice to the competition and speed the process of winnowing the wheat from the chaff. For lesser mortals bent on agreeable social golf Moor Allerton, like Ganton, is best played on a still summer's day, to enjoy the full enchantment of the game as it should be, with God and the larks above and the cares of everyday life consigned to oblivion for a few blessed hours.

Fulford, the original home of the Benson and Hedges International, is certainly the most popular Yorkshire course among the professionals. If it is not quite in the championship class it is certainly a most splendid members' course, and the narrow fairways through the woodland provide a good test for the professionals, especially on a windy day. But what makes it so popular is the excellence of the flattish greens. This means that the man with a hot putter has a chance for a birdie on every green: in one round in 1985 Ian Woosnam had ten of them, eight in a row. The potential for dramatic charges makes for the most exciting tournament golf, never more so than in 1988 when Peter Baker faced a twenty-five-footer for an eagle which would tie his score with the leader, Nick Faldo. Baker made it, and in the sudden death play-off he faced the same situation again – same green, much the same length of putt. Again he stroked his eagle putt straight into the centre of the hole for his first victory on the PGA European Tour and yet another triumph for Fulford's greenkeeping staff. Tony Johnstone repeated the double-eagle feat in the 1991 Murphy's Cup to defeat Eamonn Darcy.

The Benson and Hedges International forsook Fulford for one year in 1979 in favour of St Mellion, a new development in Cornwall. The course – although exhilarating enough for resort visitors – was not quite up to snuff for tournament play. The developers, the redoubtable Bond brothers, therefore vowed to create a championship course that would make the players' eyes pop with wonder. For their part, Benson and Hedges vowed, 'Do that and we'll be back.' Jack Nicklaus was commissioned to perform the requisite miracle. The nature of the site demanded a miracle, because a golf course cannot be constructed on a near-vertical hillside. The first challenge for Nicklaus was to create the site for the course, by blasting sizeable chunks of Cornwall into a precipitous ravine just wide enough to accommodate two trout poachers splashing along in single file. The Benson and Hedges returned to St Mellion in 1990, and in the locker room many lurid adjectives were applied to the new course. During the first two tournaments a distressingly high proportion of the contestants retired in mid-round for medical reasons, mostly bruised egos. The nature of the site presents the golfer with some novel problems, and only those with the wit to devise novel responses can hope to prosper on this wondrous addition to the tournament scene.

The island of Jersey does not fit happily in a chapter on the golf of the Midlands and northern England, but geographically it would not fit happily in any other chapter, and it is emotionally well suited to the mood of lyricism. Jersey is a citadel of creature comforts and the pursuit of pleasure, and La Moye well reflects the island's temperament. It is a fun golf course, just as the Jersey Open is a fun tournament. This judgment is not supposed to be a high-minded put-down – far from it.

After all, golf should be fun, among other things. The course is a mixture of flattish pasture on a high plateau and genuine links. It is also a mixture of excellent golf holes and some whose main function is to get the players from here to there. Again that may sound like condemning the course with faint praise, but these changes of pace and style serve a valuable purpose for tournament golf. They provide many birdie opportunities and they lull the players into a false sense of complacency, inducing them to drop their guard just as they encounter a really strong run of holes. There is nothing like the feeling that a course is a piece of cake to bring golfers into rude confrontation with the truism that golf is a humbling game. La Moye has sharp claws.

The tournament has taken the place of the old Swiss Open as the holiday event of the year. Many players take their families. Tommy Horton, latest in the succession of great Jersey professionals, such as Harry Vardon and Ted Ray, makes sure that everyone has comfortable accommodation and briefs them on the best places to wine and dine. The promoters, bless them, recklessly flout the sensible convention of 'no drink in the press room' and the machine-gun chatter of typewriters is punctuated by the trench mortar fire of popping corks. Golf is a serious business, and getting more serious year by year, but it must be hoped that there will always be room in the calendar for one Jersey Open, and preferably *the* Jersey Open.

Jack Nicklaus putting at St Mellion

The Belfry

The Belfry, near Sutton Coldfield in the Midlands, is the headquarters of the Professional Golfers' Association and host to the English Open. It has two eighteen-hole courses, the Brabazon and the Derby, which were designed by former Ryder Cup international Dave Thomas and BBC television commentator Peter Alliss, as well as a first-class hotel and leisure complex.

In 1985 and 1989 it was the setting for the Johnnie Walker Ryder Cup matches between Europe and the United States. Europe's triumph over the 7,176-yard Brabazon layout in 1985 was the first home win since 1957, and crowds flocked to a venue ideally served by road, rail and air transport. The matches return in 1993.

Above all the Brabazon is a driver's course and a bunker right must be avoided from the first tee before the approach is slotted between two more traps to a lozenge-shaped green with water to the left.

The ninth hole

At the 349-yard second a stream crosses ten yards short of the small, narrow green, which is bunkered left, right and front, and the tee shot is tight. It is also tight at the third, with a bunker right some 250 yards from the tee and the green another 215 yards distant.

You face an enormous carry to a far from generous fairway, with traps left and right, at the par-five fourth, then a lay-up short of the stream fronting the sideways-on green, but the stream across the fifth is comfortably carried unless there is a headwind.

A lake to the left threatens all the way along the 396-yard sixth, where you must fly a stream from the tee, while the 183-yard seventh demands an accurate hit to an elevated green with a vertical-faced bunker in front and more sand behind. The 460-yard eighth is a great driving hole, with the lake narrowing the fairway from the left, and requires a long, accurate second to a target beyond a stream. If you hit too far right off the tee at the ninth uphill to the clubhouse you face a second to a steeply sloping green across the edge of the lake.

The short par-four tenth, where Tour players try to drive the green

Severiano Ballesteros is reputedly the first man in a tournament to hit the green with a left-to-right drive at the much talked-about 275-yard tenth – across the water amid the trees. Most play safe with an iron and a pitch.

You must skirt two large bunkers on the left off the eleventh tee, then fly a stream fronting the uphill green at the 235-yard twelfth. Bunkers left and right must also be negotiated at the par-four thirteenth, and mounds beyond the green at the 194-yard fourteenth help to arrest bold tee shots.

All but the mightiest hitters go for a lay-up second short, right at the tough 550-yard fifteenth, while you try to cut the corner at the gentle dog-leg left sixteenth before tackling a tricky tiered green. Trees make cutting the corner at the right-hand dog-leg 575-yard seventeenth a real risk, but if you take the safety first route, a stream crossing the fairway comes into play.

The last, at 474 yards, is one of Britain's most testing finishing holes. You hit over the lake twice – often with wood both times – before wrestling with a three-tiered green. The full terrors of the hole were exposed on the last day of the 1989 Ryder Cup matches, when Seve Ballesteros, Paul Azinger, Payne Stewart and Mark Calcavecchia all found the water, enabling the matches to be tied for only the second time in their history.

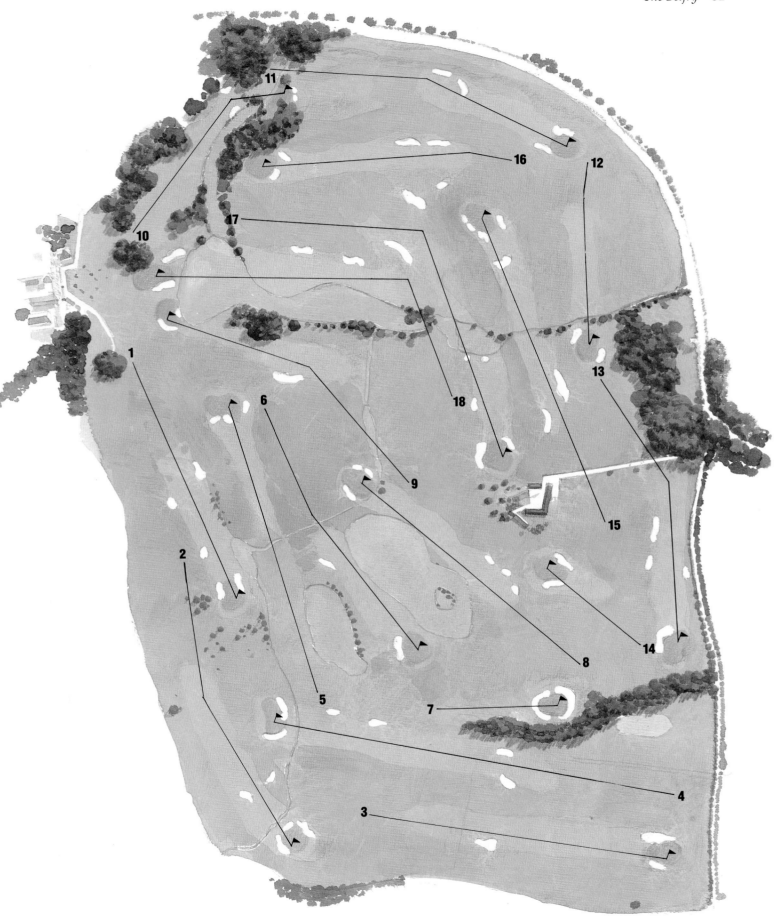

The seventeenth hole

The eighteenth hole and clubhouse

Fulford

With one exception the Fulford course in York was used to stage the Benson and Hedges International every year from 1971, when Tony Jacklin won, to 1989 – when Gordon Brand Junior took the title to secure a return to Ryder Cup action at The Belfry.

Jack Newton, Graham Marsh and Greg Norman of Australia, Lee Trevino and Tom Weiskopf of America and Britain's Sandy Lyle, Sam Torrance and Mark James have won there, and the young Englishman Peter Baker made his breakthrough in the 1988 event by eagling the par-five eighteenth to tie with Nick Faldo, then eagling it again to beat him in the play-off.

For the first six holes, club professional Bryan Hessay explains, the wind is normally right to left, while from the twelfth to the eighteenth it is generally left to right. Out of bounds on both stretches is to the left.

A row of tall trees lines the left side of the fairway at the 412-yard first, where two bunkers left must be avoided off the tee. The out of bounds can come very much into play at the 438-yard second, as Denmark's Steen Tinning discovered in round four of the 1989 Benson and Hedges event, when he hooked three three-irons and a four-iron over the fence there to run up a thirteen!

A long-iron tee shot is required at the 189-yard third, while a copse on either side of the fairway must be bisected off the fourth tee, and a big tree left and a bunker right guard the green. There are bunkers left and right at the 167-yard fifth, while the 561-yard sixth, out of range in two, demands two deadly accurate blows to set up the approach, and the 415-yard seventh demands that you aim for the left half of the fairway to open up the green.

The eighth is a 371-yard dog-leg right, with big trees ruling out corner-cutting and a sand-trap waiting if you aim too far left, and the ninth is an eminently birdieable par-five at 486 yards, with an uphill green guarded by bunkers left.

You will need a middle iron to a large undulating green, bunkered both sides, at the 165-yard tenth, while, despite its daunting 514 yards, the eleventh offers another birdie chance if you miss bunkers left and right off the tee.

Bryan Hessay recommends a one-iron and a pitch to the plateau green at the twelfth, but rates the 473-yard thirteenth the toughest par-four on the course. There is out of bounds left all the way – it's within fifteen yards of the green.

After his thirteen at the second, Steen Tinning made amends in that final round on 13 August 1989, when he holed-in-one with an eight-iron at the 161-yard fourteenth, which has a ditch and trees in front, to win a £13,000 Volvo car.

The fifteenth plays a drive and medium iron, but a one-iron is advised off the tee at the 383-yard sixteenth, aimed at the left centre of the fairway, and that is also the case at the 356-yard seventeenth, where there is a huge oak to contend with to the right. A ditch, and the tree up which Bernhard Langer once climbed to chip his ball out of it, lie just short of the green.

Drive left centre of the right-hand dog-leg 480-yard eighteenth to set up a definite birdie chance.

The fifth hole

The sixteenth hole

The eighteenth hole and clubhouse

La Moye

La Moye, a clifftop links close to the airport on the Channel Island of Jersey, has come on by leaps and bounds as a golfing test since it was first used as a tournament venue, and now there is a magnificent new clubhouse affording a panoramic view on a clear day across the course to Jersey's sister islands. Originally designed in 1902 by Percy Boomer, father of the late Aubrey Boomer, La Moye had another five holes built in 1976.

Brian Huggett, Sandy Lyle, Tony Jacklin, who lived on Jersey for several years, Ian Woosnam and Sam Torrance are among the winners of the Jersey Open there, and in 1989 Christy O'Connor Junior's victory after a play-off against Denis Durnian was the key to his Ryder Cup return at The Belfry.

The 165-yard opening hole can be a tester in a stiff breeze, the tee having been switched from behind to in front of the clubhouse, while the 518-yard second, a sharp dog-leg to the right, offers a very realistic birdie opportunity. You then turn back to play the 188-yard third to a plateau green, before commencing the down-up-down-up sequence of holes to and from the cliffs from the fourth to the seventh.

The approach to the fourth green, tucked around the corner of the hotel, is tricky, while the fifth green is tightly bunkered, with trees beyond, and the par-five sixth has a deceptive second shot.

You leapfrog over dead ground after your tee shot through the valley at the seventh, then drive over the brow of a gentle hill at the eighth, before pitching downhill to the green with its trees beyond. An elevated tee is used at the ninth, a 410-yard par-four demanding a drive across the road to the clubhouse and a testing second up to a new plateau green at eleven o'clock.

You drive between the dunes along the tenth before aiming to a high green at one o'clock, then tackle the uphill eleventh, a 497-yard dog-leg right.

The twelfth is an all carry 166-yard short hole over a sea of humps and hollows, and the thirteenth a 427-yard downhill par-four bending to the left. Overshooting the green can present huge problems.

At the 190-yard fourteenth you hit from a hilltop tee across a deep valley to a hilltop green, missing which can leave you severely stretched to save par. You must then carry your drive over rough ground at the fifteenth, with deep trouble to the right and the clifftop beyond the green.

The 479-yard sixteenth back to the clubhouse from the cliff edge is no easy birdie hole, many shots finishing short right, nor is the 428-yard seventeenth, back to the clifftop, with the difficult to judge uphill second. Hit the fairway to set up a last birdie chance at the eighteenth, where you pitch downhill to an ample green.

The eleventh and twelfth greens

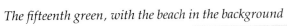

The fifteenth green, with the beach in the background

The sixth hole

The eighteenth green and clubhouse

Lindrick

Lindrick Golf Club, near Worksop, has been the setting for many men's and women's events, both pro and amateur, but none more important than the 1957 Ryder Cup matches, when Dai Rees led his men to their first victory over the Americans since 1933, thanks to a dramatic $6^1/_2$–$1^1/_2$ singles success after they had lost the foursomes 3–1.

Originally the Sheffield and District Golf Club, Lindrick, which celebrates its centenary in 1991, lies in heathland among trees and acres of gorse, and its limestone subsoil ensures excellent year-round drainage.

The first hole is a gentle left-hand dog-leg, with trees left and right and a string of bunkers on the right running up to and beside the green, while the second, a shorter par-four, is a much more severe dog-leg to the left. Unless you drive 200 yards past the end of the trees you will have no sight of the target.

It is all carry at the 163-yard third to a well-trapped green, and the par-five fourth is a dog-leg right between two bunkers with tree trouble short left of the green, a natural amphitheatre once used for prizefighting and cockfighting. The par-four fifth is ringed by sand with trees beyond, the sixth another short hole heavily bunkered on the right, and the seventh a dog-leg left around more trees.

There is plenty of fairway to aim at down the eighth, also a dog-leg left with trees and bunkers narrowing the target, but trees crowd in left and right at the ninth, which has two bunkers short of the green. A nest of sand-traps on the right, close to the third green, must be avoided off the tee at the 368-yard tenth. You aim through the trees at a green heavily bunkered front and right, with trees beyond, at the 173-yard eleventh, before tackling the 464-yard twelfth, with the encroaching out of bounds down the left all the way.

The thirteenth dog-legs left between trees and acres of gorse, with two traps at the neck in the driving area and a cluster of cross-bunkers to clear short of the green. There is then a long carry over the gorse at the par-five fourteenth, with a line of bunkers coming into play as they jut in on the left, and more short, as well as left and right, of target.

Trees crowd in left and at the rear of the green at the par-four fifteenth, and at the longer sixteenth, with its meandering fairway and out of bounds awaiting a quick hook. There are bunkers galore in the run-up to the green at the 397-yard seventeenth, back among the gorse, while the relatively new eighteenth, bunkered all around the front, is one of the few par-three finishing holes on British championship courses, at 206 yards.

The fourth hole

The seventeenth hole, with the main road running behind the green

Royal Birkdale

The Royal Birkdale links on Lancashire's Irish Sea coast were originally laid out by George Low, but in the 1930s Fred Hawtree and J.H. Taylor redesigned them, and they are rated among the very best tests of golf in the world. They have staged a multitude of major events, including the Open Championship, with Peter Thomson (twice), Arnold Palmer, Lee Trevino, Johnny Miller, Tom Watson and, most recently, Ian Baker-Finch emerging as winners; and the Ryder Cup, which ended in a draw there in 1969. With most fairways flat, and greens generally well defined, Royal Birkdale is a much fairer test than many traditional seaside links.

The first plays as a dog-leg left around a big bunker, while the second, thirty yards shorter at 418 yards, is a straight-along par-four with bunkers front, left and right and trees beyond the green. There is a long carry from the third tee, and two traps to be avoided on the right. The 205-yard fourth is bunkered left and right, and so is the 348-yard fifth, only much more so.

Bunkers left and right wait to ensure the drive at the par-five sixth, a dog-leg right to a green with trees left and beyond. From a high tee at the par-three seventh, a 156-yarder, you can expect wind problems, and the same applies at the 460-yard eighth, where you drive across a veritable ocean of bunkers to the narrowest of targets.

An angled fairway severely tests the blind tee shot at the ninth, with trouble waiting on the right. The big

The eighth hole

danger is a hook off the tee at the tenth, a sharp dog-leg left, and the same is true at the 411-yard eleventh, but a row of bunkers waits to trap a tee shot aimed too far to the right.

The 186-yard twelfth is set among the sandhills close to the sea, so beware the wind once more. At more than 500 yards the thirteenth is a testing par-five, with a long carry to an angled fairway sprinkled with bunkers, then you climb high up the dunes to the tee at the 201-yard fourteenth, last of Royal Birkdale's short holes, to hit across a valley and road to a well-trapped target.

The 545-yard fifteenth is rated among the best holes on the course. You must hit the fairway to be in a position to attack the green over a mass of fairway sand-traps. Arnold Palmer took an adventurous route at the sixteenth in the 1961 Open, and a plaque in the right rough marks the spot from which he crashed a muscular recovery to the green.

It was at the 525-yard seventeenth in the 1969 Ryder Cup that Open Champion Tony Jacklin holed a 'tram-liner' to draw level with Jack Nicklaus in the final single. To get there he had to drive through a forbidding 'tunnel' between high dunes.

At the heavily bunkered eighteenth, played as a 474-yard par-four in the English Open in 1988, Nicklaus and Jacklin halved, Nicklaus conceding Jacklin's final putt to ensure that the whole match was tied in character-istically sporting fashion.

The third hole

The fifth hole

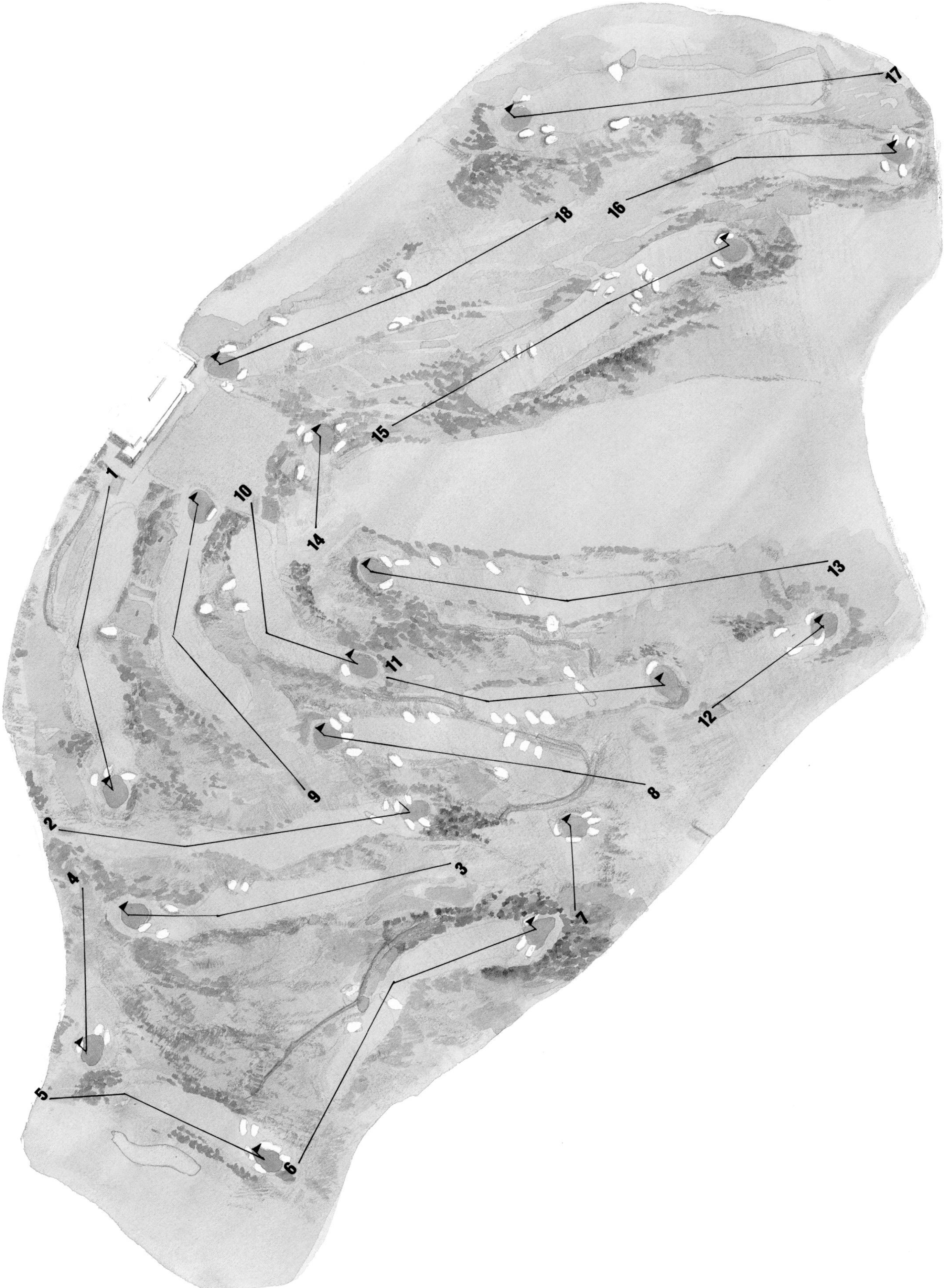
1
2
3
4
5
6
7
8
9
10
11
12
13
14
15
16
17
18

An aerial view of the seventh hole

Royal Lytham and St Anne's

When Severiano Ballesteros won the 1979 Open on the Lancashire links of Royal Lytham and St Anne's they called him the 'car park champion' because of repeated dramatic recoveries from wide of the fairway – one, indeed, from a car park. When the Spanish star won the third of his Opens back at Lytham in 1988 he followed a much less circuitous route.

Bobby Jones, whose amazing 'mashie' shot from a bunker at the seventeenth is recalled by a plaque, was the first Open winner at Royal Lytham in 1926. Bobby Locke, Peter Thomson, left-hander Bob Charles and Gary Player were also winners there, but perhaps the most memorable victory of them all was Tony Jacklin's in 1969 – the first Open triumph by a Briton since Max Faulkner in 1951.

It is not one of the most attractive Open settings, with houses all around, a railway line running down the right of the opening holes and no view of the sea, but it does have a grand old clubhouse with the Dormy House behind.

Lytham is the only major championship course in Britain which opens with a par-three – David Graham and Lanny Wadkins had holes in one there in the last two Opens.

Trees separate the course from the railway right at the 420-yard second, as they do at the third, a 458-yard par-four with bunkers all the way down the left. You play the par-four fourth, a dog-leg left, from a raised tee, and must hit your tee shot on the right to set up the approach to a green ringed by five sand-traps.

The 212-yard fifth is guarded by six traps, and tee and green are elevated either end of a 180-yard carry, while the par-five sixth, a slight left-hand dog-leg, tempts you

to cut the corner, However, a bunker with trees beyond bars that route. Big hitters going for the green should beware nine bunkers in their path.

The railway comes back into play down the right at the 551-yard seventh, where there are bunkers left and right in driving range as you head for a large but well-protected green, and at the 394-yard eighth, with its generous fairway and steep, bunkered bank sixty yards short of the plateau green.

Buildings beyond the green distract the eye at the 162-yard ninth, whose green is ringed by bunkers, and you must slot your tee shot between two sandhills at the 334-yard tenth before playing the huge 542-yard eleventh. This has four fairway bunkers within driving range, trees left to ensnare the second shot and more trees behind a tightly trapped target.

The 201-yard twelfth, only back nine par-three, is played out of the trees, while the thirteenth has ten bunkers down the right but, like the fourteenth, the drive is not too terrifying. You must avoid bunkers left and right off the tee at the demanding 468-yard fifteenth, with its crop of cross-bunkers short of the green, and the drive is blind over a ridge at the par-four sixteenth, which has trees and bunkers left and more bunkers short and either side of the green.

No fewer than eighty-two of Lytham's 191 bunkers are on the last six holes, and eighteen of these are on the 453-yard seventeenth, most of them running up the left and crossing the fairway at the neck of the left-hand dog-leg. Stay right or your second is blind.

Seven cross-bunkers threaten the drive at the last, and more ring a green set right under the clubhouse windows.

An aerial view of the eighth and ninth holes

The par-three ninth hole

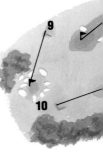

The fifteenth hole

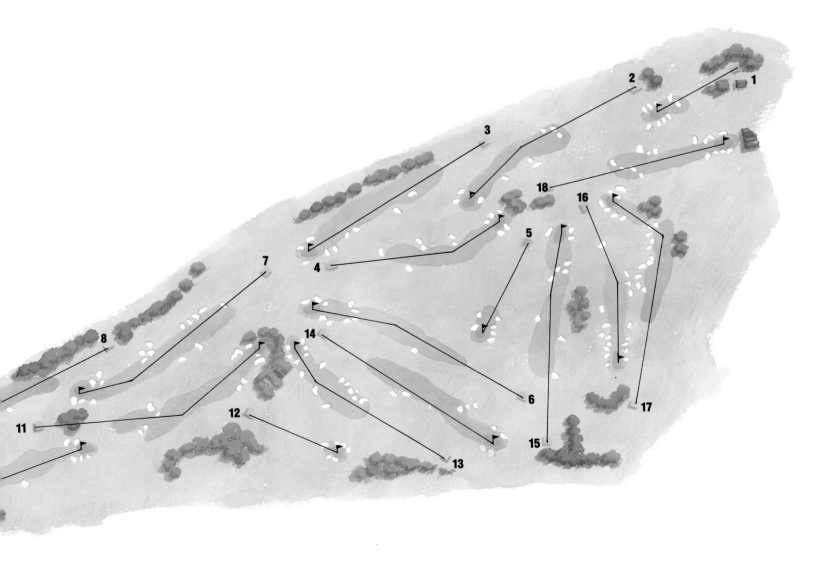

The thatched starter's box, with the clubhouse behind

Royal St George's

When the links of Royal St George's at Sandwich on Kent's English Channel coast were re-introduced to the Open Championship rota in 1981, after a thirty-two-year lapse, American Bill Rogers won with a score of 276 – precisely fifty strokes better than J.H. Taylor's winning aggregate when the Open was staged there for the first time outside Scotland in 1894.

Harry Vardon fired a winning 310 in 1899, Walter Hagen scored 300 when triumphant in 1922 and Henry Cotton 283 in 1934, helped by a record sixty-five, which inspired the 'Dunlop 65' golf ball.

After Bobby Locke's first Open win there in 1949 the Open stayed away from Sandwich until traffic problems were solved, but after Rogers's victory, Sandy Lyle became the first British winner of the Open since Tony Jacklin in 1969 when he won there in 1985.

Many Amateur Championships, as well as Walker Cup and Curtis Cup matches, have been played at Royal St George's, of which Bernard Darwin once wrote, 'as nearly my idea of heaven as is to be attained on any earthly links'.

A big cross-bunker threatens the approach at the 445-yard first and, having cleared two more large bunkers off the second tee, you face a difficult-to-judge pitch over a bank. The 214-yard third plays a long iron over daunting rough to a far from generous target, and was introduced by architect Frank Pennink among several other improvements in the 1970s.

You veer sharp left after driving over one bunker and steering clear of three more on your left at the uphill fourth, and at the fifth you drive between the dunes, aiming to stay right of a cluster of bunkers in order to get a good view of the green over more sand at eleven o'clock.

After turning on your heel to play the 156-yard sixth you face the long par-five seventh, with plenty of fairway, albeit hidden, in which to land your ball, as you play beside the road leading to the adjoining Prince's Golf Club.

The eighth, ninth and tenth are solid par-fours with well-bunkered greens, the tenth perched high in front of you. The eleventh is a long, heavily trapped par-three back down towards the coast road, the twelfth a dog-leg right with the green heavily protected in front, the thirteenth long and narrow with three big angled cross-bunkers short of a green hard up against the Prince's clubhouse.

Out of bounds on the right threatens as you fire over the dunes from the tee at the daunting 508-yard fourteenth, before deciding on your strategy to negotiate the 'Suez Canal' crossing the fairway some 160 yards short of the flat green.

The fifteenth is a long par-four over, between then over more bunkers to a narrow green, and the short sixteenth is where Tony Jacklin was seen live on television holing-in-one with a seven-iron in the 1967 Dunlop Masters. Finally, it is uphill to the heavily guarded seventeenth with trouble all the way, then downhill over cross-bunkers to the eighteenth, with its infamous bunker at five o'clock.

The sixth hole

The third hole

The two huge bunkers on the fourth hole

The bell on the first tee

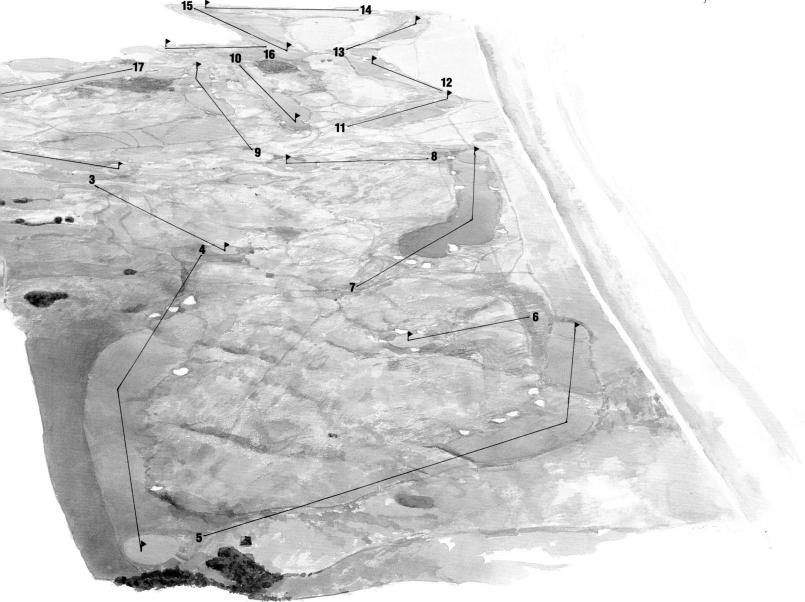

St Mellion Golf and Country Club

The spectacular Jack Nicklaus course at St Mellion, sited just beyond Plymouth at Saltash in Cornwall, was the first to be built in Britain by the great man. Since its official opening in July 1988, when Nicklaus and Tom Watson played Sandy Lyle and Nick Faldo for the St Mellion Trophy, it has swiftly established a reputation as a layout of the highest quality. Nicklaus courses are renowned for their toughness and St Mellion is no exception, $1^{1}/_{2}$ million cubic metres of earth having been moved in order to construct it.

Brothers Hermon and Martin Bond, the farmer-owners of St Mellion, commissioned Nicklaus in 1982 to add his layout to their original eighteen holes, on which the 1978 PGA Cup matches and 1979 Benson and Hedges International were staged. The Nicklaus course encircles the original, running through deep, wooded river valleys and steep gorges, and offering unparalleled natural spectator galleries, and the Benson and Hedges International has been played there since 1990.

The downhill first is a not too difficult opener in favourable weather conditions, but the second, a 540-yard par-five off the championship tees, is a severe dog-leg right around the trees, with out of bounds on the right.

A sheer drop of more than 100 feet along the right edge of the par-four third narrows the fairway dramatically as you hit from an elevated tee, while the 185-yard fourth is played through an avenue of trees to a green densely bunkered on the right.

The 354-yard fifth is a truly dramatic hole. Your tee shot must carry 170 yards across a lake. Then you turn left at right-angles and fire across a meandering stream to a green tucked into the trees. The inevitable stream and trees lie to the right of the sixth, then to the left, even more claustrophobically, of the left-hand dog-leg

The first hole

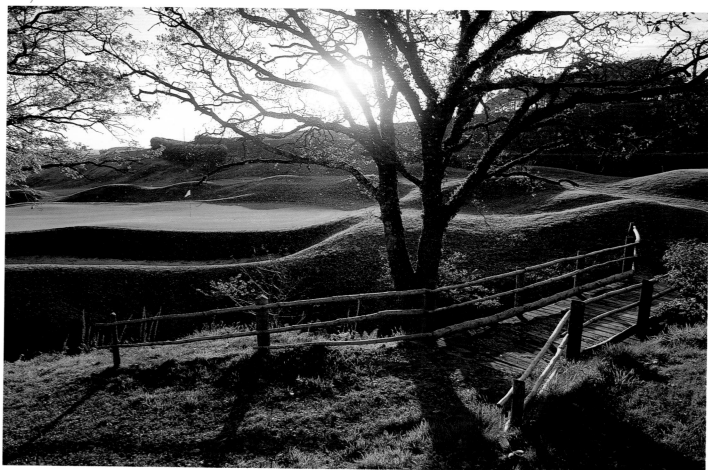

The ninth hole

The uphill sixth hole

seventh. The eighth is an all carry par-three of 140 yards and the ninth, back up to the clubhouse, a 410-yard par-four demanding a long carry from the tee.

The tenth dog-legs to the right around the trees, the eleventh, a par-three with trees down the right, requires the tee shot to clear a lake fronting the green, and the 545-yard twelfth was hewn out of the forest and threads its way over a lake, and beside and across a stream between the trees.

The par-four thirteenth and par-three fourteenth, although both well-bunkered, offer some relief from the crowding trees, as does the par-four fifteenth if you keep to the left. There is a hefty carry at the par-five six-teenth, with three big bunkers waiting to swallow the drive, and five more lying menacingly short and left and right of the green.

A large tree in mid-fairway must be negotiated at the seventeenth, with the road running down to the right, and you drive across the road up an avenue of trees, then veer right to play the last, whose green is tucked teasingly beyond and to the right of another lake and surrounded by spectator mounds.

The par-three fourteenth hole

A view from the side of the seventh hole

St Pierre Golf and Country Club

For the 1989 Epson Grand Prix, won by Severiano Ballesteros, the St Pierre Course at Chepstow, just across the Severn Bridge from England, was altered so that the 237-yard eighteenth, a spectacular par-three across the lake to the clubhouse, became the sixteenth, with the tenth becoming the seventeenth and the ninth the eighteenth. The belief was that in a match-play event – as the Epson Grand Prix was then – the eighteenth (now the sixteenth) would come much more into play. Too often matches had been over and done with long before reaching St Pierre's *pièce de résistance* – a panoramic television hole. But conversely many stroke-play championships have come to a thrilling climax on the hole, and it reverted to being the eighteenth for the Murphy's Cup event later in the year.

At the first hole, a 576-yard par-five between large trees, Ballesteros hit two mighty blows to within a few inches of the flag for a winning eagle in the Epson final against Denis Durnian in 1989, but an out of bounds fence to the right and trees short left can bother lesser mortals. The second has some huge oaks on the right of the fairway and the green is raised. The short third, played uphill, also has an elevated green and tends to play longer than its 135 yards, while at the 417-yard fourth you must miss a bunker right from the tee.

You must carry a steep dip to a narrow green at the fifth, then hit from an elevated tee down to the liberally bunkered 165-yard sixth, before enjoying driving from the top of the hill down to the seventh fairway below, where you face a virtually blind second to a small, tightly trapped target.

The 309-yard eighth, with huge trees all the way up the left and another big one in the right half of the fairway, is driveable, but it is prudent to lay up. The ninth is a long and demanding par-four, with a bunker right and trees left to contend with from the tee and bunkers short of the target to deceive the eye.

A good drive will almost reach the green at the 362-yard tenth, but you must not be short with your second or it will kick left, while the main danger for the drive at the eleventh, whose green is at the crest of a slope, is a bunker on the right. Two extremely big and accurate hits are required to get near the green at the 545-yard dog-leg twelfth, and the 219-yard thirteenth is a real tester of a par-three from a high tee.

Accuracy is at a premium through the trees at the 521-yard fourteenth, as it is at the 375-yard fifteenth, where the target from the tee is between a big tree left and a row of four bunkers right. Then you pitch down to a green guarded by four bunkers and the lake left and beyond.

A giant chestnut tree 150 yards out on the right must be negotiated at the sixteenth, a dog-leg right. The seventeenth is also a slight right-hand dog-leg, played from an elevated tee. Go too far right and your approach is over a towering tree. Then it's the famous eighteenth, which demands that you carry your ball all the way to an elevated green, with out of bounds left.

The seventeenth green, with the eighteenth behind

The fifteenth hole

SPAIN

No country in continental Europe has contributed more to the PGA European Tour than Spain. For many years Spain had produced outstanding players, such as the Miguel brothers, Ramon Sota and Angel Gallardo, but it was the emergence of Severiano Ballesteros which really awakened the world of golf to the potential of Spanish professional golf. In the 1970s, when the European Tour was in its formative stages, what was needed above all was a superstar who would excite the imagination of sponsors and public. That superstar burst upon the world of golf during the Open championship of 1976 at Royal Birkdale. Ballesteros did not win but the swashbuckling manner of the teenager's play, his fearless, fighting spirit, his exciting power and the sheer guts which he displayed in coming back in a burst of birdies and eagles after a disaster gave notice that here was a player who was going to take the world of golf by storm. Ballesteros was box office. Apart from pulling in the crowds and the TV cameras, Ballesteros performed an even greater service to European golf by inspiring the other players to believe in themselves. He was not content to play second fiddle to the mighty Americans, and that supreme confidence rubbed off on those who played alongside him week by week.

No man, it is said, is a prophet in his own country and it took a long time for Spain to recognize the heroic stature of Ballesteros. Since he did not kick a football, or ride a racing bicycle, or fight bulls, he made little impact on his own countrymen. Slowly, long after the rest of the world had hailed his genius, Spain began to take notice of this alien sport. Historically golf in Spain had been confined to a tiny minority of the rich and privileged in a handful of exclusive clubs, or had been provided as an amenity for tourists on the Costa del Sol. All the country's professionals, including Ballesteros, were graduates from the ranks of the caddies at these two very different styles of golf club.

The ninth hole at Valderrama

So the situation when the European Tour was formed was that the old established Spanish Open continued as usual, being taken to a different part of the country each year and being played as an annual diversion for the benefit of the local club members. Subsequently commercial sponsorship was pioneered by the oil company, Cepsa, with the establishment of the Madrid Open. This was most frequently played at the Real Club de la Puerta de Hierro with its hilly course, heavily wooded with sombrero pines, its palatial old clubhouse and its polo field, which was used as a practice ground by the golfers.

Commercial considerations grew stronger, with the resort courses getting in on the act, most notably the new development at La Manga on the coast of Murcia. This ambitious tourist development, sited on an old citrus farm along the rocky coast, possesses two fine courses (which are rather incongruously planted with avenues of palm trees as a change from the ubiquitous pine) and took the Spanish Open for five years for promotional purposes. Since then the Spanish Federation has reverted to its policy of moving the championship around.

El Prat, host to the newly inaugurated Barcelona Open, stands as a monument to a remarkable genius, Javier Arana, who ranks among the greatest of European golf course architects. Arana worked only in Spain and his trademark was a solitary tree strategically sited in the middle of a fairway. More to the point, this former amateur champion stamped every course with his profound understanding and love of golf, investing every hole with an interesting challenge. At El Prat the canvas for his artistry was a featureless strip of coastal plain, situated by the sea but not linksland in the common meaning of the term, and he used a profusion of sombrero pines to create a woodland golfing adventure. It is a pity about Barcelona airport just over the fence, because the roar and stink of jet airliners take the edge off a masterpiece.

The view over the course from the clubhouse patio at Puerto de Hierro

Two other Arana courses come into the Tour's programme from time to time: Club de Campo in Madrid, another woodland course on dramatically plunging and swooping country, and the incomparable El Saler near Valencia, one of the glories of European golf. El Saler is a true links, with elements of woodland on the inland holes, and the most comprehensive test of golf most of the players will meet in a year. Many people rate El Saler among the greatest of European courses and, as such, a very welcome addition to the Spanish Open roster after years of neglect. Mind you, Bernhard Langer was not exactly enraptured with the place after three rounds of the 1984 Spanish Open. He was not in the sunniest of moods when he returned to his room after being fined for slow play, and his spirits sank even lower when he discovered that his briefcase had been stolen. Twenty years earlier some pros carried nothing but their clubs and a shopping bag containing a few clean shirts when they went abroad. Indeed, one pro had to discard his dirty linen before returning home in order to make room for the bundles of inflated lire he had won in Italy. But the 1980s saw the emergence of the briefcase as the essential addition to the player's luggage, to carry tickets, credit cards, diary and the mass of correspondence which is one of the penalties of

success. Langer is not a demonstrative man, more of an internal burner, and when he began his final round he released his frustration by inflicting grievous bodily harm on his golf ball. Take that! And that! The normally composed and conservative Langer found, to his delight, that his aggression was paying dividends. He forgot his troubles and became absorbed in his round, prospering more and more as he progressed. At the end he had surged to the front with a score of sixty-two, a total which no pro would have believed possible on such a demanding course. A small loss had been triumphantly turned to a large profit by the finest golfing performance of the decade.

A short distance inland from El Saler, between the sea and the city of Valencia, lies the golf club of El Escorpion. Gary Player might well describe it as the best golf course he had ever seen – of its kind. Such diplomatic persiflage will not do for an objective analysis of El Escorpion's qualities, unique though they may be. It lies on the site of an old citrus plantation which had been divided into plots, like a chess board. Unfortunately, not all the plot owners were willing to sell to the golf club, so the course contains a number of square islands, producing holes with ninety-degree dog-legs. On the plus side, it offers a rare opportunity to combine golf with the scrumping of oranges and it proved a popular choice for the 1980 Spanish Open. To be sure, this popularity was due primarily to the magnificence of the clubhouse, one of the truly great clubhouses of European golf. It is a conversion of a large farmhouse, built in the sturdy, fortified style common in the days when Moorish invaders were a constant threat. Add to those noble surroundings a ladies' section devoted to the preservation and celebration of the glories of Spanish cuisine, and a house committee with a profound appreciation of the greatest vintages of Rioja, and any technical deficiencies in the golf course are put into civilized perspective.

Another development in Spain is a surge in interest from the tourist industry, with resorts seeking exposure through the medium of professional golf. The Mallorca Open has come into the schedule, a welcome pipe-opener to the season at the beautiful Santa Ponsa course, and so Spain has become an exceedingly popular and important factor in the Tour's programme, with half a dozen major promotions a year. This spate of interest in the game was doubtless a factor in the decision of the Tour's sponsor, Volvo, to take its inaugural Masters tournament to Valderrama in 1988.

Valderrama began, like most courses along the Costa del Sol, as part of a property development. First came Sotogrande, a high-quality residential development in conjunction with a Robert Trent Jones course which quickly earned a reputation as a major additon to Spanish golf. When all the villas were sold the course, as is usual under such schemes, was taken over by the members and the developers moved across the main coast road into the low foothills to create New Sotogrande. Again Robert Trent Jones was commissioned to create a course of championship calibre, and a number of villas were built. Then a consortium of golf enthusiasts led by Jaime Ortiz-Patino bought New Sotogrande, changed the name to Valderrama and completely transformed the place. Trent Jones was recalled to revise and refurbish the course, the original schemes for property development were scrapped and the project took an entirely new direction: the aim being to create an exclusive private club devoted to the traditional virtues of golf. Volvo, with its insistence on nothing but the best, had found a host of like mind for the European Tour's flagship tournament.

The players arriving for the inaugural Volvo Masters were astonished at the condition of the course. Many of them had never seen such immaculate fairways, and those who had played in the US Masters declared that these were even better than Augusta National's. The greens were as fast and true as those encountered at an American Open championship. The difficult course, made even more testing by the brisk winds, presented the golfers with their sternest challenge of the year and, the ultimate test of a golf course, the cream quickly rose to the top, with Nick Faldo gaining a narrow victory over Severiano Ballesteros and Sandy Lyle. Who could ask for more? Actually, Mr Patino immediately asked for more, demanding more course improvements and

Crowds at Santa Ponsa watch play at the 1988 Mallorca Open de Baleares

The beautiful course at Las Brisas lies between the Mediterranean and the Andalusian mountains

even better conditioning for the next Volvo Masters.

Ballesteros, the tireless crusader, reflecting on the massive contributions made to European golf by Spain and the Spanish players, took the opportunity to press Spain's claim to host the Ryder Cup match. Nobody could argue against his submission that the Ryder Cup would have to be played on the Continent before long and that when the day came Spain would have to be at the head of the queue. Valderrama would be one obvious candidate and so would Las Brisas, just along the coast.

This is another Trent Jones course, on the plain between the Mediterranean and the foothills of the Andalucian mountains. It is a strong course in its intrinsic design, with plenty of water in the Trent Jones tradition, but the difficulty of a golf course depends as much on the way it is presented as on its physical features. Ballesteros was co-promoter of the Spanish Open of 1987 and, conscious of the conditions to be encountered in the forthcoming Ryder Cup match at Muirfield Village, Ohio, he insisted that the greens be hard and fast. It may be felt that there was an element of special pleading in that policy, since the tougher the conditions, the better would be the chances of the more ac-

complished golfers, such as Ballesteros himself. It is true that self-interest is often a strong factor when players complain about course conditions, and the less gifted strikers are the most vociferous campaigners for watered greens. The converse, however, does not apply. Making a course more difficult may help the star players, but that is surely a good reason for turning off the water, since the object of tournaments is to identify the great players.

An outcry about the unplayably fast greens went up after the first round, and Ballesteros's sixty-four in the pro-am, the most telling vindication of the conditions, was dismissed as a freak round. The greens had to be watered to prevent the grass from expiring. Ballesteros was critical of the watering, but it was rather the waters of the lake on the fifteenth hole – into which he hooked his drive on the last day for a double bogey to finish two strokes behind Nick Faldo – which thwarted him.

The influence of Ballesteros is to be felt in another area of European golf. His international successes have tended to make his fans adopt him, particularly in Britain where he is accepted as 'one of us' – a relationship which he appreciates because he receives the recognition denied him for so many years by his own countrymen. So British fans, anxious to be associated with golfing success, see Ballesteros as not so much Spanish as European, since this label makes him one of us, rather than one of them. In fact, Ballesteros is first and foremost a Spaniard and if anything his pride in being Spanish increases as his lifestyle becomes more cosmopolitan. He wants Spain to be the leading golf nation in Europe, with the best courses, the best players and the best tournaments. He uses his influence to that end and since that influence is extremely powerful he will make it happen. He used it to bring the national championship to his home course, Pedreña, where it all started for him as a caddie. Again he insisted that the course should be prepared with soft fairways and hard, fast greens. Massive rains the previous week frustrated that intention, although the intervention of the weather, usually regarded as being under the control of God, did not deter Ballesteros from publicly castigating the Tour officials. This was the first Tour event to be played at Pedreña and many players were anxious to see a course which Ballesteros had frequently compared favourably with Augusta National. Most were disappointed by the reality, a glaring example of trying to compress a quart into a pint pot, albeit an attractive pint pot of roller-coaster fairways lined by mighty pines and designed with all the skills of Harry Colt. But the final judgment had to be that, as at El Escorpion, the ancillaries were the best of Pedreña, notably the opportunity to stay in the beautiful city of Santander and travel to the game by ferry.

Ballesteros has now started building courses and promoting tournaments, and these may deflect his enthusiasm from Pedreña. In particular his development at Novo Sancti Petri, on the Atlantic coast near Jerez, could well come into the reckoning for major golf promotions – and very welcome too for those who enjoy a *fino seco*, chilled but not iced, before dinner. Spain is sure to remain an exciting growth area for the European Tour for years to come. In the 1970s the problem for the Tour was to find sponsors; the problem for the 1990s will undoubtedly be to find enough weeks in the year to accommodate all the potential sponsors.

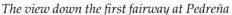

The view down the first fairway at Pedreña

El Prat

José Maria Olazabal won the Catalan Open at El Prat in 1986, his first full season as a professional; Des Smyth, Sam Torrance and Severiano Ballesteros won there the previous three years. But the longest route to victory on this palm-crowded championship layout beside the sea, a short drive to the south of Barcelona, was taken by Britain's David Whelan in 1988. He had to go four extra holes before emerging triumphant in a play-off against Nick Faldo, Mark Mouland and Barry Lane.

Fly in for a tournament or holiday round at El Prat and you may get a sneak bird's eye preview, for the big jets often make their final approach to the nearby international airport over the course, whose par-four opening hole has trees to the right and bunkers to the left in the driving area, but offers a real birdie chance.

The short par-four second is one of the easiest holes on the course at 270 metres, and at the par-three third more likely to come into play than the broad expanse of water between you and the green are the bunkers right and left of the putting surface. Hole number four offers another good birdie opportunity, but don't push your drive out into the lake to the right.

Favour the left side of the fairway to set up a scoring chance at the fifth, a gentle dog-leg right, but beware the bunker, while at the long-short sixth the lake short left and five strategically placed bunkers conspire to reduce birdie chances.

The seventh, a par-four, plays as a dog-leg left around the trees, with bunkers narrowing the steeply rising entrance to the green. You drive back across the water you encountered at the third at the eighth, at a narrower point, then fire into a two-tier green, with palm trees coming into play if you stray off line, and there is another steeply undulating two-platform putting surface awaiting you as you play up the par-five ninth beside the beach.

The tenth demands a tightly controlled tee shot, with trees crowding in on both sides of the fairway and two meticulously placed bunkers on the right, and a tall tree blocks the left side of the fairway as you play towards the green at this par-five.

Big bunkers right and left front and the lake beyond call for careful club selection at the short eleventh, while at the par-five twelfth trees galore left and right demand care and attention all the way.

Miss the bunker right by too much at the left-hand dog-legged thirteenth and you must negotiate a bunker left of the green. The fourteenth dog-legs the other way, with palm trees a constant threatening factor as you play to a triple-tiered green – one of the toughest holes on the course.

The par-five fifteenth is the longest of El Prat's holes, with an undulating green presenting plenty of problems, while at the par-four sixteenth it is woods all the way down the left that threaten, and more obstructions if you stray too far right.

Trees crowd in claustrophobically around the green at the par-three seventeenth and a large frontal bunker adds more problems, while the eighteenth is a fine finishing par-four, dog-legging to the left around dense woods, with a bunker in the driving area on the right and a tricky two-tier target to hit.

A view over the well-watered course towards the sea

The second hole

The par-three fifth hole

El Saler

It was fitting that in April 1989 West Germany's Bern-hard Langer should end a long, lean spell with victory in the Peugeot Spanish Open at El Saler, near Valencia, for it was there in 1984 that he produced one of the truly great rounds – a ten below par record sixty-two – over one of Europe's truly great golf courses for his first win in the event.

Until that championship little was known inter-nationally of the course that Javier Arana sculpted out of rugged linksland beside the Mediterranean. Now this gem of a golfing test, with its huge rolling greens

and ninety-five bunkers, its giant dunes and fickle, sometimes fearsome sea breezes, ranks among every connoisseur's top-ten. With its on-site *parador* (state-run hotel), it is increasingly proving a mecca for golfing pilgrims.

The first hole, out towards the entrance to the club, is a gentle left-hand dog-leg to a well-guarded green, where a drive too far right presents big problems. Bunk-ers on both sides of the fairway demand an accurate drive at the par-four second, and a wickedly sloping green adds to the hole's problems.

The par-three seventeenth hole

It's about turn then, and back down the par-five third, which dog-legs left uphill to a green guarded along the right by sand. You must avoid hitting into the two big sand-traps located in the right hand-corner of the dog-leg.

Hole four is an all carry par-three to a two-platformed green nestling in the midst of trees, while hole five is a par-five up over the brow of a hill, with trouble to be found left and right, where Herr Langer took six in his final round in 1989 after having buried his ball in a bush.

At 415 metres the sixth, a dog-leg left, is a real tester, requiring a long straight tee shot to a sloping fairway if the green is to be hit in two, whereas the par-four seventh, so long as you sidestep the bunkers to the left off the tee, presents a comfortable passage.

The eighth is a real links hole with out of bounds (the beach) left and a two-tier, steeply sloping target below a high dune, while at the par-three ninth the out of bounds is to the right and there are three big bunkers. Mark McNulty holed-in-one with a five-iron in the 1989 Open.

The first hole

The fifth hole

Don't be too far right off the tee at the tenth or you may be blocked out by a tall pine, while at the par-five eleventh – one of the longest holes on the course at 520 metres – a pine and a bunker confront the shot to the green.

Bunkers and the sheer size of the green demand accuracy at the short twelfth, and accuracy is again at a premium on the short par-four thirteenth – off the tee and to a green with bunkers front and trees beyond.

You must fly a bunker to the right off the tee at the fourteenth, while at the next, a 520-metre par-five, avoiding the trees flanking the generous fairway is a must. Out of bounds left puts a premium on a solid drive as you enter the home straight, and a two-tiered green protected by three bunkers permits no relaxing.

The club's course notes describe the par-three seventeenth as 'a decisive hole'. Thick rough and a nest of five bunkers severely punish waverers. Fittingly, the eighteenth is a great finishing hole, with the wind often a powerful factor. There is out of bounds left, bunkers and thick rough right and at 430 metres the hole requires a long and accurate second.

The par-three ninth hole

The first hole

La Moraleja

Just off the main Madrid–Burgos highway, a few minutes drive from the centre of the capital, La Moraleja is the work of Jack Nicklaus, and a picturesque and varied test of golfing skills it has turned out to be. The Spanish Open was played there in 1986, with Howard Clark the winner, and it was chosen in 1988 to stage the first Benson and Hedges Mixed Professional event, with Europe's male and female stars linking up and Mark McNulty partnering Marie Laure de Lorenzi to a famous victory.

A strikingly elegant clubhouse looks down over the eighteenth to the adjoining first hole, a gentle dog-leg left with a bunker short, right of the green, the only real worry. The second is an excellent par-three of 176 metres, with a stream running the length of the hole left and the slightly elevated green well protected by bunkers and trees. The onus is on the correctly shaped tee shot according to the pin placement.

You play uphill all the way to the third to an elevated green guarded by a deep bunker to the left, then turn to the left to play from an elevated tee down to the course's toughest par-three at 195 metres. The only way in is the aerial route.

The fifth is a dog-leg left with a huge bunker waiting to devour greedy golfers trying to bite off too much, three more traps waiting for the drive which veers right, and a stream beyond the green.

You dog-leg right, then left at the gently uphill sixth, picking your way between prettily shaped sand-traps, and only the very longest hitters will get up in two at this 472-metre par-five. Fire your drive over the bunker at the corner of the seventh, a dog-leg left, then face a tricky downhill second to a green with sand on the left and water on the right and beyond.

The eighth dog-legs the other way, so aim to be left and long to get a good view down an avenue of trees of an angled, elevated green, then hope for a birdie four at the 475-metre ninth, with its generous driving area. Fairway trees hamper your view of a green set between large bunkers.

A view from the back of the fifth hole

The uphill third hole

The sixteenth hole

Great precision is required at the par-four tenth, named 'El Terror', because of the narrow fairway and a green surrounded by Spanish oaks, and there is no let-up at the eleventh, with out of bounds to the right and trees guarding a long, narrow green.

Keep left with your tee shot at the par-five twelfth, if you want to go for the green in two at this 486-metre hole, which has a lake biting in from the left before the green and out of bounds beyond. So long as you don't cut your drive into the lake you will face a short pitch across the water to set up a birdie at the 312-metre thirteenth, and there is another clear-cut scoring chance at the 288-metre fourteenth, provided you miss the cavernous bunker on the left.

The fifteenth is a straight along par-three, with houses on the right, but you face an awkward recovery if you stray offline. You hit downhill but play your approach uphill to the well-trapped sixteenth, with out of bounds beyond, while at the scenic short seventeenth your nerve is tested by a long tee shot over a lake.

A long drive is a must to have a hope of reaching the 461-metre eighteenth in two, and if you drive left the lake comes very much into play. An outstanding finishing hole.

The eighteenth hole and clubhouse

The thirteenth hole

Las Brisas

The World Cup of Golf was played at Las Brisas, near Marbella on Spain's Costa del Sol, for the second time in November 1989. Jack Nicklaus and Johnny Miller won for the United States in 1973, and the Spanish Open was played there in 1970, 1983, and 1987, when Nick Faldo kept his nerve to master the glassy greens, whose slopes and pace are one of the features of the course. Ian Woosnam won the inaugural Mediterranean Open – reduced to 54 holes because of rain – in 1990.

Views down to the coast, around the millionaires' playground of Puerto Banus, and inland to the majestic Sierra Blanca are spectacular from a course designed by Robert Trent Jones and opened in 1968. The great American architect's trademarks – a profusion of water hazards, large, decoratively shaped bunkers and big undulating greens – abound on the course, most of which can be seen from the hilltop clubhouse.

At the par-four first a drive left or right ends in trouble. The approach is over the edge of a lake to a green with water to the left and rear. A straight hit from the tee is again at a premium up the second, if you are to drive beyond the lake left and trees and buildings right, before bearing right to hit to the green.

The par-five third is a tester at 460 metres, as is the par-three fourth, with lots of trouble short left, at 185 metres, while the fifth, at 530 metres, is a real trial of strength and stamina, with bunkers awaiting wayward drives. At 350 metres the sixth offers birdie possibilities, but it is not for the faint-hearted, the second shot having to be played over a water inlet and a bunker to a green flanked to the left by a lake.

Bunkers crowd round the green at the short seventh, while the par-five eighth unusually offers two routes to the green after you have driven across the lake. The safer shot is the shorter one, sharp right back across the lake, followed by a pitch to the small green, but the brave take the longer direct line over trees, water and sand. Mis-hit at your peril.

The ninth is a birdie hole at 324 metres, as is the tenth, a dog-leg left, while the 190-metre eleventh hole, played from an elevated tee to a small green, bunkered on both sides and with a lake curving round the front and left side, demands a well-struck long iron, perhaps a wood.

At 475 metres the twelfth, like the eighth, offers two routes to the target after a drive across the water. You can go straight on, then turn sharp left for a short pitch to the green over a ditch, or try to traverse the length of the lake, plus a bunker, and get home in two.

The thirteenth is a dog-leg to the left through the trees, and it is back through the trees to the dog-leg (to the right) par-four fourteenth. Also a dog-leg to the right is the 390-metre fifteenth, which meanders through an olive grove. In the 1973 World Cup Jack Nicklaus boldly drove over the trees and the out of bounds right to set up a short birdie pitch. But not everybody can carry the ball 250 metres!

The 205-metre sixteenth demands a carry over a lake to a steeply sloping green, and is out of reach for many when into the wind, while the short par-four seventeenth requires a precise approach to a small water-ringed target.

Placement of the drive, with the lake biting in from the left and bunkers right, is the prime consideration at the eighteenth, then you finish by hitting up to a two-tier elevated green.

The first hole

The third hole

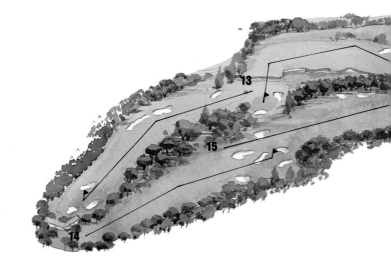

The fifteenth hole

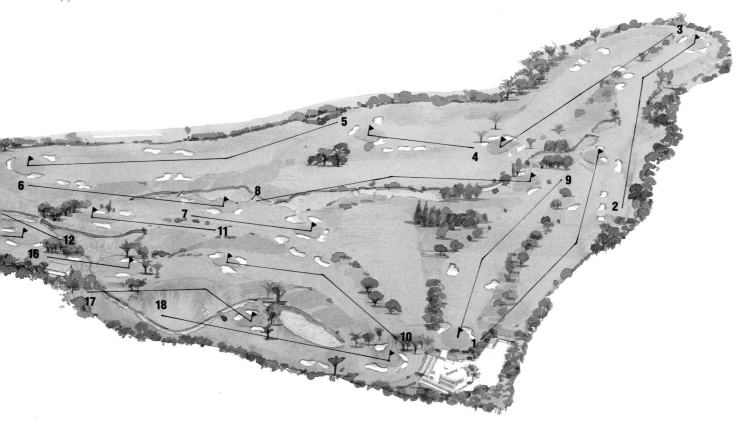

Pedreña

Sailing across the beautiful Bay of Santander to play Severiano Ballesteros's home course of Pedreña in the 1988 Peugeot Spanish Open was a fairytale experience for most of the competing professionals, with the first tee but a short stroll from the point of disembarkation.

Perhaps not surprisingly, Ballesteros, whose brother Manuel now lives in the old family home overlooking the course, fared badly that week, as helicopters ferried the world's press to view the luxurious house he has built for himself nearby, with its practice greens, swimming pool and tennis court. He claimed the course was playing too easily, and certainly Mark James's winning aggregate of 262 – eighteen below par – was low.

At 331 metres the opening hole is none too tough, but if you stray into the bunkers or deep rough left of the tee you will struggle. Water to the right at the short second awaits only the wildest tee shots, but a big bunker between lake and green can be a real problem.

A view over the seventeenth hole back across to the town of Santander. The course is normally reached by ferry.

Bunkers in the landing area and big trees to the right must be skirted, and a bunker fronting the green must be flown, in order to set up a birdie chance at the par-four third.

The 412-metre fourth is rated the toughest par-four on the course. A light fade from an elevated tee is demanded to the right-hand dog-leg, then an accurate long iron to a green heavily bunkered short right as well as left.

Drive and sand wedge are generally all you need at the wide-open 286-metre fifth, but bunkers in mid-fairway and woods to the right demand precision from the tee at the sixth, and club selection is the problem as you aim at a two-tiered green over guarding sand-traps.

An offset green with sand along both sides tests your accuracy at the par-three seventh, and you must not be distracted by the view of the River Cubas at the eighth. Fairway bunkers to the right can be unforgiving.

The first hole

The seventeenth hole

The par-five ninth is often played into the wind, so getting home in two can be tough. Land short right down a bank and you face a blind third. Then a hilltop target faces you at the 190-metre tenth, with big trees to your left and a steep slope to the right, while bunkers short, right and left await big hitters bidding to get home in two at the long eleventh.

The 153-metre twelfth is the easiest par-three on the course. The uphill thirteenth, despite its narrow green, is another birdie chance at 354 metres, and so is the 315-metre fourteenth, with its superb view of the ships at sea beyond.

Sheer length at 211 metres tests you at the par-three fifteenth. It has no bunkers but there are big cypress trees to the right and awkward sloping pitching areas left if you miss the target.

Thick rough and a bunker block the right-hand passage to the long sixteenth, while two concealed midfairway bunkers lie in wait as you take in the view at the downhill seventeenth. Tee as well as green are elevated at the par-four home hole, with the land falling away sharply to the left from the green.

The sixteenth hole

The first hole

Real Club de la Puerta de Hierro

From its elegant hilltop clubhouse, which stands in spacious grounds, Real Club de la Puerta de Hierro, only a few minutes' drive from the centre of Madrid through the university campus, commands spectacular views across the valley. It looks towards the rival Club de Campo and beyond to the often snow-capped mountains.

Besides the 6,347-metre par-seventy-two championship course – on which Severiano Ballesteros, winner of the Madrid Open there three times, fired a record sixty-three in 1980 – there is another eighteen-hole layout, plus lavish polo and tennis facilities.

The first hole is a panoramic par-three across a valley in front of the clubhouse, with three big bunkers guarding the green. Many a sudden death play-off has been decided here.

There is trouble all the way along the left side of the par-five second, with the fairway sloping towards dense woods, while the two-tiered green, protected by bunkers left and right, offers some teasing pin positions.

You drive over an extensive carry to the steeply downhill par-four third, then fire steeply uphill to a green with a veritable sea of sand below it to the right.

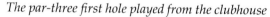

The par-three first hole played from the clubhouse

The palatial clubhouse

Tee shots steered too far left down the dog-leg fourth end among the trees and prevent a clear approach to an elevated green, while at the par-five fifth the problem off the tee is presented by bunkers left and right. Go for the green with two mighty blows and you risk falling away short right into more sand or trees.

Trees abound left and right, as you hit down over an expanse of sand-traps to the picturesque par-three sixth, which presents a marvellous amphitheatre for spectators, then you drive over the road to the brow of a fairway sloping down to the right. A real birdie chance.

The eighth offers even more generous birdie opportunities at 273 metres, but your drive over the trees must be accurate, and big hitters who go for the two-tiered green risk an array of bunkers and an unkind ricochet into deep trouble beyond.

You drive down a narrow, wooded valley at the ninth. Arrive safely off the tee and a well-bunkered, large two-tiered green is the target. At the tenth you drive uphill over a brow, avoiding a bunker on the right, then hit to a generous but heftily bunkered green, while the short eleventh is not so short at 198 metres, with trouble waiting up the wooded bank to the right and below the green left in the shape of three big sand-traps.

Accuracy, above all, is at a premium at the heavily wooded twelfth, with a bunker right waiting to catch the drive, and more trouble round the green. Fortune can favour the brave at the driveable 281-metre downhill thirteenth, but the green has three platforms and three protective bunkers.

Don't stray left at the dog-legged fourteenth or you will be in the woods, and the same applies to the par-five fifteenth, where the choice as you face your second is whether to play short of two big cross bunkers or try to fly them.

The sixteenth offers a good birdie chance to accurate hitters, and you must be up at the 159-metre seventeenth with big bunkers beckoning short right and centre as well as trees. The longest hole on the course is the last, at 550 metres, but the fairway is wide and the green large.

The seventeenth hole

The first hole

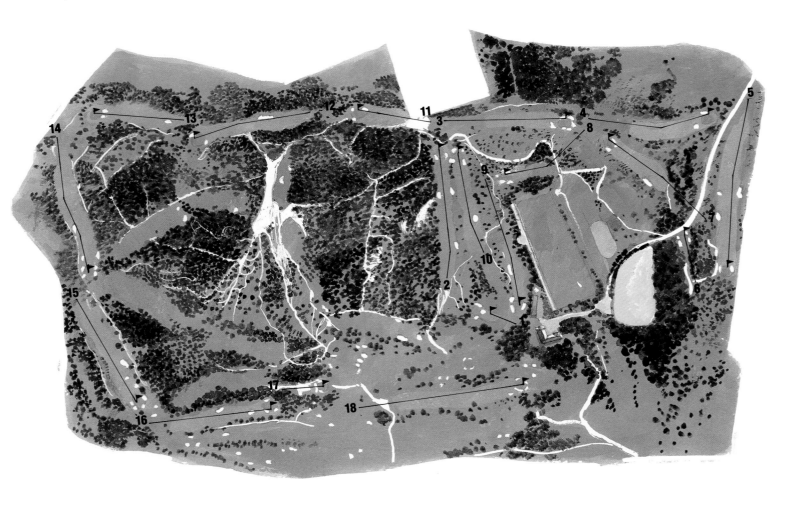

Santa Ponsa

Santa Ponsa is sited some sixteen kilometres from Palma, capital of the island of Mallorca, on the Andraix highway in the important tourist centre of Calvia, with its four kilometres of attractive coastline and large capacity yacht basin. Folco Nardi designed the course, and another architect, Pepe Gancedo, has prepared plans for a further thirty-six holes in an area which commands magnificent views out over the Bay of Santa Ponsa.

As contestants in the Open de Baleares have found, the opening par-four demands precision from the tee to bisect the two big fairway bunkers, and the drive should be kept to the right to avoid a small tree left of centre in the fairway. Care is also needed with the approach, with a big bunker to the left of the green.

Cut the corner too tight at the 520-metre second, a ninety-degree dog-leg to the right, and you can tangle with a steep drainage ditch or even the out of bounds. It is a long carry to the green over a lake and it could be wiser to lay up in two.

The short third hole presents no insuperable problems, but trees to the left and right come into play at the left-hand dog-legged fourth hole. There is also a bunker situated 170 metres out, and you face a blind uphill second to a tight target. A par-four feels like a birdie here.

At 310 metres, the fifth offers a real birdie chance, but the sixth, at 450 metres, is a tester, with an uphill second having to clear a stream crossing the fairway fifty metres short of the green.

Probably the prettiest hole on the course is the par-three seventh. You fire downhill through a gap in the trees, taking care to leapfrog the lake short left. Four historic stone columns among the trees, towards which the fairway slopes right, must be bypassed at the uphill eighth. Long hitters must beware the stream crossing the fairway, before firing to a tight elevated green.

Bunkers left and right will catch stray drives at the uphill ninth, but there are none at the tenth, one of the longest par-fives in the world at 590 metres. Here the problem is water left and right, linked by a stream across the fairway, as you hit towards the green.

The lakes should not bother you as you turn back up the eleventh, with a birdie opportunity, but a par will be more than welcome at the 220-metre uphill twelfth.

Out of bounds left is the only worry at the downhill thirteenth, but beware a slice into the pond as you play blind to the green, while at the fourteenth a tricky green presents the only real problem. The last par-three on the card is the fifteenth hole, well protected by bunkers and trees, and then there are three dog-legged holes to finish.

The 400-metre sixteenth veers ninety degrees to the right and has out of bounds left and trees and a lake to the right. The bold will drive over the water.

At 320 metres the seventeenth affords a big birdie bonus, but pars are most welcome at the uphill 420-metre home hole, where a bunker to the right, surrounded by fig trees, must be missed off the tee, and a tricky two-level green must be negotiated.

Valderrama

Formerly Sotogrande New and sited beyond the main Gibraltar–Malaga road in the hills high above Sotogrande itself, Valderrama was remodelled by designer Robert Trent Jones, at the request of Club President Jaime Ortiz-Patino prior to the first Volvo Masters in autumn 1988, to turn it into a true championship test. So it proved, as Nick Faldo, Severiano Ballesteros, Sandy Lyle and Ian Woosnam took the first four places.

Fittingly, you set out on this steeply undulating, panoramic course from elevated tees, playing from a narrow driving area to a tree-framed, contoured green, well guarded by bunkers. The par-four second plays as a right-hand dog-leg around central trees in the middle of the fairway, while a tiny elevated green, sloping back to front, is the target at the 156-metre third, with big trouble left and long. Driving down from an elevated tee at the par-five fourth, you must avoid big bunkers on the left, then steer clear of the lake to the right of a three-tiered green surrounded by cork trees.

Only the most accurate tee shots will keep you well clear of trees left and right as you turn back along the par-four fifth. A cork oak forces you to play your short second to the left. The tree-surrounded tee at the pretty short sixth is much higher than the steeply tiered green, with its profusion of bunkers. You can get some tough pin positions here.

Woods to the left must be avoided from the tee at the par-four seventh, then a nest of bunkers short right of the green. Overshoot at your peril. Par-fours tighter than the 319-metre eighth, which dog-legs gently left, are hard to find. Stray into the trees left or right and you will probably have no shot to an elevated green guarded by a huge front bunker.

The par-five eleventh hole

The twelfth is an extremely difficult long par-three

The sixth green at Valderrama

The clubhouse overlooks the Robert Trent Jones course

Five bunkers, one with a tree growing in it, and a sloping target present the problems as you play back to the clubhouse up the ninth. Then the par-four tenth is a dog-leg right, with a huge lake lurking down the slope to the right. Drive down an avenue of cork trees to pitch to a well-bunkered, subtly sloping green.

It is a long uphill clamber to the par-five eleventh, with its Mediterranean backdrop and the tendency for balls to veer to the right towards gaping sand-traps. Drink in the intoxicating view before hitting to the 200-metre twelfth, hemmed in by trees and bunkers and tilting tantalizingly front to rear.

From the thirteenth tee you must track left of trees to the right, centre of the fairway, then negotiate a small elevated green, which tilts to the right. No sand, but no walkover. Plenty of room for the tee shot at the fourteenth, but the target, heavily bunkered to the front, lies at an angle and brims with tricky undulations.

Hit your tee shot over the trees to the longest of the par-threes at the fifteenth, then tackle a tight tee shot down sixteen to a fairway sloping right to left and a testing second to a sloping, well-trapped target. The seventeenth is a double dog-leg par-five and you must keep left to avoid a blind third, and new improvements are under construction.

Dog-legged, too, is the final hole. Drive between the trees, then face a long iron to a green bunkered on three sides, with a severe downslope at eleven o'clock.

The fifth green

The first hole

Club de Campo

Britain's Max Faulkner, Open Champion in 1951, was the first winner of the Spanish Open at Club de Campo, close to Madrid, in 1957. Sebastian Miguel won there in 1960, Scotland's Sam Torrance in 1982, Rodger Davis in 1990, followed by Eduardo Romero in a seven-hole play-off with Severiano Ballesteros in 1991.

It lies across the valley, within clear view of the clubhouse at Puerta de Hierro, regular venue for the Madrid Open Championship, and it was at Club de Campo that Spanish Ryder Cup stars like Mañuel Pinero, José-Maria Canizares and Antonio Garrido attended the country's famous caddie school – learning the 'three Rs' as well as the rudiments of the Royal and Ancient game.

The opening hole is a spectacular dog-leg to the right measuring 460 metres, with a well-protected, gently sloping green, while the fairway at the 410-metre second is flat, and you must land your drive on the right, close to a big bunker, to open up a long, two-level green guarded by a big bunker short left and two more to the right.

You must fly your tee shot over a stream to the green at the 205-metre third, well protected by trees and sand-traps, and you fire over a stream again at the 470-metre fourth and try to land your ball on the upper platform to afford a view of the two-tier target beyond a fairway falling away to the right.

Aim for the left half of a fairway bordered by trees on both sides at the 377-metre fifth to set up the second shot to a green sloping slightly to the right. Then the 407-metre sixth is a dog-leg left towards a hilltop, double-platformed green, which is well protected by bunkers; a decision not to cover a stream in the driving area here was controversial.

The 490-metre seventh is a par-five, dog-legging to the right along a fairway falling away left towards another well-guarded green. The 358-metre eighth also dog-legs gently right as it winds uphill to another split-level, well-bunkered target, while the short ninth (155 metres) demands the tee shot be struck across a deep valley to another two-tier green.

Bunkers and trees are again in evidence around the green at the 370-metre tenth, another slight right-hand dog-leg, while trouble awaits the underhit tee shot at the 195-metre eleventh, which is protected by sand left and right. Two tall trees in the fairway define the driving area at the 438-metre twelfth, whose spectacular green affords a splendid view of Madrid.

The 430-metre thirteenth is a downhill dog-leg right, similar to the first, but the green is more heavily guarded by trees and traps, while the 505-metre fourteenth hole generally plays very long and is a double dog-leg fringed by trees with a difficult-to-judge third shot.

You play uphill at the 350-metre fifteenth, steering clear of a big bunker on the right from the tee, before trying to thread your approach between two greenside bunkers.

And you must aim to land your drive on the left again, close to the bunkers, to open up the approach at the 398-metre sixteenth to a green with three gentle slopes on its surface. A tree on the right can create problems for the second shot.

Bunkers and trees afford the green plentiful protection at the 142-metre seventeenth, but provided you keep away from bunkers right the 321-metre last hole, with its large green, presents few complications.

The sixth hole

The par-three third hole

The short ninth hole

The uphill fifth hole

ITALY

For the visitor who flies to Italy from London to play golf the journey takes about a hundred years, back into an era when the lower orders knew their place and the gentry kept up appearances. In most places around the world a golf club is just that, pretty much like any other golf club, but in Italy golf is gloriously and preposterously Italian. When the PGA European Tour first ventured into Italy the players and officials, mostly of modest origins themselves, ran headlong into a clash of cultures. Where else could it happen that Brian Barnes, preparing to play a shot in the Italian Open, should find his line impeded by a novel immovable obstruction in the form of a spectator standing implacably two yards from his ball? Barnes suggested, politely enough in the first instance, that it would be more convenient for both of them if the *signor* moved aside. 'I am a member,' said the spectator. 'This is my club and I can stand where I like. I like to stand right here.' Where else could a competitor in the Open, penalized for identifying his ball in a bunker, run screaming from the course and return with the Italian rule book pointing out the heading to the rule: '*Identificare la bolla*'? Where else could the tournament committee sit in voluble argument for six hours trying to make the draw for the pro-am because they could not decide who was most worthy to play with Tony Jacklin? Where else could a player obtain a ruling from an official wearing a referee's badge and driving in a cart marked *arbitro*, and then be disqualified on the grounds that this dignitary was not an official referee, just the President of the Italian Golf Federation?

Yet it is surely true to say that for players, officials and press alike the Italian Open is one of the favourite weeks of the golfing year. And this popularity has very little to do with the fact that amateurish and eccentric administration has given way to efficient professional organization. Rather it is due to the national attitude to golf which insists that the game, like eating, taking a

The eighteenth hole at Monticello

mistress or driving fast cars, is supposed to be one of the supreme pleasures of life. And golf in the Italian context is much more than the actual playing, but embraces the aesthetic and sensual delights of dressing up, dining, luxuriating under a hot shower, lounging around in comfortable surroundings and swapping lies about how well they played and how unlucky they were. We all like these things but only the Italians pay such attention to detail in planning the frills of golf.

It is a pity in a way that tournament golf has grown so big, because large crowds need vast car parks and tented villages, and easy access, and so some of the delightful small clubs have been lost to professional golf. The dining-rooms of Garlenda, Villa d'Este and Florence are sadly consigned to the realms of nostalgia. Rome's course on the Via dell'Acquasanta, with the period charm of a club established at the turn of the century, lacks only length as a championship test, and the capital will in future have to watch its major golf at Olgiata and the new Federation course of Le Querce, or at one of the new golf developments.

One fact most people know about Rome is that it is built on seven hills, and this gives an indication of the countryside on which Olgiata is built: undulating, with plenty of trees and a clubhouse fit for a Doge's palace.

A significant development in Italian golf, and a growing sign of the times, was the opening of Le Querce, inaugurated with the staging of the 1991 World Cup. This is a purpose-built championship course with full spectator amenities, and was commissioned by the Federazione Italiana Golf as the regular home of the Italian Open championship. The rating of golf courses is altogether too subjective an area for instant judgments. Only time will reveal the true quality of Le Querce, but it does have one immediate, if peripheral, advantage. Competitors can stay in Rome – with all the attractions implicit in the principle that man doth not live by golf alone – and can conveniently commute to the course on the *autostrada*.

Monticello, in the north near Lake Como, has become a regular championship course. It is a new development, designed as a weekend retreat for the wealthy businessmen of Milan and Turin, and extremely luxurious. The land is flat and featureless and so the course, long enough to test the biggest of hitters, will need some years of maturing before the saplings grow large enough to play their part in the strategy of the course and in giving it character and beauty.

For a small island Sardinia has contributed greatly to the growth of professional golf and will doubtless continue to do so, particularly at Pevero, one of the outstanding courses of Europe. Two architects inspected the site in the precipitous mountains on the Costa Smeralda and pronounced that it was impossible to build a course on such terrain. Robert Trent Jones, however, relished the challenge. He blasted rock into the narrow valleys to create areas wide enough for fairways and then proposed to import shiploads of topsoil. But an idea came to him. He had pioneered growing grass on sand, previously thought to be impossible, and it occurred to him that crushed rock was sand. He sent for a rock-crusher and experimented. It worked and the developer of this exclusive resort, the Aga Khan, was saved half a million dollars as a result. It is a unique course, in that the fairways are flanked by steep walls of rock thickly covered with dense bushes, the *maquia*, which traditionally provide sure cover for kidnappers hiding from the law.

The first time the Italian Open was played at Pevero there was a strong wind and the field of fifty tournament professionals in the curtain-raising pro-am lost eighty-one balls between them. One pro ran out of ammunition during the championship and had to wade through a lake picking up golf balls between his toes in order to complete his round. For lesser mortals the loss of a few golf balls is a small price to pay for the breathtaking views of the Mediterranean from the clifftop holes.

The other Sardinian course, and the first to host a championship, is Is Molas in the south. The land hereabouts is a gently sloping plain and rather featureless compared with the wildness of the hinterland. The task of creating a golf course was entrusted to the remarkable civil engineer and unashamed golf addict, Piero Mancinelli, educated at Wellington, and a one-time rugby football international and wartime bomber pilot with the Italian Air Force, who transferred his allegiance and served with Britain's Eighth Army in the desert. One further item of biographical detail, although not strictly pertinent to his credentials as a golf course architect, is that he is one of the few people who can conduct a long-distance communication without the benefit of a telephone. The site precludes Is Molas from being particularly exciting or inspirational, but it is a large, technically sound and fair test for the pro-

fessionals. Fittingly, its first championship in 1976 was won by the talented Baldovino Dassu, the first native-born winner since the 1950s and the prime of the formidable Aldo Casera and Ugo Grappasoni.

Is Molas has a special place in the lore of the formative years of the Tour, and the incident of the phantom referee referred to earlier was a prime example. It occurred during the third round of that 1976 Italian Open when Sam Torrance hit his drive over a drainage ditch bordering the sixteenth fairway. Neither Torrance nor his playing companions, Billy Casper and Eddie Polland, had copies of the local rules with them, an unbelievable but not uncommon omission among professional golfers. The pertinent local rule stated clearly that a ball over the ditch was out of bounds. The situation was complicated by the fact that red and white posts had been driven into the ground on the out-of-bounds side of the ditch, prima facie evidence that the ditch was in bounds. Because of the rocky nature of the ground the stakes could not be driven tight against the ditch and Torrance's ball lay between the edge of the ditch and the line of white stakes. He consulted his playing companions who both gave the opinion that the ball was in bounds. While they were discussing the problem a buggy drove up containing three officials of the Italian Golf Federation. The senior among them, the acting President of the federation, indicated that the ball was indeed in bounds. Torrance duly dropped on to the fairway under penalty and played on. When Torrance left the eighteenth green he was confronted by the referee, Arthur Crawley-Boevey, who showed him the local rule: over the ditch was out of bounds. Torrance was disqualified. Confusion was now replaced by pandemonium which raged for three and a half hours, until common sense, natural justice and the rule of equity finally prevailed and Torrance was reinstated.

This misadventure did at least have a happy ending, unlike the saga of Brian Sharrock of Wigan who missed the cut in Madrid and decided to drive to Is Molas. Since he had won only a meagre £75 the previous year he had to watch the pennies, and the trip would also give him a chance to see more of Europe. The first section of the journey, to Barcelona, passed without incident and he enjoyed a good night's rest. Next day he drove on to Marseilles and encountered his first problem: there was no ferry to Sardinia as he had been led to expect. There was however, he was assured, a ferry which sailed from Corsica. Sharrock parked his car, dug into his dwindling cash resources and bought an air ticket to Corsica. When he arrived he learnt that there were no ferry sailings on Sundays. If he waited for the Monday ferry he would not arrive in time for the pre-qualifying round.

Faced with this insoluble dilemma he did what any professional golfer would do in the circumstances: he repaired to a waterfront bar and ordered a large one. A good barman dispenses advice and sympathy, spiritual as well as spirituous balm, and once he learned of the young Englishman's predicament he suggested a solution: a private charter. As luck would have it, his cousin had a suitable craft and would certainly be willing out of the goodness of his heart, and for a suitable consideration, to undertake the perilous crossing to Sardinia. Negotiations were conducted and the initial quotation of £100 was generously reduced to a mere £80. Sharrock was put ashore at a point which the boatman assured him was just a hop and a step from Is Molas golf club. The boat disappeared with suspicious speed. A kindly motorist gave him a lift – a mile up the road to a bus stop. It was here that Sharrock realized why Corsicans have their unenviable reputation for banditry: he had been landed in northern Sardinia. Undaunted, our hero took a bus to the station, a slow train to Cagliari, a taxi to Is Molas and arrived at midnight, having spent fifty-six hours and £185 more on the journey than it would have taken by air.

Fate has a disagreeable habit on those occasions when it gives you a good mugging; just as you are enjoying the relief that at last the battering is over, the boot comes flying in for one final cruncher. Because of the inclement weather and the small number of entrants, the pre-qualifying round was cancelled and all entrants had places in the championship. All Sharrock's rush and aggravation had been in vain. The tale of woe ended with him disqualifying himself when he realized that he had followed a wrong procedure with a provisional ball. Now all he had to do was to get himself back to Marseilles and drive to Paris in time to miss qualifying for the French Open. It is a great life, being a tournament professional.

An example of the Tour outgrowing the old, traditional courses is the Lido di Venezia, short and old-fashioned and cramped for space. But what memorable times it provided in the early days of the great European golfing adventure. Imagine staying in Venice, taking a trip across the bay in a *vaporetto* to the Lido, playing your round and then returning to the architectural treasury of that fabulous city. Small wonder that some Americans and other overseas players prefer the European circuit to their domestic tours. Akron, Ohio, was never like this. A good argument can be made that playing in Europe, with its variety of courses and extremes of weather, produces a more rounded and resourceful

golfer; there can be no doubt that it produces a more rounded character. But the Tour has outgrown the Lido and now Venetians must drive fifty kilometres inland to Albarella to watch the big-time golf. Certainly it is a better, and fairer, test for the professionals, but nobody would call it romantic. The price of progress is a switch to the newer, longer courses such as Molinetto, Milan and Monza, a splendid course which upholds the Italian golf tradition of great cuisine, while the old-timers sigh for the good old days.

While in nostalgic mood, mention must be made of the Ugolino Club near Florence, if only because it was selected for the Open championship by popular demand from the press tent. Jack Statter, the golf correspondent of the *Sun* newspaper, had during the war served in the desert campaign as an RAF armourer. One day an Italian soldier who had become detached from his company surrendered to Jack. Instead of sending the man to the prisoner-of-war pens, Jack, in his typically generous and unconventional style, signed the Italian on to the ration strength of his motley party of bomb-loaders. The unofficial recruit to the RAF was a restaurateur in Florence and he ended the war happily trying to make the unit's field rations into palatable meals. Afterwards the two friends regularly exchanged Christmas cards, and the agreement was that if ever Jack visited Florence he and his friends would be fêted with the meal of a lifetime. So the golfing press tirelessly pestered officials of the Italian Federation to stage the Open in Florence. There was also a patriotic duty, it was pointed out, to introduce golfers to the glories of Italian culture, a consideration which far outweighed objections that Florence did not have a suitable golf course. Finally the lobbying paid off and the Open was scheduled for Ugolino in 1983. Throughout the war Jack had carried with him a battered copy of Fowler's *English Usage*, and daily reading of this work had made him a master of syntax and grammar; when he fell ill, on being informed that he had cancer of the colon, he told the surgeon, 'You are the first person who has ever been able to fault my punctuation.' Sadly he died before the championship and, despite strenuous enquiries by Mario Camicia among catering associations, it proved impossible to find Jack's wartime friend. So the great feast never took place, although the bean soup in Ugolino's clubhouse went some way towards compensating for the loss.

Le Querce

Le Querce is situated about forty-five minutes' drive north of Rome – provided that the notorious Roman traffic is in your favour! – and is the first development by the Italian Golf Federation. Designed by Jim Fazio, it represents exactly what a Federation looks for in a course – something that will test the best but, when played from a variety of tees, will provide an enjoyable examination for those not so gifted.

With one eye on the future, the course has been designed with excellent practice facilities, including a three-hole practice course. In addition to this, the Italian Golf Federation has developed a school at Le Querce which will educate the next generation of Italian professional golfers and greenkeepers. All in all it is a far-sighted project, and one will leave Le Querce with an appreciation of the excellence of its maintenance.

A water hazard threatens at the first hole

A tricky 541-metre par-five opens the proceedings, with water threatening the second shot before pitching up to a small, slightly elevated green.

The second hole, which is a short par-four at 330 metres, demands perfect judgment of length with the second shot to its elevated green, since only the top half of the pin is actually visible to the player from the fairway.

A well-struck mid-iron should find the heart of the green at the par-three 169-metre third hole, but beware of trouble waiting to the right. And the tee shot at the fourth will frighten the best of players; many will reach for the one-iron to avoid the water on the left of the fairway at this 395-metre hole. The second shot is made just that little bit more difficult by the fact that the fairway slopes from right to left.

A wayward tee shot to the right at the 397-metre fifth will be penalized by heavy rough, while the second shot will test a player's mid-iron accuracy. Longer hitters may be tempted to cut the corner at the dog-leg left sixth hole but, at 360 metres, a one-iron, nine-iron will normally suffice.

The seventh hole is an excellent par-five, which at 514 metres can be reached in two on a calm day. The green is very long, giving a wide variety of pin positions. Then the 351-metre par-four eighth requires a tee shot across the large ravine that runs through the course. It must be carefully placed between the fairway bunkers before a short-iron second shot is played to an undulating green that requires a delicate putting touch.

The ninth is a lovely short 150-metre par-three over a fold in the ground, giving a good chance for a 'deuce'. But beware – anything hit short will come back off the green by forty metres. The tenth hole requires a carry over the ravine at 180 metres, again to be avoided as it swings down to the left of the fairway at this 374-metre hole. A good drive will leave an eight- or nine-iron over another ravine to a green, which must not be missed short or left.

The eleventh is an uphill, 371-metre par-four with a severely sloping green awaiting the second shot. And the long, downhill 197-metre par-three twelfth hole demands that a long iron or wood be struck to an extended, but narrow, target. The thirteenth hole, at 337 metres, is a beautiful dog-leg, with the angles created by a huge tree on the right-hand side of the fairway.

The par-five fourteenth turns back towards the clubhouse and its entire length runs along a ridge. On a calm day it can be reached in two (490 metres), but again accuracy is the key here if par is to be held.

A long, 412-metre par-four fifteenth hole demands two well-struck shots to a large green. The hole dog-legs to the right, but the short line is defended by heavy rough; whereas the sixteenth is a superb hole whose character comes from its length, 343 metres. Most players will play a one-iron or three-wood to leave themselves with a full-length pitch to a well-bunkered green.

At 197 metres, the long par-three seventeenth hole has bunkers on either side of the green, and a ravine awaiting the sliced shot! To finish – a long uphill par-five, 498 metres, with 'instant death' awaiting anything that is hit vaguely left. The green itself is on two levels, segregated by a one-metre rise, which can play havoc with the silkiest of touches.

The sixth green

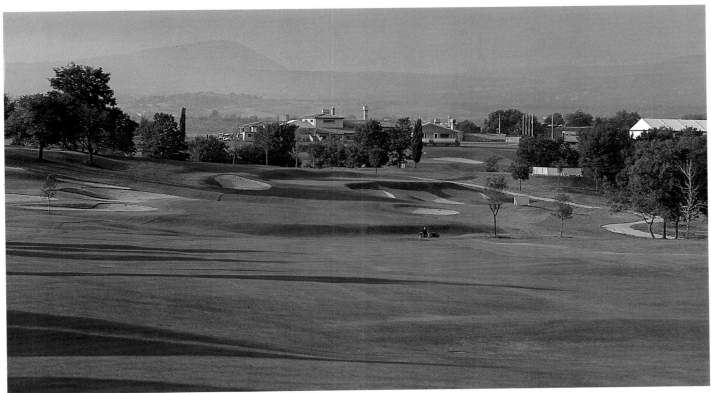

The long par-five seventh hole

The tenth hole

A view of the sixteenth hole

The seventeenth hole

Milano

Monza, home of the Milan Golf Club, is perhaps better known for its Grand Prix race track. It is a favourite forest playground for the Milanese.

Sandy Lyle of Britain and Spain's José Marie Canizares were Lancia Italian Open Champions there in the 1980s, and the championship returned to the venue in 1990 after three years at Monticello, Como.

With out of bounds beyond the wire fencing to the right along its whole length, and woods on both sides of the fairway, the 456-metre first is no easy opener. Bunkers to the left at the corner of the gentle right-hand dog-leg can trap the unwary.

Out of bounds right and woods left and right again appertain to the par-four second, which has a raised green defended by wide bunkers on either side, while three large bunkers protect the front and sides of the slightly raised and convex green at the 179-metre third.

The fourth goes the other way and is a 317-metre par-four, which dog-legs slightly right around a wood with three big bunkers in the driving area left, while the fifth is a dog-leg left surrounded by high trees, with bunkers on both sides at the neck of the 'bend'. A bunker left at 180 metres and two right at 200 and 220 metres put a premium on an accurate tee shot at the sixth, which also dog-legs left towards a green crowded with trees and sand-traps.

You hit out of the woods to a slightly raised green at the 183-metre seventh, which has two big bunkers in front, then you tackle a sharp dog-leg right, wooded on both sides, where a line tight to the trees right is recommended off the tee to set up the approach to a three-tier green guarded by four bunkers.

The ninth back to the clubhouse is a long par-five at 508 metres, whose green is defended on the left by two grass bunkers; the tenth an uphill par-three of 202 metres, with bunkers left and right short of a green hemmed in by trees; and the eleventh a dog-leg right with out of bounds right, trees both sides and bunkers left and right approaching the green.

Four bunkers short of the green and a ditch long left guard the tree-shrouded par-three twelfth, while the par-four thirteenth, with out of bounds right and a bunker left at 180 metres, just short of a drop in the fairway, is another tester.

The fourteenth is a pronounced dog-leg right with bunkers strewn across the fairway in the driving area, and out of bounds right and beyond a green guarded by tall trees right and bunkers on three sides. Trees left and a bunker at 220 metres right put a premium on a straight drive at the fifteenth. You drive out of the woods from an elevated tee at the par-five sixteenth, then hit to a raised green with out of bounds behind.

The wooded par-four seventeenth has two bunkers right to catch the faded tee shot and a raised, well-bunkered green, while raised ground at the corner of the left-hand dog-leg eighteenth bounces the ball to the left to set up the approach to a green with out of bounds twenty metres beyond.

The thirteenth hole

The eleventh hole   **Overleaf:** *The eighteenth hole*

Monticello

American Billy Casper was the first winner, in 1975, of the Italian Open at the Circulo Club of Monticello, which, as its name implies, has a circular clubhouse, of ultra-modern design.

Just a few minutes off the *autostrada* from Milan (half an hour's drive distant) by the beautiful lakeside town of Como, with the Alps and Switzerland beyond, Monticello also staged the Italian Opens of 1987, when Sam Torrance beat José Rivero in a play-off; 1988, when Aus-

tralian Greg Norman, lured to Italy by the offer of a fifth Ferrari to add to his collection, finished as champion; and 1989, when Ronan Rafferty took his first seventy-two-hole Tour title.

The drive to the opening par-four hole must bisect two large sand-traps, and the second shot avoid bunkers left and right of an ample green, while the second, a dog-leg right, requires the tee shot to land left of centre fairway to afford a clear entry to the green.

The seventh hole

You hit over a water-filled ditch at the par-three third to a target guarded by big bunkers right, then tackle a 502-metre par-five, which dog-legs sharply to the right. Try to bite off too much and you could end up in the trees right, while two big bunkers left await the too-safe drive.

The par-four fifth is another dog-leg right, with bunkers at the neck, left, and a lake beyond on the left is another worry. The same lake awaits as punishment for a quick hook off the sixth tee. At 203 metres the seventh would be a testing par-three even if the green were not on an island in the lake. A nerve-stretcher this, especially in the wind.

Only a weak fade will flirt with the water at the par-four eighth, where the second shot, if you miss the fairway, can be tightly demanding. The ninth, at 511 metres a par-five, is not too demanding if you land your drive in the fairway.

A bunker left can trap the tee shot at the tenth. You should be safely short of the fairway trap at the par-five eleventh, then you fly your second over two streams which cross the fairway.

Bunkers left and right in the landing area at the left-hand dog-leg twelfth must be negotiated, while traps either side of the green at the thirteenth, a long short hole at 223 metres, must be bisected.

The fourteenth is a long par-five, veering right between the trees with bunkers front, left and right of the green and trees beyond, while bunkers left off the tee are the chief hazard at the fifteenth.

A tough finishing stretch gets under way with the 393-metre sixteenth, which curves left, with the lake tight to the fairway on that side and a road and ditch beyond it to the right.

You must hit over the road and ditch to the well-bunkered short seventeenth, then keep right off the tee to miss a big bunker at the last. End in the rough right and you face a testing second over a big greenside sand-trap.

The eighteenth hole

The par-three seventh hole

The eighteenth green and clubhouse

The tenth hole

A tall tree guards the sixteenth green

Ugolino

The club is situated in the Chianti hills nine kilometres south of Florence, above the market town of Grassina. On clear days excellent views of the city can be seen from the course. Golf has been played in Florence since 1889, and since 1933 at its present site, on a course unchanged since it was designed by Blanford & Gannon, the English architects. For the tournament the two 9-holes are reversed, which offers a tougher finish along with better viewing for spectators.

The 203-metre first hole requires a slightly downhill tee shot to a narrow green, which is cut into the side of the hill. There are bunkers to the front left of the green, and a deep cavernous bunker on the right, together with a lake that awaits the loose shot – a tough opening hole. The uphill tee shot at the 350-metre second needs to be long and high. There is out of bounds on the left of the fairway, marked by the greenkeepers' sheds, and also behind the green, which is guarded by two bunkers on each side.

Out of bounds runs the full length of the right-hand side of the 469-metre third hole, although the fairway slopes from right to left. The green is approached by a slight dog-leg from left to right.

The next five holes at Ugolino are situated on the other side of the main road, under which a golfers' underpass has been built. The fourth hole, at 340 metres, requires another uphill tee shot, with the front of the green again guarded by bunkers, both left and right.

With a slight dog-leg to the right, and a narrowing fairway, at the 325-metre fifth many players take an iron from the tee, rather than risk the driver. And the short sixth, at 148 metres, is another uphill tee shot, with large bunkers front and left of the green. The seventh hole has possibly the flattest, and widest, fairway on the course, to which players drive across a public right of way. At 335 metres, the narrow green is protected by trees on the left and a large bunker on the right.

A large tree in the middle of the fairway at driving distance, out of bounds and a lateral water hazard on the right-hand side dominate the 476-metre eighth hole. Having successfully negotiated the tee shot, the second shot is to a slightly elevated green. Then it is back under the road to the ninth, which is a 294-metre severe dog-leg to the right around tall pine trees. The majority play an iron for safety from the tee, although the brave may

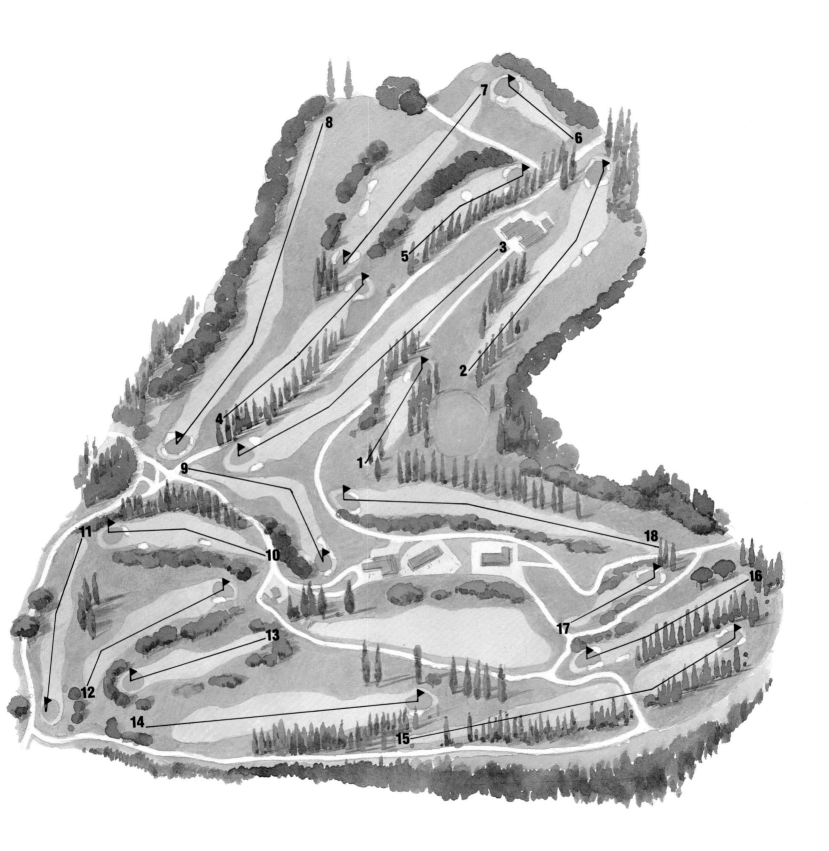

cut the corner. The green is situated right outside the clubhouse.

From an elevated tee, the 305-metre tenth hole requires a tee shot over the main driveway of the club, to a right-to-left sloping fairway. The green is again narrow, guarded by bunkers to the front right and left. The eleventh requires an uphill tee shot to a severely right-to-left sloping fairway. At 258 metres, the very long and the very brave may attempt to drive the elevated green – but out of bounds waits behind and to the right of this very wide, but narrow in depth, green.

An inviting drive from an elevated tee is on offer at the 298-metre twelfth hole, which is a slight dog-leg up to a steeply elevated green. Although the tee and green are on the same level at the thirteenth, a deep depression lies between the two, so the full 199-metre distance must be hit.

Another depression at the fourteenth requires a long carry with the tee shot to reach the flat of the fairway at the 398-metre hole. The green is again narrow with trouble lurking on the right-hand side. Then a very narrow fairway at the 472-metre fifteenth hole, with out of bounds on the right-hand side, must be hit if the green is to be reached in two. The second shot has to be hit over some tall pine trees situated on the corner of a slight dog-leg.

At the sixteenth, long hitters can attempt to drive the well-guarded green at 280 metres. However, with the hole being uphill and having a tall tree directly in front of the green, few will reach the putting surface. The seventeenth, the shortest hole on the course at 130 metres, is played from an elevated tee to a pear-shaped green.

A very narrow, tree-lined fairway makes the final drive at the 461-metre eighteenth hole quite formidable, with a solitary pine tree some 300 metres from the tee making the second shot to an elevated green an interesting proposition.

The first hole, a long difficult par-three to start

The long, narrow eighteenth hole, dominated by pine trees

The elevated second green

The short sixth hole

The long par-five eighth hole

The seventh green

BELGIUM

Professional golfers are inveterate complainers. Fault-finding seems to be an occupational disease and, it must be admitted, the stress of international travel, the complications of different currencies, different languages and lifestyles did justify moments of discontent in the pioneering years of the PGA European Tour. In addition the insular British were quick to find fault with foreigners and foreign ways in those early days simply because they were foreign. There were misunderstandings and embarrassments and the Tour staff had to acquire the skills of diplomacy in addition to their qualifications as unofficial travel agents, interpreters and administrators. It was all part of the tourist syndrome which might be summed up in the expression: 'These people don't understand the meaning of an honest pint of ale.'

In time, as the visitors discovered that continentals did not eat their young and that they did in fact understand and respect the Rules of Golf, the mood changed. Living together, playing together and sharing the discomforts of travel together united the nationalities into a cosmopolitan whole. Instead of national cliques, with the Spaniards sticking together in one closely knit brotherhood and the Italians forming another national coterie, the players began to form friendships not on the basis of ethnic backgrounds but on the basis of common interests. Baldovino Dassu dined with Michael King, and the Welshman Brian Huggett and the Belgian Donald Swaelens, of fond memory, became inseparable. The Brits picked up smatterings of European tongues and the Europeans in self-defence learned English. It was the sensible solution to the communications problem to settle on one language and English was the obvious choice. In many ways the European Tour mirrored the progress of the EEC's faltering early progress, before natural doubts and suspicions became allayed and everyone began to work together.

The ninth green and clubhouse at Royal Waterloo

The assimilation of the polyglot tribe of golfers was a smoother process in Belgium than elsewhere owing to the ambassadorial influence of the late Donald Swaelens, who had been a popular and regular competitor in Britain for many years, and even more so of the great Flory van Donck. It is curious that the name of van Donck is virtually unknown outside Europe, especially among younger golfers. Prior to the publication of the book *The Fifty Greatest Post-war Golfers* the selection panel met to consider nominees and van Donck's name was put forward. Half the panel had never heard of him. Yet the tall and courtly figure of Flory van Donck was a giant of the game during the post-war era, a prolific winner and a fine advertisement for professional golf and for Belgium. Most of the senior players of the new PGA European Tour, such as Neil Coles and Christy O'Connor, were his friends, and he smoothed the way for the golfing invasion of Belgium. The Belgian custom of serving chips with everything also helped to make the British golfers feel at home.

Another helpful factor was the historical link between Belgium and Britain. Nobody with the slightest feeling for the past could fail to be warmed by the resonances emanating from the name of Belgium. Few British families have not lost a relative in battle on Belgian soil fighting for the common cause, and dull indeed of soul would be he who could approach Waterloo without humming the opening bars of the 1812 Overture. On the first visit to Royal Waterloo most of the players made a pilgrimage to the battlefield, and by the end of the week they all knew the very glade on the course where the Scots Greys had assembled before their charge against Napoleon's Guards.

Dull also of soul would be he who could look out over Royal Waterloo without a feeling of impatience to lace on his spikes and get at it. There are some open holes but it is mainly a forest course of the best type, which is to say that the finest elements of the course were started some 300 years before anyone thought of making a golf

The eighteenth hole at Royal Waterloo

course. Avenues of majestic trees define the fairways which swoop up hill and down dale, and for the spectators the sting of excitement comes in the tail. When Harry Colt and C. H. Alison designed Royal Waterloo in 1923 they worked on the sound, if currently unfashionable, principle of letting the land dictate the sequence and nature of the holes. That consideration far outweighed any notions of mathematical symmetry of two halves of par-thirty-six, each containing two par-threes and two par-fives to break up the staple diet of par-fours at regular intervals. In this case the topography suggested that the round should finish with a run of three successive par-fives and so that is what they built. To the average long-handicapper this arrangement might loom as an arduous penance after fifteen more or less manageable holes, but to the professionals, to whom length is a minor consideration, a par 5-5-5 finish offers the prospect of birdie-birdie-birdie with the even headier prospect of replacing one or all of those birdies with eagles. Of course, the pursuit of those birdies can also involve the slightest pressing with the driver to set up the most favourable approach shot, resulting in those abominable sixes and sevens, but such negative thoughts must be held at bay.

So tournaments at Royal Waterloo invariably produce sporting echoes of the thundering hooves of the cavalry in that pivotal contest just down the road which changed the direction of European history. In 1988 the players were introduced to a new battlefield, Bercuit, also near Brussels, a course distinguished by not yet having been honoured with a royal prefix, putting it in the minority among Belgian golf clubs. For students of

golf it can be described amply enough in three words: Robert Trent Jones. It is young enough (1965) to be in the modern idiom, but old enough to be fully matured. For many years Trent Jones was the bogey man of golf architects among professional golfers, of a calibre somewhat short of greatness. He was, they said, a sadist who hated golfers and got his jollies from watching the humiliation of the pros. Ben Hogan set the unfortunate example of Trent Jones denigration. When Hogan tamed the 'monster' Oakland Hills, a course revised by Trent Jones, to win the 1951 US Open, Mrs Trent Jones offered him her congratulations and was considerably taken aback when he gruffly replied, 'If your husband had to play his own courses for a living you would starve.' In recent years the professionals have come to appreciate the genius of Trent Jones, and in a poll of PGA European Tour players one of his courses was voted the best they played all season. It is true that his courses do not permit much margin of error and they also require acute judgment in course management, selecting the most favourable target areas and planning what type of shot to hit. But are not those the very requirements necessary to produce a worthy winner? Golf, after all, does not begin and end with hitting the ball. It involves, or should involve, thought and character as well as motor skills, and Bercuit provides just such an examination.

Belgium and Holland offer good examples of an attitude, universal in modified forms, which pays lip service to the idea of golf for everyone, while at the same time defending the exclusivity of the game and thereby hindering progress. Perhaps that rather complicated

thought can be better expressed by an example. The butcher and the baker are members of a fashionable golf club. The candlestick maker deplores the snobbery which deprives him of the chance to play golf. Eventually he is admitted into membership of the club and immediately becomes the most virulent snob, jealously insisting that the club must 'maintain its standards' and keep out the riff-raff. He has achieved the social cachet of golf club membership and the last thing he wants is to have it diluted by an open-door policy. Hence golf clubs vie with each other in exclusivity in a social hierarchy which reaches a pinnacle in the aristocracy of the game, the handful of clubs for which membership is by invitation only. Getting into those clubs is like becoming a fellow of All Souls College or being admitted into the Order of Merit. The golf club tie becomes a tribal symbol proclaiming a man's social standing, and within the subtle pecking order of the game an exclusive tie and a thirty-six handicap are infinitely 'better' than a down-market tie and a scratch rating. To some extent this may be a harmless conceit, except that this exclusivity tends to be based on wealth rather than on virtue, so the snobbish clubs generally have the better courses.

That situation presented both a challenge and an opportunity to a Dutch entrepreneur, Freddie Hooghiemstra, and his partners. They recognized that Holland and Belgium were prime areas for golf development and they believed that since neither country had a tradition of cheap and nasty public golf amenities, they might start a tradition of high-quality amenities for newcomers to the game. They began with a comprehensive indoor range, on the grounds that stimulating interest in golf would provide a market for club and course development. The decline in agriculture simultaneously made available land, often associated with ancient châteaux suitable for conversion into superb clubhouses.

Others had the same idea, one splendid example being Golf de la Tournette on the motorway between Brussels and Paris. Two courses have been built on the wooded park of a great seventeenth-century château. An imaginative innovation of this development was to engage two golf course architects, the distinguished William Amick to create an American-style course of championship calibre, and Martin Hawtree to design and build a shorter and rather less testing English type of course.

This flurry of course development, not just in the Low Countries but throughout Europe, signified much more than the obvious fact that continental Europe would quickly increase the percentage of golfers per head of population compared with the British Isles. It meant that the legions of continental recruits to the game would start on modern courses with driving ranges and all the amenities for practice and tuition. The players would thus enjoy a huge advantage over their counterparts in the British Isles, where most of the courses were built during the early part of the century, when the Corinthian ethic decreed that practice was tantamount to cheating. British and Irish golf thus faced the challenge of remodelling both their courses and their attitudes if they were to compete realistically with the Continent in producing the champions of tomorrow.

The eighteenth hole and clubhouse

Royal Waterloo

As its name suggests, the Royal Waterloo course outside Brussels, designed in 1960 by Fred Hawtree, is laid out on the very battlefield where Napoleon and the Duke of Wellington fought it out in 1815.

Another Englishman, Gordon J. Brand, followed Wellington to victory in the Volvo Belgian Open there in 1989, and Ireland's Eamonn Darcy was champion in 1987, when storms reduced the event to fifty-four holes. That victory earned Darcy his place on Europe's Ryder Cup side, and he played a vital role in the first victory on American soil at Muirfield Village by beating Ben Crenshaw in the singles. Two Swedes, Ove Sellberg and Per Ulrick Johansson, won in 1990 and 1991 respectively.

The par-four first offers a swift birdie opportunity, provided you don't stray into the bunker at the corner of the right-hand dog-leg off the tee, while the even more acutely dog-legged par-four second presents another good chance. But beware the three bunkers running up the right side of the green.

The 489-metre third has a plantation of new trees to influence your tee shot, then you play out to the right across a string of bunkers to a big green with more bunkers left and right.

The 173-metre fourth has a big bunker to the left and three in a row to the right of the target, and there is a sand-trap in mid-fairway awaiting the unwary tee shot at the par-five fifth, which plays very long into the wind, with more bunkers left and right and trouble beyond.

There is out of bounds all along the left at the sharply dog-legged left par-four sixth, with a bunker waiting for the too-straight tee shot, while four bunkers are ranged around the green at the 147-metre seventh hole, with out of bounds menacing beyond.

A bunker to the left can trap the tee shot at the 328-metre eighth hole, but this is a genuine birdie opportunity, whereas – in contrast – the par-five ninth green, on top of the hill, is very difficult indeed to hit in two, with big bunkers waiting to swallow anything offline.

If possible attack the green at the 368-metre tenth from the right half of the fairway, before facing the longest par-four on the course, the 388-metre eleventh, a sharp right-hand dog-leg with lots of trouble on the right. The 176-metre twelfth is a panoramic affair, but don't lose sight of the bunkers left and right of the target and the trouble beyond.

You must keep left of jutting trees as you drive down the narrow 373-metre thirteenth towards a well-trapped target, then it is uphill at the 358-metre fourteenth, another tree-narrowed hole with a huge bunker right of the green and one short centre to make judgment of your approach tricky.

Encroaching trees pose a problem at the 147-metre fifteenth, while the 439-metre sixteenth hole demands a long drive down the right and a long, accurate second. Then you can contemplate a double birdie finishing flourish.

The seventeenth is a long and deceptive par-five, well bunkered left and right by the green, and the eighteenth another par-five, with three big bunkers waiting to swallow the sliced approach.

The ninth hole

The sixteenth hole

The downhill dog-legged third hole

SWEDEN

The current vigorous growth in professional golf in Scandinavia owes much to two exceptional men, a tennis player and an ice hockey star. The young Bjorn Borg was a phenomenon, the despair of his coaches and tennis theorists because he invented a private game of his own, which he called 'Hit it back over the net'. Style and correct technique meant nothing to Borg, whose exceptional reflexes, wonderful eye and outstanding athleticism enabled him to conquer the world of tennis with this simple philosophy. Needless to say, he became a huge hero in Sweden, a country which breeds an enthusiasm for sport of quite abnormal intensity because of the short summer playing season. It is debatable whether sport is a suitable medium for the expression of a national identity but, human nature being what it is, every nation likes to think of itself as a master race, and Borg certainly gave the Swedes good reason to harbour such a conceit. The Swedes' vision of themselves as a nation of supermen had already been nourished by the likes of world heavyweight champion Ingemar Johanssen and the multi-talented Sven Tumba, who perfectly fitted the ideal of a Norse god among men. Tumba represented Sweden at international level in five sports: ice hockey, skiing, football, skating and golf, and in a popularity contest it would have been a toss-up between Tumba and the King.

Tumba well understood the national craving for sporting success, and when he grew too old for the energetic sports at which he had excelled, he devoted his full attention and enthusiasm to golf, a game which he played with enormous verve and power – including, unfortunately, the putting. He opened a golf centre in the middle of Stockholm, on the grounds that the first essential was to provide facilities to introduce his countrymen to the game, and then he turned his attention to tournament promotion. Since there was no tradition of major golf sponsorship in Sweden in the early

The eighteenth hole at Drottningholm

1970s, Tumba realized that the only way to create a major tournament was to persuade many sponsors to contribute amounts of such modesty that they could virtually be provided from petty cash, without involving the companies in all the paraphernalia of market research and board meetings to approve special appropriations. It was all done on the old boy network. Tumba would ring up the chairman of a company and say, 'I want you to send me a thousand crowns for a golf tournament.' Usually the name Tumba was enough to extract an immediate commitment. If the chairman enquired what his company would receive in return, Tumba explained that the firm's name would be emblazoned on a caddie jacket. If the player survived the pre-qualifying round the jacket would be paraded around the golf course in front of a huge gallery for at least two rounds. It might even be picked up by the television cameras. Some businessmen wanted a guarantee that their jackets would at least get into the tournament proper. Certainly, replied Tumba, you can have the caddie jacket of an exempt player for 5,000 crowns. But if you want to be sure of getting the company name on television, you would be better off having one of the big name players at 10,000 crowns.

By ruthlessly exploiting his celebrity status Tumba thus enrolled hundreds of sponsors, each putting in different amounts for different parts of the action, and the first really successful example of multi-sponsorship was launched on to the European Tour in the form of the Scandinavian Enterprise Open. Admittedly, those early SEO promotions had something of the appearance of the Spithead Review, with flags and banners and advertising hoardings all over the course, but at least professional golf had been launched in Sweden as a major spectator sport. Since the most modest level of sponsorship involved a ticket for the sponsor, the house was well and truly papered and large crowds guaranteed, albeit largely of perplexed businessmen curious to see what they were getting for their money.

Putting on the eighteenth green during the PLM Open at Ljunghusens

The nature of the Swedish landscape imposes a certain sameness on Sweden's inland courses. Farmland is far too precious for golf, so most of the courses are built among the pine forests, where only a thin layer of earth covers the rocky landscape. And none of the early SEO courses, Drottningholm, Bokskogens, Vasatorp or Linköping, had been built with the requirements of tournament promotion in mind. If the SEO was to develop into a major sporting occasion it would have to have a purpose-built facility and this is exactly what Tumba set about providing. With his usual energy and enthusiasm he drummed up the finance and created the Sven Tumba Country Club along the shore of a mighty lake at Ullna, near Stockholm. Visiting stars who came to play the SEO were invited to give their suggestions for refining the original design. Someone, for instance, suggested that a lone tree in the seventeenth fairway constituted an unfair hazard, and Tumba went out that evening and cut it down. Lee Trevino thought that it would add a certain zest to that same fairway if a promontory was built into the lake to accommodate what would be almost an island green; when he returned the next year the new green was in play. Just how good a course it may be is a matter of individual opinion, but there is universal agreement that it is exceptionally beautiful, particularly along the run of lakeside holes, and wonderfully exciting with a high potential for disaster on almost every hole.

The SEO thus made for spectacular and gripping television, thereby providing an enormous boost for the tournament and its sponsors. There is, however, a dismal economic truth in that expression about easy come, easy go. Tumba, who had only to lift a telephone to raise finance for the tournament, was obviously unable to employ the same technique on behalf of a private club. At the same time he was unable to restrain his expensive ambitions for improving the course. Mr Micawber's sage observation was that if annual expenditure exceeds annual income by sixpence then the result is unhappiness. In this case, the shortfall was rather more than sixpence and something had to give. Tumba and the club went their separate ways and the tournament moved to Drottningholm.

The success of the SEO naturally excited the interest of big business, notably PLM, the giant manufacturer of cans and packaging. The company experimented with minor tournaments before taking the plunge in 1986 with a full-blown European Tour event, to be rotated around three remarkable courses on the southernmost tip of Sweden.

Of these Falsterbo is the oldest and most celebrated, a flattish but by no means featureless links course bounded on the one side by the Baltic and on the other by the Straits of Denmark. In the early days of the club's existence the caddies, seeking somewhere to try their hand at this curious sport, obtained permission to play among the tracery of backwaters just over the club's fence. They laid out their course, which soon became an independent club in its own right, Flommen. And just two miles inland a new course, Ljunghusens, was built on open heath; and so this little corner of Sweden became a thriving golf resort, especially popular for the fact that golf can be played in the moderate southerly climate virtually all year round.

In the event Flommen proved to be less than entirely suitable for a major golf promotion, leaving the tournament to introduce Bokskogens into its trinity of venues. Bokskogens was an obvious choice, being close by, near Malmö, but it was also a happy choice because it preserved PLM's policy of rotating the tournament around different types of golf course. It now had a classic links in Falsterbo, an open heath in Ljunghusens and a typically Swedish woodland course in Bokskogens. For the veterans of the Tour it was a welcome return to a happy hunting ground of the early 1970s, for Bokskogens had twice hosted the SEO. The players liked Malmö, because it was so accessible from Copenhagen airport by hydrofoil, because the town was compact enough for it to be easy to sort out the best bars and restaurants, and because the golf course was very much in the British tradition.

Tony Jacklin certainly found it to his liking in 1974 because he ended a lean spell with a comfortable victory there. This was during Jacklin's fractious period, when he complained *ad nauseam* about his lost putting in terms which suggested that his putting was a precious object which had been stolen in the night by evil spirits. One felt that he might imminently offer a reward for its safe return. As a result of this attitude he was hyperconscious of cameras and crowd disturbances. He could detect the untimely click of a Leica at fifty paces, and since the local smudgers (press photographers to the uninitiated) were unfamiliar with the conventions of golf, he spent an inordinate amount of time during the first round stepping away from his ball with a look of martyrdom and giving lectures on the niceties of the game. He even did impromptu photo-sessions, inviting the cameramen to click away as much as they liked while he went through the routine of putting, complete with simulated expressions of delight or disappointment, before announcing, 'Now, please, hold your fire while I do the real thing.' And it worked. Next day he enjoyed the courtesy of complete silence and scored a course record sixty-five to set the foundations of his victory.

In the standard reference book which lists every club in Europe courses are graded in four categories: great course, interesting course, holiday course and recommended course (but not too highly recommended, apparently). Falsterbo very properly is in grade 1, along with the magnificent Halmstad, but some of the other courses in this top category give rise to the feeling that Drottningholm has been rather harshly judged, damned with faint praise by its second-grade rating as an interesting course. It is certainly in interesting hunting country near Stockholm, with the interesting royal summer palace on the grounds, and on the Tour's first visit in 1973 it produced some interesting weather, in the form of stupendous thunderstorms which played hell with the playing schedule. Even making allowances for a certain sameness about Sweden's inland courses (and one can sympathize with adjudicators getting the feeling that they will go mad if they see another stand of pine trees or another outcrop of granite), Drottningholm has golfing merits which surely deserve better than that label of 'interesting', normally employed in golf as a polite euphemism for bloody horrible. Eamonn Darcy's backlift is interesting, as are some of Gary Player's more eccentric pronouncements, or a casserole of leftover paella. Perhaps the SEO's return to Drottningholm on a regular basis will bring the course to the judges' attention and persuade them to reconsider their verdict.

Tournament golf is now an established element of the Swedish sporting scene, and an attempt may be made to assess the prospects of Sweden doing in golf what it has achieved in tennis. The Swedes are impatient for success and people in golf are continually being asked how long it will be before a Swedish player might win a place in the Ryder Cup team, or win the Open championship. Such questions cannot be answered, of course, but the pace of golfing progress has been phenomenal. Thanks to the pioneering work described above, Sweden, along with Denmark, and to a lesser extent Norway, has become Europe's hottest growth area for golf. The Swedes have become a nation of golf nuts not far short of the Japanese in their fervour. As a result there has been a spate of new golf developments and the creation of the most comprehensive junior training programme in the world. The single-minded drive for golfing success has not always met with the unconditional approval of the ruling bodies, in respect of the rules of amateur status, but the interim results have been impressive. Sweden is now a powerhouse of European amateur golf, and a solid base of club and amateur golf is the essential nursery of the professional game. It is, in short, only a matter of time before Sweden follows the example of Spain in producing a Severiano Ballesteros, or Germany in producing a Bernhard Langer, or Britain in producing a Sandy Lyle, a Nick Faldo or an Ian Woosnam. Swedish professionals have already made a marked impact on the European Tour and the Swedes can assert with confidence, 'You ain't seen nothing yet.'

Drottningholm

Drottningholm, sited within walking distance of the royal palace itself and reachable by boat from central Stockholm as well as by road, has been the setting for five Scandinavian Enterprise Opens, with left-hander Bob Charles winning the first of them in 1973 and Severiano Ballesteros and Ronan Rafferty those of 1988 and 1989; and the inaugural Scandinavian Masters in 1991, won by Colin Montgomerie.

It is a basically flat, heathland course, largely open from the first to the eleventh but then wending its way through woodland coming home. Natural spectator vantage points abound on the front nine, and there is a charming hilltop clubhouse and restaurant.

Only the timid follow the left-hand dog-leg route to the green at the short par-four first, which was originally the eighteenth and plays from the road up to the clubhouse. The direct route is diagonally across a lake and the professionals regularly drive the green. Woods to the left await a hooked drive at the second, and there is more trouble over the green. At the third, a left-hand dog-leg, the tee shot must not be short or the approach must flirt with more trees in the run-up to the green to the left and beyond it. The fourth is another par-four of similar length, this time a dog-leg right with bunkers left and right, and more traps and trees around the green.

You drive diagonally to the fifth fairway, then veer to the left. Hit too straight and long and three fairway bunkers are waiting. The par-three sixth is tucked into the trees so you must not be offline, but it is back into open country after driving out of the woods to the gently dog-legged (to the left) seventh. Bunkers left of centre can trap your tee shot, and two nestling up to the green at five o'clock claim fading approach shots.

Another par-five follows at once, and at 515 metres players face a long second down the hill and across a road to a green bunkered left and right and set at an angle. At 150 metres the short ninth seems not too frightening. It's uphill, though, with bunkers short and right and a bank running away beyond, and the sloping surface demands some bold cross-green borrows.

Trees short right and bunkers long left are the hazards to avoid off the tee at the par-four tenth, where you get to a long, narrow green beyond more bunkers overhung by more trees.

Not too much trouble awaits you as you drive with the road to your right down the par-four eleventh, then it is through the woods to play down to the picturesque right-hand dog-leg twelfth. Next turn sharp right through the clearing for the 145-metre thirteenth, with steeply banked woods to the right and a big bunker short left.

It is a longish walk to the tee at the fourteenth, an ample-fairwayed par-four, which dog-legs right, while the fifteenth is a dog-leg left, a little longer and with tree trouble lurking left of the green. The par-five sixteenth is a long slog at 490 metres, and if your second is too far to the right you face a blind third over a tall tree.

At 160 metres the picturesque par-three seventeenth is not too awesome, but many pros came unstuck here as they made errors of judgment, hitting from an elevated tee in the woods to a well-bunkered target with trees to the right and beyond

Plenty of room to drive at the 510-metre eighteenth, but even the best players find it a long haul in two, many coming up short right or left, then facing a tough pitch over sand from the rough.

The par-three sixteenth hole

The ninth hole

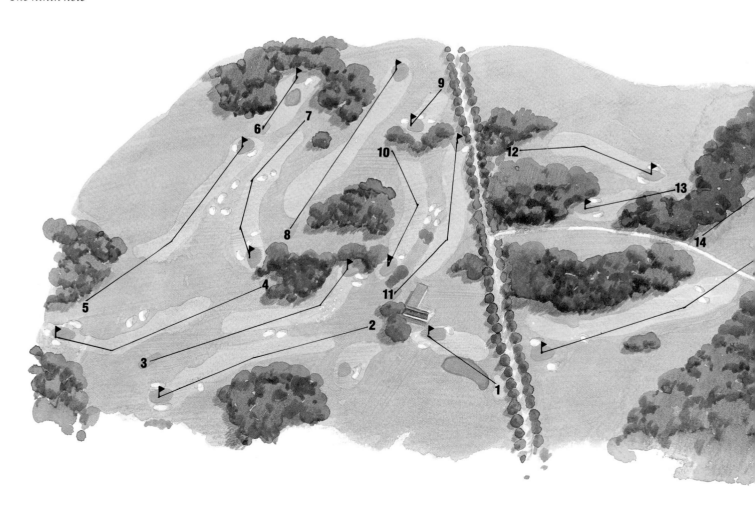

The third hole

The eleventh hole

15

16

17

Falsterbo

Falsterbo, flanked by the similar courses of Flommen and Ljunghusens, all of which have hosted the PLM Open, is rated among the great links layouts of Europe.

Situated at the southernmost tip of Sweden, where the Sound and the Baltic meet, it boasts beautiful seaside turf, gentle sand dunes and no fewer than ninety-two sand bunkers. The bird life is a delicious bonus.

The club was founded in 1909, and cattle and horses originally roamed the land. Gunnar Bauer re-designed the course in 1930 and although it has been lengthened from 5,585 metres to 5,895 metres over the years, the par has been shrunk from seventy-five to seventy-one. A lighthouse dominates the links, sometimes reduced by flooding to as few as eleven holes in winter, and coastal erosion is a perennial problem.

Trees and bushes to the left and out of bounds right confront the nervous golfer on the first, a testing par-four. Out of bounds to the right and ponds short and long left and beyond the green stare back at you on the tee at the 160-metre second, not to mention three large bunkers wrapping themselves around the front and right of the target.

The out of bounds continues all the way down the right at the narrow par-five third, which has a pond halfway up on the left and acres of rough around it. You must carry a big cross-bunker with your shot to a steeply two-tiered green.

Push out your tee shot at the par-four fourth and you are in the *flommen* or sea-water lagoon. This is rated one of the best golf holes in Sweden, with water very much coming into play again to the right, short and beyond as you hit for the green. A real nerve-tester.

You must steer clear of the water to the left and right of the par-four fifth hole, with a mid-fairway ridge waiting to bounce your ball either way, and there is more water to be found short left and beyond the well-bunkered green.

Plans are afoot to bring the lake at the short sixth more into play, but at present trees left and beyond and out of bounds right of the raised green are the hazards. The short par-four seventh in front of the clubhouse is one of the original holes: not too demanding a tee shot, but you need a very precise pitch to negotiate a bevy of bunkers.

It is all carry to the 175-metre eighth, while at the ninth the option is to try to fly the road crossing the fairway and risk tangling with a big bunker, or to play short and face a long second. Out of bounds, followed by water, await the pushed drive at the tenth, and it is all carry over water to the short eleventh, with a stream left and bunkers right ready to engulf the errant drive at the twelfth and a sandy grave short of the green.

Sheer length at 530 metres is a tester at the par-five thirteenth, and the short fourteenth, at 220 metres, is no cakewalk. Go for it in two at the 480-metre fifteenth, and you must avoid the pond short left.

The sixteenth, with the beach to the right, affords a real birdie opportunity, but you are usually hitting into the wind to a sloping target. A the seventeenth you hit off the tee with your back to the very 'join' between the Baltic and Oresund, with a pond awaiting a hook and a long narrow green to contend with, while the often downwind eighteenth presents you with a tiny target hard up to the shoreline dunes.

The seventh green

Overleaf: *The sand dunes protect the eighteenth hole*

The seventh green and clubhouse

Bokskogens

You approach Bokskogens, opened in 1963, from Malmö, twelve kilometres or so distant, through dense beech forests, although it is by no means a woodland course.

The course is a basically flat, open parkland layout, whose water hazards are largely confined to man-made ponds, edged by woods, with individual trees strategically preserved to guard greens or shape drives and approaches.

The downhill 350-metre opening hole offers a generous birdie chance, with a murky pond at drive's length to the right presenting the only real problem. Big bunkers must be negotiated at the 190-metre par-three second, while the par-four third presents no special problems.

A battery of greenside bunkers and a steeply rising,

double plateau putting surface have to be contended with at the fourth, where the drive must find the left half of the fairway.

The fifth, at 508 metres, is a monster of a par-five. Long hitters going for it must avoid drifting right into water and trees. Come up short right and you must play blind to a triple-tiered green.

Beautiful Lake Yddingen lies immediately to the right of the pretty par-three sixth hole, where the tee shot is over a pond to a tree-ringed green. However trees, shrubs and tall reeds hide the lapping waters from the player's view.

You fire out of the trees to the par-four seventh, where the premium is on accuracy in your approach to a tiny, well-trapped green. Next a bunker and a pond strategically sited to the right of the par-four eighth fair-

The short par-three tenth hole

way wait for the pushed tee shot, while bunkers left are the problem awaiting the tee shot at the enormous uphill par-five ninth, especially into the wind. A genuine three-shotter this.

Back at the picturesque stone clubhouse, with its raised practice putting green, you turn sharp left to tackle the 145-metre tenth. Here a Volvo car, on offer for an ace during the PLM Open, was parked on a raft floating on the pond fronting the green.

The par-four eleventh tests a golfer's accuracy from tee to green. The left side of the fairway must be favoured off the tee with a tall tree guarding the green right front, and a pond short right, while no problem to the pros, lies in wait for errant handicappers.

The pond bisecting the long twelfth is easily flown in two by the pros, who can comfortably reach the green with the wind behind, and even club golfers can hope for birdies at the par-four thirteenth and fourteenth, although long drivers should beware the pond biting in on the right.

Not until you almost reach the steeply sloping green can you enjoy a view of Lake Yddingen at the short fifteenth. Then a gentle fade off the tee is the right shape for the sixteenth which has trees right and left, while length and accuracy from the seventeenth tee are essential to afford a clear view of the green, as you turn at right-angles left to fire over a paddock to a tiered target.

There is out of bounds all the way left at the tough par-five home hole and a copse short right below the green if you come off your approach: a grandstand finishing hole to a course which, incidentally, boasts another intermingling nine holes.

Barsebäcks Golf and Country Club

Barsebäcks, the venue for the 1992 Scandinavian Masters, is situated approximately forty-eight kilometres north of Malmö. The tournament is to be played over a composite eighteen holes from both the Old and New Barsebäcks Courses, giving a par of seventy-two over a challenging test of 6,675 metres. This composite course combines seven holes from the New Course – designed by Donald Steel and opened in 1989, and running through the pine trees – and eleven of the more established holes along the sea front on the Old Course, which was built in 1969 and designed by the late Ture Bruce.

The first hole, at 305 metres, plays as a straight hole with trees to go over 220 metres from the tee. A small green is guarded by a bunker on the right-hand side, but the hole provides a relatively easy start. The 358-metre second hole is characterized by having trees running all along its left-hand side from tee to green, and beyond the green. The long par-five third hole, at 510 metres, is a dog-leg left over a big pond, followed by the short 180-metre fourth where the green is guarded by a kidney-shaped bunker on the right.

The longest hole on the course, the 520-metre fifth, has pine trees running along the right-hand side, and a bottle-neck created at 250 metres from the tee. The next two holes are dog-legs – the sixth at 410 metres to the right, and the seventh at 365 metres to the left. Coming to the short eighth hole, you face an iron shot for the 150-metre carry over a pond in front of the green – this is normally played into the west wind.

The last hole on the front nine is the longest par-four at 425 metres, with a green well-guarded by both trees and two bunkers. It is also the first of three seaside holes, with the tenth at 400 metres dog-legging left, and the eleventh a 375-metre dog-leg right.

The last seven holes of this composite course run through the pine trees. The twelfth, a 510-metre par-five, needs two straight shots to a sharp dog-leg left, with a wedge remaining to a difficult green hidden in a corner. Donald Steel is the man behind the last six

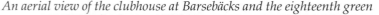

An aerial view of the clubhouse at Barsebäcks and the eighteenth green

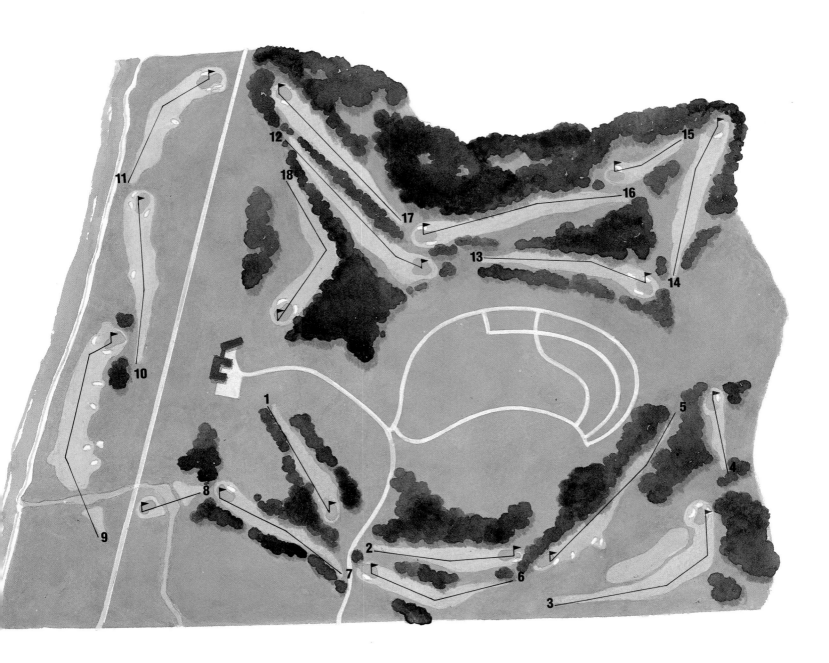

holes, starting with the thirteenth, a 385-metre slight dog-leg right to a well-guarded green with three big bunkers and a severe slope.

The fourteenth is a straight hole, at 395 metres, with a greenside bunker on the right, and the short fifteenth at 175 metres has bunkers on both sides of the green. You need a long drive at the 414-metre sixteenth hole in order to reach the narrow, but 50-metre-long, green, with bunkers on both sides.

From the tee at the seventeenth hole you can see through the pine trees behind the green 400 metres away to the sea. The right club is needed for the approach shot, because the green is 69 metres long and guarded on the left by a bunker. The final hole, at 385 metres, is a sharp dog-leg right at 229 metres, approaching a reasonably large green. In order to cut the corner you need a very long and high tee shot over the pine trees.

Ullna

Sven Tumba, Sweden's most famous sporting all-rounder, created the course at Ullna with a little bit of help from his friends, with stars such as Arnold Palmer, Gary Player and Tony Jacklin advising on particular holes.

On a balmy summer's day the course holds no terrors, but when the waters of the nearby lake start making waves, as the wind whips up, beware – Ullna, with its trees and ponds and rocky outcrops, not to mention the lapping lake itself, can turn into a fearsome card-wrecker. Sandy Lyle once ran up double figures at the first.

The opening hole is an uphill par-five through the trees, the second a much more comfortable par-four, dog-legging uphill to the right, with most of the trouble in judging your second.

Hole number three is a spectacular par-three, played steeply downhill from the woods across a pond to an island green with the lake waiting thirstily beyond – a memorable short hole.

The fourth offers a chance for the longer hitter, placing his tee shot close to the lake on the right, to carry a second shot some 190 metres across the water to the green. The more cautious player plays around the left-hand side of the lake.

The 190-metre short fifth down below the clubhouse demands that a tee shot be struck right across the water, often through a stiff breeze, to a big, semi-island green:

another remarkable hole. Tumba then relented briefly with a forgiving short par-four sixth, although, after a far from demanding tee shot, you must again aim at a water-ringed target with your next.

Then it is back inland and a climb up the dog-legged seventh to the top of the hill, then back down again, like the Grand Old Duke of York's marching armies, to the eighth.

Back you go up the hill to the ninth, and back down again, bearing to the right to pitch to the green beside the trees at the 400-metre tenth. Then it's off to the woods via the par-four eleventh, 165-metre twelfth, the monster par-five thirteenth (545 metres) and fourteenth (550 metres) holes, and the eminently birdieable (provided you are accurate) short par-four fifteenth hole.

Lake Ullna comes back into play with a vengeance as you turn down the home straight, this time, of course, to your left. Your tee shot is across the water at the 180-metre sixteenth, and from a tee backing on to the lake at the seventeenth you steer your tee shot up over the hill, then pitch down to a target virtually lapped by the waves – a shot to test the nerve as the tired golfer heads for home.

It is goodbye to the lake as you bear inland again to play all the way up the hill again to the eighteenth, with the premium on a well-judged second to a green sloping right to left.

The par-five fourth hole

The par-three third hole

SWITZERLAND AND AUSTRIA

When the PGA European Tour first began, the Swiss Open was played in the week immediately following the Open championship, and it fulfilled a most important purpose: it was winding-down week. After the intensity and strain of the Open championship the players and officials appreciated the opportunity to relax in the idyllic surroundings of the Alps at Crans-sur-Sierre. It became a tradition to take wives and families along and the tournament took on the atmosphere of a golfing wakes week. The tournament organizers fostered this spirit by organizing *raclette* parties, handing out tickets for the ski lifts up to the Pleine Morte, the glacier from which the peaks of all the mighty Alps can be viewed, and providing nightly dancing and entertainment in the Sporting Club. The golf was keenly contested as usual, but for once it did not loom as the be-all and end-all of life, rather as one element in a golfing holiday.

Some of the more lurid and hilarious episodes in the never-to-be-written book of the off-duty life of the PGA European Tour were enacted at Crans, including the incident of the well-known golfer who stood calmly drinking a pint of beer in a fashionable bar while clad only in his underpants which, to complete the unconventional picture, he had draped over his head. As for some of the motoring stories, of runaway cars whose brakes failed from over-use on the hairpin bends of the road down the precipitous slope to the Rhône valley, yet another book could be written on the subject of Golfers and the Suicidal Tendency.

Inevitably the Swiss Open had to keep pace with the march of progress, however, and some of the delightful informality was consigned to the realms of nostalgia, because serious money demands a serious approach. And Switzerland's prize money became very serious indeed under the impetus of a remarkable man, Gaston Barras. In this part of Switzerland there are three dominant families, or tribes: Barras, Bagnoud and Bonvin. Gaston Barras was a modest dairy farmer and milkman in the 1960s, when Crans was a picture postcard village

known only to hikers and the handful of golfers who arrived every year for the low-key Swiss Open. But he had an entrepreneurial spirit and boundless energy and he was determined to put Crans firmly on the map, which is exactly what he did. Agence Barras led the development drive which turned Crans into a fashionable winter sports centre of a quality fit to be selected for the skiing world championship, and he promoted Crans as a year-round resort by exploiting its attractions for golfers.

He attracted major sponsors, such as Ebel and Canon, upgraded the tournament to the European Masters and engaged Jack Nicklaus to create a second championship course. In short, he transformed the runt of the European Tour's litter into one of the richest events in the European calendar. Crans may not be a diamond among golf courses but it has the most spectacular setting of the Tour, and the most exciting potential for low scores and dramatic charges. It was here that José Maria Canizares equalled the world record of twenty-seven strokes for nine holes, where Baldovino Dassu went round in sixty and where, almost certainly, the sixty barrier of the European Tour will be broken.

Since the course is under snow for half the year, and used as nursery ski slopes, it takes a long time for the course to be brought into good condition each year, and so the timing of the European Masters is a matter of delicate judgment. Too early, as was previously the case, and the grass on some of the greens does not develop sufficiently for a good putting surface; too late, and the weather can disrupt the proceedings. But when nature co-operates and the sun shines there is no more exhilarating place to watch and play golf. And between shots there is that magnificent panorama of towering, snow-capped peaks above and the silver ribbon of the Rhône shimmering in the heat haze below. The rarefied atmosphere gives the golfers the bonus of 10 per cent extra distance, which tempts the big hitters to go for the short par-fours. When the shots come off, and the par-fives yield up their quota of birdies and eagles, and the putts run truly, then the competition crackles with excitement and you feel that this is how all golf tournaments should be.

As to the future, things move slowly in this part of Switzerland because the risk of avalanches makes this a most sensitive ecological area, where the felling of a single tree almost requires a special Act of parliament. But some day, probably in the early years of the new century, the European Masters will surely move across the road to the new Nicklaus course and into a new era. And, no doubt, many will sigh for the good old days with their cherished traditions, such as the tournament staff dropping into the Hôtel des Mélèzes alongside the seventh tee for coffee and croissants with strawberry jam and a cheery '*Bonjour*' from Madame Lamont. Progress has its price but there is no stopping it, just as there is no stopping M. Gaston Barras.

Austria, meanwhile, has been slow to discover golf, or possibly golf has been slow to discover Austria. Either way, it has fewer than 5,000 players distributed around its twenty courses, half of which have only nine holes. The most venerable of them is Wien, close to the city centre of Vienna and enclosed within a race track.

For many years it was Austria's only course and its quality was not such as to generate mass enthusiasm for the game. Most of the courses have been constructed since the war, and Austria has never become a popular destination for golfing tourists. This is a pity, because Innsbrück-Igls is an outstanding course and Murhof, designed by Bernard von Limburger, is another undiscovered gem. And Semmering is an extraordinary golfing fantasy, where you play on mountain meadows situated high in the Alps, and where there is one short hole where the green appears like a pocket handkerchief, seemingly vertically below the tee. This hole offers the rare opportunity to give the ball a sharp clip with a putter off the tee and let the law of gravity do all the rest.

The building of Jack Nicklaus's Gut Altentann at Salzburg gave Austria its first course of genuine championship calibre, and the inaugural Austrian Open for the 1990 season put the country on the PGA European Tour's itinerary. And now, no doubt, golf fever will enslave yet another nation. That will be no less than fitting, because for years golf professionals have been exhorting their pupils to swing to the tempo of the waltzes of old Vienna.

The par-three sixteenth hole at Gut Altentann with Jack Nicklaus and Tony Jacklin at the official opening

Golf Club Crans-sur-Sierre

Low scores are common on one of the highest courses in Europe – Crans-sur-Sierre, perched on an Alpine plateau in the great Swiss ski resort, with the Rhône Valley way below, and home of the Canon European Masters – Swiss Open.

There are birdies and eagles galore to be bagged amid the snow-capped peaks, as the professionals wing their drives vast distances through the thin air at altitude, against a backdrop as spectacular as any in the world.

José-Maria Canizares of Spain shot twenty-seven for nine holes in 1978, Italian Baldovino Dassu sixty for eighteen holes in 1971, Sandy Lyle 127 for thirty-six holes in 1983, Swede Anders Forsbrand 192 for fifty-four holes in 1987 and Canadian Jerry Anderson 261 for seventy-two holes in 1984.

The first is a downhill par-five of 475 metres – very much a birdie hole for the professionals – while the second, coming back towards the town, is a 395-metre

A general view over Crans-sur-Sierre dominated by the snow-covered Alpine range

par-four with bunkers fronting a green tucked into the trees.

You drive from an elevated tee in the trees across a road to the tight 170-metre third hole, with steep banks on either side, then you must steer clear of trees right and left as you drive blind at the downhill fourth – which is rated a par-four despite its 460 metres.

The fifth is a tricky little dog-leg at right-angles around the wood on the right, while the sixth hole is an even shorter par-four at 299-metres, with trees hemming you in all the way up the hill to a well-bunkered green.

From the seventh tee, which is to be found in front of the Hôtel des Mélèzes, players get a spectacular view of the Rhône Valley stretching away to the right. The big hitters can drive the green 289 metres distant, but bunkers located in the hill up to the putting surface await shortfalls.

Overleaf: *The eleventh hole*

The seventh hole

The eighth is a 173-metre par-three, and the ninth a monster of a par-five at 579 metres, all uphill and bending slightly left, with a big pine barring the way to the green if you play too far left. Then it is all downhill from an elevated tee at the par-four tenth, and across the slope to the well-bunkered 194-metre eleventh before facing a downhill second to the 352-metre twelfth.

The 190-metre thirteenth plays long up the hill, then you face two big par-fives – downhill all the way at the 524-metre fourteenth, then back up the fifteenth with the green often out of view as you hit your approach.

Five-birdie finishes are common at Crans, with the sixteenth, through the pines, a par-four of only 299 metres, the seventeenth, at 324 metres, also virtually driveable, and the eighteenth, at 350 metres, none too demanding, as long as you drive straight and true and don't overshoot the target, with a big bunker and out of bounds lurking.

The first hole

The seventh hole

Gut Altentann Golf and Country Club

The PGA European Tour broke new ground in 1990 by staging the first Austrian Open on the new Jack Nicklaus-designed Gut Altentann course near Salzburg, with a tournament won by Bernhard Langer in a play-off with Lanny Wadkins. The following year the title was won by Mark Davis of England.

Woodland and water are strong features of this creation by 'the golfer of the century' in Henndorf. You tee off beside Lake Wallersee at the first towards a dual fairway. It is a 351-metre par-four offering a real birdie opportunity. Hole two is a 460-metre par-five dog-legging to the left, with a wide landing area protected by a big bunker left. With the green tucked beyond another bunker, it will prove a genuine three-shotter for most.

The third is a 424-metre dog-leg right around woods, with the approach played across a ditch, and the fourth a 181-metre par-three with a veritable desert of sand to the left. You must fire over a ditch crossing the fairway, then veer right to play to the green at the 332-metre fifth, while the par-four sixth, in the reverse direction, offers a wide landing area for the tee shot, but a huge lake adjoins the right side of the entire hole.

The seventh has a much narrower target from the tee between the lake, again on the right, and sand, and you must hit over the edge of the water to the green. There is also trouble aplenty on the left at the left-hand dog-leg eighth, a 466-metre par-five, with trees left and behind the green, and you must hit the length of a lake at the 153-metre ninth.

The tenth is a dog-leg right between the trees, the eleventh an even more acute dog-leg left, with a huge sand-trap along the left of the fairway, and the twelfth is a par-three, with trees down the right as well as sand.

You head back towards the tenth green at the par-four thirteenth, and the fourteenth resembles the eleventh in layout, while the very long par-five fifteenth dog-legs to the right towards a green whose entrance is acutely narrowed by bunkers and trees. The green at the 172-metre sixteenth is guarded all along the left by a lake with tree and sand to the right.

You face trouble all along the left at the left-hand dog-leg 365-metre seventeenth, while the par-five finishing hole is long and fairly straight, provided you avoid problems left and right off the tee.

The twelfth hole

Overleaf: *Views over the Gut Altentann course*

The 1990 Austrian Open

PORTUGAL

The story of tournament golf in Portugal is faintly biblical, in that it divides into two testaments – the old, pre-European Tour testament being firmly based on the charming little course just north of Lisbon, Estoril. Between 1953 and 1974 the twin plateaux of the Estoril course overlooking the Atlantic Ocean at Cascais were the country's golfing capital, a club with a strong Anglo-Scottish atmosphere because of its expatriate membership and its popularity among visiting golfers from Britain. It was the exclusive home of the Portuguese Open championship whose honour board contains the names of Eric Brown, Peter Alliss, Ken Bousfield (twice), Max Faulkner and Lionel Platts, as well as the leading continental players of the time, including both the Miguel brothers of Spain, the legendary Flory van Donck of Belgium and, three times, Ramon Sota, uncle of Severiano Ballesteros. It was thus an important crucible in the development of European professional golf.

Then followed the tourist boom, with the emphasis switching almost exclusively to the Algarve coast, to Frank Pennink's Vilamoura, Henry Cotton's Penina and Vale do Lobo and to Quinta do Lago. Golf, sensibly enough, was recruited as a promotional exercise to publicize the delights of the new playground of the sun-seekers. It was fortunate, both for Portugal and for golf, that Frank Pennink, who pioneered so much of continental course construction, was the architect selected to create Vilamoura, because he set a standard which those who followed had to emulate or exceed. Pennink followed the time-honoured precept of designing a course through a forest of sombrero pines on undulating ground, which represented a severe challenge off the championship tees but which could be enjoyed by less gifted holidaymakers from the middle tees. It became a popular attraction among the tourists, but some idea of its intrinsic golfing quality can be judged from the winning score, 287 by Brian Barnes, when the Portuguese Open was played there in 1979.

Henry Cotton had a similar site for Vale do Lobo, although he also had the priceless advantage of access to a stretch of the spectacular clifftops where he created the feature hole: the short seventh, or sixteenth in the later routing, played across a deep ravine. It remains one of the most memorable holes in Portuguese golf, a veritable graveyard for medal cards and a source of pocket money for the small boys who scavenge for lost golf balls at the base of the cliff.

Cotton faced a completely contrasting challenge when he was commissioned to design a championship course for the Penina Hotel. Here was a flat and featureless swamp, once a paddy field, presenting numerous problems for the architect. Cotton drained the swamp with a network of ditches and lakes, using the spoil to elevate tees and greens and to add a little movement to the fairways. The key to Penina, and its sister north course, was a comprehensive programme of tree and shrub planting. This area of Portugal was once a Moorish province, and the name Algarve means 'The Garden'. Cotton turned Penina into an arboretum of native and foreign trees which grew quickly in the benevolent climate into mighty avenues, and he adorned the scene with a profusion of flowering and decorative shrubs. He made the course enormously long, with gigantic tees, to provide maxiumum flexibility in the setting of the tee markers to accommodate changes in wind direction. This is an excellent idea, although architects do not often have the luxury of the extra land at their disposal. However, there was an embarrassing sequel when Penina was first used in major competition. On the eve of the inaugural Algarve Open someone went out at dead of night and moved all the tee markers right back to the furthest extremity of the championship tees, creating a monster of a course such as Cotton had never intended to be used in his most mischievous dreams. Play was well advanced in the first round before the enormity of the sabotage was discovered, and the golfers toiled in the sun with fairway woods and long irons at hole after hole, cursing the sadist who had set up the course. Not surprisingly the tournament was won by the old pro, Bernard Hunt, a man of unflappable temperament who once had his four-iron struck from his hands by a lightning strike, picked up the club, made par on the hole and did not think to mention the incident during his post-round interview. The culprit who had stretched Penina to its full 6,837 metres was never publicly identified.

The prolific American architect, William Mitchell, was engaged to design Quinta do Lago, three loops of nine holes now extended to thirty-six holes, for an ambitious resort development next to Vale do Lobo. The property was the finest golfing site that any architect had been presented with in Portugal and, no less important, Mitchell was not constrained by a miserly budget. The roller-coaster contours of the dense coastal pine forest gave him ample scope to exercise his genius, and he created twenty-seven holes which were quickly acclaimed both for their golfing qualities and their immaculate condition. For years, however, they were undiscovered gems – undiscovered by all but a fortunate few who were privileged to play them in glorious isolation.

The reason for this exceptional state of affairs was the Portuguese revolution, which put a stop to development just as the foundations of the clubhouse were being laid, leaving twenty-seven holes in the middle of an otherwise virgin forest. The revolution was blessedly non-violent, at least in the Algarve where life continued in its habitual tranquillity. Henry Cotton gave golf lessons to the revolutionary guards who occupied Penina, until life became intolerable when the caddie

master became leader of a workers' committee and occupied his office, appropriating his stock of golf balls and generally making life miserable. The Cottons left for Spain. At Vilamoura a sergeant and a platoon of soldiers arrived without warning one morning, lined up all the golf club staff and invited them to denounce the capitalistic crimes of the golf director, David Green. When Green came upon this curious assembly he reverted momentarily to his military persona, barked in his best Sandhurst voice, 'Attention! Left turn! Quick march!', and the soldiers scuttled off with their tails between their legs. At Faro airport visitors had to fill in forms of baffling complexity, a bureaucratic innovation which backfired because the armed guards were even more baffled than the visitors and languidly waved through frivolous passengers who had signed declarations that they were leaving the country bearing millions of roubles.

In due course democracy was established and life slowly moved forward. Hotels and villas were completed at Quinta do Lago, plus another course, São Lourenço. Robert Trent Jones put his distinctive imprint on Portuguese golf with a new course at Troia on the coast south of Lisbon, which won high praise from the straight-hitting professionals in the Portuguese Open of 1983. Those who hit wayward drives were less enthusiastic because, beyond the range of the fairway sprinklers, balls ran into what were effectively unraked bunkers on either side of the fairways. With Portugal's entry into the European Community, golf benefited from the stimulated economy. A number of new golf developments have made the country one of Europe's major growth areas for the sport.

It is universally accepted that the growing strength of the PGA European Tour derives in large part from the variety of courses and conditions that the golfers are required to play. For that reason, the inauguration of the Atlantic Open in 1990 was doubly welcome. Estela, on the exposed Atlantic coast of Portugal north of Porto, is something of a rarity in being a new links – and a pretty good one, too. The players loved it at first sight. Being a modern design, it is fair – in that the problem is clearly presented with none of the blind shots so commonly encountered on ancient links. It also enjoys, if that is indeed the word, spanking winds off the ocean strong enough to tear the superfluous yardage charts from your hand. So, glory be, the players have to go through a time warp back to the days when golf was a game of eye, and feel, and instinct, and inventiveness. It is courses like Estela (which also played host to the 1991 Portuguese Open) which make the Europeans such imaginative shot-makers and which, incidentally, win Ryder Cup matches.

Henry Cotton with the Penina Hotel and golf course in the background

The ninth hole

Overleaf: *The eighteenth hole*

Penina Hotel

The late Sir Henry Cotton, three times Open Champion, proved himself a golf course designer as well as a golfer of extraordinary skill when he created the Penina championship course on the Algarve coast, between Portimão and Lagos, in 1964.

From what was originally flat swampland he produced a magnificent test of golf, with woods and water coming into play on almost every hole. At full stretch it measures 6,837 metres, but with some tees 90 metres long it is possible to reduce this to manageable proportions.

The course, to which another British architect, Dave Thomas, recently added some refinements, is sprinkled with strategically placed bunkers, and now that the thousands of trees planted in the 1960s are mature, all the holes are well defined.

At the par-four first, away from the magnificent Penina Hotel, which offers clients a further thirty-six holes to play, you must negotiate a gentle left-hand dog-leg, flanked by a stream and sprinkled with bunkers. Keep right off the tee at the second, with a ditch and out of bounds left, then veer left to fire over a moat fronting the green, before tackling the straight-along third with its elevated green.

The fourth is a par-four ringed by sand-traps, the fifth a par-five curving severely left across a ditch and bunkers to the green, the sixth and seventh shortish par-fours, the latter with a stream and two fairway bunkers to be leapfrogged and a pond to the left.

At 221 metres the par-three eighth to an elevated green is no easy ride, while the ninth, dog-legging sharply to the left round the trees, then playing uphill over sand and water, is a hole to make you think. So is the tenth, a par-five which plays as a right-hand dog-leg around tall trees, while a trio of bunkers on the left, not to mention the trees, force you to steer right up the eleventh.

You must hop over a wide moat with your approach to the elevated green at the twelfth, flirt with the lake to your right and bunkers left as you play the testing thirteenth, then steer clear of the water, once more to the right, as you head up the par-four fourteenth.

There is plenty of trouble waiting to the left as you play straight along the narrow par-four fifteenth before tackling one of the best short holes in Portugal. From the championship tee, the sixteenth is a formidable hole, with a water-filled ditch crossing diagonally in front of a green, well-bunkered left and right, then hugging the left side of the target.

The seventeenth and eighteenth holes are par-fives, offering birdie opportunities if you still have your wits about you, but neither is anything approaching a walk-over.

You must drive the wide water hazard at the seventeenth, then carry it with your second shot down the eighteenth, with its green sloping up towards the hotel beyond three big bunkers, and trouble situated both left and right.

Quinta do Lago

Quinta do Lago in the Algarve is the quintessential holiday golf complex, with hotels, restaurants, bars, beaches, sailing, tennis, riding and a host of other sporting activities expertly catered for, and an international airport – with northern Europe's major capitals only a couple of hours away – just down the road.

Its C and B nine-hole loops add up to one of the most admired championship tests on the PGA European Tour calendar. Four of the first five Portuguese Opens there produced first-time winners, in the late Salvador Balbuena of Spain, Tony Johnstone of Zimbabwe, Britain's Warren Humphreys and Australian Mike Harwood.

The fifth hole

For the 1989 Portuguese Open – Tournament Players' Championship – the B loop comprised the outward nine and the C the homeward nine. Previously the course went out on the C loop and returned on the B, with the opening hole a right-hand dog-leg par-four between the trees, diving down, then rising to an elevated green.

You play the par-three second from a hilltop tee out across a deep valley to a large green on the opposite hill-side, with a big bunker right and a steep fall-away left, while the third is a sharp right-hand dog-leg par-five around the trees and a big bunker climbing up to a hill-top target guarded by two front bunkers.

The sixth hole

Keep to the right of a deep bunker to set up a good birdie chance at the 325-metre fourth, before tackling one of Europe's more thrilling tee shots away down to a broad fairway with a lake biting in from the right, before aiming at an angled green at the par-four fifth.

The long short sixth (200 metres from the back) is one of the toughest par-threes on tour, especially with the wind against – all carry over a huge lake. At the par-four seventh you face a blind second downhill towards the lake, after landing your tee shot on the high right-hand side of the fairway, then it is back across the lake from the tee at the eighth, a marathon uphill 510-metre par-five, before playing the left-hand dog-leg 413-metre ninth, where the pros hit over the bunker at the corner and lesser mortals keep to the right.

The par-four tenth plays down a valley fairway then up to a large green, bunkered at the front, and the eleventh is a 500-metre par-five, uphill after hitting from an elevated tee. At the twelfth underhit approaches could finish in the lake left. There is no water at the 171-metre thirteenth, but bunkers left and right must be avoided.

A big bunker and trees to the right are the worry at the 505-metre fourteenth, which bends to the left round more trees to climb up to a green bunkered front and right, while at the down-and-up par-four fifteenth you must miss the bunker left, around which the hole dog-legs.

All the trouble is on view as you look down from a high tee to the well-bunkered 182-metre sixteenth. At the next, dog-legging to the right around the woods, avoiding driving through the fairway into more trees is the first problem, and judging your approach to an elevated green the second.

Finally, a big bunker right and two more under the trees at the corner of the left-hand dog-leg confront you as you hit down and then up at the 355-metre eighteenth hole.

The fourth hole

The eighteenth hole

FRANCE

France has the oldest tradition of golf in continental Europe, the course at Pau having been inspired by Scottish officers of Wellington's expeditionary force, who played golf in the fields here at the end of the Peninsular War and returned on holiday with their clubs. Their informal course was established as Pau Golf Club in 1856. The Pays Basque country at the foot of the Pyrenees was a popular resort area for the English gentry, and Biarritz can claim the distinction of being the first municipality to recognize the importance of golf as a tourist amenity. It turned out to be a most fortuitous beachhead for golf's invasion of the Continent because the Basques, renowned for their sporting prowess, adapted easily to this alien game. Until well into the last quarter of the twentieth century every French golf professional was a Basque, including the redoubtable Arnaud Massy who became the first overseas player to win the Open championship, in 1907. Basques also dominated French tennis (Borotra, Lacoste), just as they supplied the vast majority of France's gifted rugby players.

While golf in the Pays Basque developed as a game for all, in the tradition of Scotland and Ireland, it underwent a social transformation when it spread to the capital. The clubs which evolved around Paris, mostly in the fashionable Versailles district, took their lead from the grander British clubs, such as the Honourable Company of Edinburgh Golfers and Sunningdale. Naturally the French introduced their own distinctive style to the game. Golf was chic, a word which can seldom have been employed to describe Muirfield, and this quality of designer golf, with its emphasis on correct form and elegant dress, has become a French tradition, although the development of the game in the provinces has been much more down-to-earth.

The French Open is one of the oldest championships in the world (founded in 1906) and it had a long tra-

dition of British participation, and winners, well before the advent of the European Tour. So for France, at least, the influx of the Tour in the early 1970s was merely an extension of a well-established process. The French Golf Federation saw it, however, as an opportunity to popularize the sport by taking the championship around the country. This evangelism was undoubtedly effective in bringing golf to the notice of the provinces, but, while these forays to Lyons, Le Touquet and La Baule were sporting successes, the expansion of the Tour created an economic imperative for financial success. The championship had to attract large crowds and this inevitably meant a return to the capital, to Chantilly, St Cloud, St Germain and La Boulie.

This period of expansion also brought the new course of St Nom la Bretèche into prominence with the inauguration of the Lancôme Trophy. The Lancôme started as a promotional exercise, for the sponsor and for the game, with invitations to the great players of international golf. What began primarily as an exhibition developed, however, by progressive stages into a full-blown tournament, until its final metamorphosis into the Tour's Tournament of Champions and one of the brightest jewels in the crown of the European Tour.

The course at St Nom has matured along with its tournament and has become one of the best liked – perhaps respected is the better word – among the players. The land is basically rolling pasture and, like all courses built on strong clay soils, has been slow to come into its own. But as the trees have grown, so the sound design has become defined, and today St Nom is a solid test with an exciting dramatic potential to reward outstanding play, particularly over the closing holes. Storming finishes, especially from such masters of the charge as Severiano Ballesteros, have become the hallmark of golf at St Nom.

As for the older championship courses, Chantilly probably stands supreme, although it says much for the quality of Parisian golf that the choice is by no means an

The par-three seventh hole at St Nom la Bretèche

easy one. Chantilly enjoys the blessing of a sandy soil and is essentially heathland, combining the advantages of linksland's clean lies with a moderate inland climate. St Cloud, St Germain and La Boulie are more spectacular in their topography and, some might say, more beautiful in the glory of their woodland. But for an examination of great players, which is, after all, the purpose of the European Tour's courses, Chantilly identifies the week's best golfer with the greatest certainty.

St Cloud and St Germain are both Harry Colt courses, a sure guarantee of their golfing pedigree, and were built in the early part of the century. They occupy similar, undulating terrain and St Cloud, the more open, is historically the easier test for the professionals. Flory van Donck won the French Open here in 1957 with a score of 266, which tells us as much about his exceptional skills as it does about the golf course. Greg Norman gave notice of his exciting potential in 1980 with a thrilling last round, which included an eagle at a par-five compiled with a drive, a nine-iron and a short putt on the way to a total of 268. The members of St Germain may have permitted themselves a few smiles of satisfaction at such humiliation of their neighbouring course, doubtless expressing the sentiment that the pros would never make a fool of their forest course. In thirty years nobody had broken 270 in the championship. But golf can be a humbling game for spectators no less than for players, and in thirty years there had not been a golfer like Severiano Ballesteros. In the 1985 championship at St Germain he was irresistible. The young Spaniard was still in unstoppable form and that week he made his supercharged style pay off handsomely. His first round was far from flawless, but his recovery shots following wayward drives were immaculate, as was his putting. He had a sixty-two and in the third round played even better, albeit for less reward. For a stretch of nine holes he played golf which it is impossible to imagine could ever be bettered. He eased off in the last round for a 263.

Ballesteros did it again the following year at La Boulie, another fine forest course near Versailles, giving notice of his intentions with a sixty-one in the pro-am. By this stage of his career his reputation had transcended golfing circles and excited a much wider audience as a sporting phenomenon, in much the same way that Arnold Palmer had become a national institution for millions who had no specific interest in golf thirty years previously. The crowds flocked from Paris, many of them unversed in the conventions of the game. It is quite understandable that sports fans accustomed to the exuberance of football and rugby matches should fail to appreciate the devastating effect that a camera click, or a whispered aside, or even a gentle scratching of the nose, can have on a golfer. Ballesteros contained his emotions for as long as he could but, after a second blatant intrusion into his concentration, he threw his ball at a photographer, a regrettable reaction but not without educational value. Ian Woosnam was also affected, to the extent that he switched from golf to hockey, patting his ball to and fro while his playing companions tried frantically to keep track of his score. Their consensus was that he had taken six putts and incurred eight penalty strokes for striking a moving ball, giving him a score of sixteen for the par-three third.

Of course, the Tour is not confined exclusively to Paris these days. Tournaments regularly return to the Pays Basque, frequently to the quaint old club of Biarritz. This is a clifftop course, exceedingly short and therefore always liable to yield exciting low scores. Biarritz must be a strong contender for the distinction of providing the Tour's first round below sixty, but whoever achieves that feat will have to work hard for it. The course is no pushover, since what it lacks in length it makes up for in cunning, and the smallest lapse can ruin a card. For genuine golfing quality, however, nearby Chantaco is a better bet, and no doubt this fine course will again host a major European event.

Le Touquet is a high-class links, a rare type of course for continental Europe, although there is plenty of natural scope for new links courses, particularly along this stretch of the Channel coast. The club – where P.G. Wodehouse once lived and drew inspiration from the visiting British bright young things for his characters – has two courses, a shortish forest course of considerable charm and the championship links which can prove to be a real handful when the sea breezes blow. It might be expected that tournaments at Le Touquet would be happy occasions because everything about the place is right. It is easily accessible, offers plentiful accommodation to suit every taste and pocket, and has a fine course. There is nothing, in short, to ruffle the feathers of the players; yet nearly every tournament here in recent years has involved some fractious rules dispute of impenetrable complexity. During the Open of 1976 one player complained that his two playing companions were colluding (playing the old buddy game, in the words of the plaintiff) by marking, but not lifting, a ball on the green in order to assist the other's

chip shot. The committee took more than an hour to sort that one out under what is now Rule 16 (Putting Green), later conceding that the judgment, while correct, might more appropriately have been given under the old Rule 9 (Advice and Assistance). The championship ended on a cheery note, at least, with the victory of Vincent Tshabalala, the first black South African to win a major event in Europe since Sewsunker Sewgolum won his third Dutch Open in 1964. The other South African players clubbed together and presented Tshabalala with a live goat, the traditional symbol of Bantu celebration. It was a heart-warming gesture of inter-racial brotherhood and was seen as a victory against apartheid and, it was hoped, the forerunner of more successes by black South African professionals. Those hopes proved ill founded. Tshabalala was selected for South Africa's World Cup team, but was persuaded to withdraw by black activists.

At the risk of giving diplomatic offence to the independent Principality of Monaco, the course of the Monte Carlo Open may be included in this review of

Crowds surround the eighteenth hole at St Nom la Bretèche

French golf. After all, Mont Agel is actually in France. When Americans ask why European professional golf has enjoyed such a resurgence, one element in a complex answer is likely to be a reference to adaptability, to a variety of different courses and conditions. Mont Agel is a case in point. One test of such adaptability is a reversal of the natural order, in that the clouds, normally an overhead feature of everyday life, often appear underfoot, creating the impression that the course is resting on a bed of cotton-wool.

Sometimes the cloud is too dense and the players have to be recalled, returning like wraiths through the mists. And then there are occasions when the sun shines and the sky is the same vivid blue as the Mediterranean, just as the tourist brochures promised, and the course takes on its full enchantment of Alpine beauty. And what a sight is revealed, as you look almost vertically down the mountainside, at the risk of suffering from vertigo – a hazard which does not complicate the lives of those who play their golf on courses such as Doral, where mounting two steps on to a tee represents a major change of levels. Looking down on the rooftops of Monte Carlo, the golfer must resist the temptation to tee up a ball and whale it into the wide blue yonder, to zap the casino in revenge or to bomb the yachts of the plutocrats in the harbour.

Another requirement of adaptability arises from the nature of the Alpine course. Tournament professionals talk a great deal about concentration, but the reality is that in practice they concentrate fully only on a handful of exceptionally challenging holes. For the rest they play on auto-pilot, allowing their minds to roam free and enjoy the view.

The pros are commonly depicted as soulless specialists whose artistic capacity is limited to the vision of a two-iron held up against a crosswind from a cuppy lie. Such is far from the case, but at Mont Agel they do not take in much of the view because there are no holes which can be played on auto-pilot. The gradients of the Alpine fairways mean that every shot has to be carefully planned and shaped, and so for once the pros really do have to concentrate fully for all eighteen holes. This is another call on their adaptability and the reason, far more than the nature of the terrain, why they find it a tiring course. Ian Woosnam, who makes a habit of producing an absolutely astonishing performance about once a month, certainly did not suffer from lethargy when he equalled the PGA European Tour record score of sixty here in the Torras Monte Carlo Open of 1990.

Although denied, as yet, the stimulus of a great golfing hero in the mould of a Ballesteros, a Langer or a Lyle, the French have taken to golf in unprecedented numbers, and during the 1980s the rate of development of new courses accelerated to the point where golf in France was growing faster than anywhere else in Europe. The impact of this growth was evident in the inauguration of the Cannes Open on the new Cannes Mougins course, a trend sure to develop as more new courses attract tournaments of the European Tour and of the thriving domestic circuit of the French PGA.

The eighteenth hole and clubhouse at Cannes golf club

José Maria Olazabal plays his second shot to the fourteenth hole at St Nom la Bretèche

There are obvious parallels between the PGA European Tour and the European Common Market, and an equally obvious conclusion that the Euro-golfers have done considerably better than the Euro-politicians in terms of co-operation, economic growth and success in the international market.

The prospects in the longer term suggest that the rapid expansion of golf in France, Germany, Spain and Scandinavia must bring in its wake fundamental changes in the balance of the PGA European Tour. For how much longer, for instance, will there be a preponderance of players from the British Isles making up the tournament fields? For how much longer will Britain host the lion's share of tournaments? Every factor – growth, climate, new sponsorship and suitable courses – suggests that the European Tour will become more and more oriented towards the Continent, and the Mediterranean area in particular. In short, it will become more European. In the light of professional golf's success in forging secure links between the nations of Europe, that is a prospect which can be faced with considerable equanimity.

Cannes Mougins Country Club

Former British amateur international and 1991 Ryder Cup team member Paul Broadhurst won the 1989 Credit Lyonnais Cannes Open without hitting a shot on the final day – when play had to be abandoned after storms flooded the course in the hills above the resort – following stars such as Severiano Ballesteros on to the victor's rostrum. Mark McNulty won for the second time in 1990 and David Feherty in 1991 on his way to clinching a Ryder Cup place.

The course, with its handsome stone clubhouse and pro-shop and lovely setting, is only a short drive down the *autoroute* from the airport of Nice Côte d'Azur, and is a popular stop on the PGA European Tour.

Out of bounds left and a stream and lake to the right menace the drive down the long par-four first, and the stream meanders on through the trees beside the green. The 190-metre uphill par-three second demands an accurate long iron shot to a tiered green bunkered left and right, with big trouble beyond and to the right. Two tough starting holes and one of the most severe starts of any course played on the Tour.

Out of bounds gardens left at the gently dog-legged third must be skirted, along with a big bunker right, while at the parallel fourth you face an uphill approach to a tricky green. Miss the long green right at the 126-metre fifth and you end up bunkered or way down the bank. This is also true of the par-four sixth, where you drive down from a high tee, trying to cut as much as you dare off the corner of the left-hand dog-leg, then fire uphill over two big bunkers.

The 501-metre seventh comes all the way back below the fifth and sixth, with a long bunker short left and trees to the right ready to thwart attempts to get home in two, while the eighth, a much shorter par-five, makes the return trip, threatening pushed approaches with a watery grave. Almost right-angular is the ninth, which has a huge rock at the corner of the left-hand dog-leg to frighten off the greedy. The tenth, too, is a dog-leg left, with trees left and right of the driving area urging prudent use of a long iron off the tee.

You play up over a ditch to the well-bunkered par-three eleventh, with its mountain backdrop beyond, then tackle another left-hand dog-leg offering the option of boldly hitting *au-dessus* the handsome château in the trees left, to set up a short iron pitch, or taking a safety first route. The par-four thirteenth is a similar shape with a ditch crossing the fairway short of two sentinel trees, then hugging the fairway left.

Four tall poplars and a huge sand-trap guard the right half of the fairway at the par-five fourteenth, and a water-filled ditch at the edge of the trees all the way down the left veers right to cross in front of the green, making a two-shot attempt to hit the target a dangerous affair.

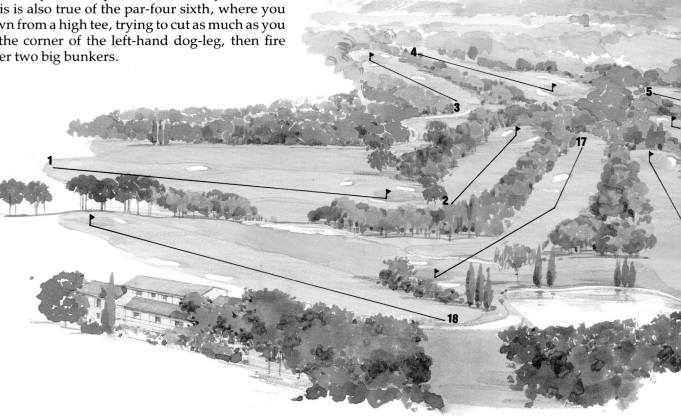

The seventeenth hole

It is water all the way down the right at the 151-metre fifteenth and out of bounds left, but you should be able to hit out beyond the stream along the left at the right-hand dog-legged par-five sixteenth.

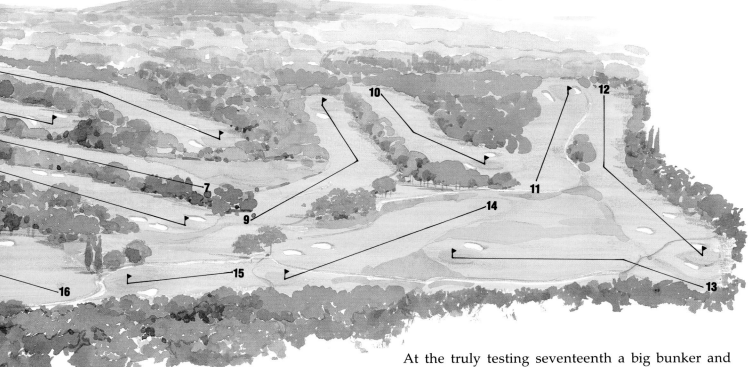

Overleaf: *The tenth hole*

At the truly testing seventeenth a big bunker and trees right must be negotiated before flying a wide water hazard fronting the green. The trouble – a pond and trees – is also on the right at the uphill eighteenth.

Fairway bunkers protect the eighth hole

Golf de Chantilly

Bert Gadd, Henry Cotton, Roberto de Vicenzo (twice), Peter Oosterhuis and Nick Faldo (twice) have carried off the Peugeot French Open title at Chantilly, which lies forty kilometres north of Paris and is a Mecca for tourists, with its magnificent château and legendary horseracing.

The club was founded in 1908, with the celebrated Tom Simpson being commissioned in the 1920s to re-design and improve the championship course, known as the Vineuil, in its serene forest setting.

With its large practice ground and putting green and acres of space for hospitality and exhibition units, Chantilly proved ideal for the staging of a modern open in 1988 and 1989.

A drive over a valley at the par-four first is followed by a long second, which must avoid bunkers on the right all the way to the green. A hooked tee shot to the second, a dog-leg left, lands you in the trees. Hit too straight and you are bunkered. The approach is to a raised green rising sharply from front to back, with trouble beyond.

The short third is ringed by woods and well protected by sand-traps, while you drive down a long avenue of trees at the par-four fourth, then aim for a narrow-necked green. Drive too far left at the narrow fifth hole and your approach is hampered by the trees; there are also trees on both sides and beyond at the par-three sixth hole.

The seventh is a much more open hole, dog-legging slightly right, with bunkers the main worry, but the eighth has trees along its full length to the left and a nest of cross-bunkers two-thirds of the way to the green.

Bunkers right and a copse of pines await the pushed tee shot at the 526-metre ninth, while at the tough par-four tenth cross-bunkers creeping out from the left must be negotiated from the tee and the drive guided far enough right to afford clear passage to the green around trees and sand.

A hook or a slice could find tree trouble at the gently dog-legged eleventh, and there is an even greater premium on accuracy at the twelfth, where you drive to the left of a big sand-trap to set up the correct approach to a green, with a steep fall-away left down to the fourteenth green. The thirteenth is a lay-up dog-leg left, dense forest to the left from the tee having to be given a wide berth before you fire at ten o'clock across a valley to a perilously well-guarded green.

You send your tee shot plunging downhill to the valley bottom at the 200-metre fourteenth, with its ring of protective bunkers, then clamber up the wooded slopes beyond to drive out towards the fifteenth fairway, hooking at your own risk, with woods on the left, careful not to push your shot into a copse at the brow of the hill before aiming at the big two-tiered green.

At 200 metres and all carry the short sixteenth, well-bunkered right and front, is a tough start down the home straight, while the seventeenth, where Denis Durnian double-bogeyed after leading all the way to lose out to Nick Faldo in 1988, has cross-bunkers and more sand beyond to ensnare the tee shot and trouble aplenty around the green.

The eighteenth, one of Europe's longest finishing holes at nearly 550 metres, rolls away downhill between woods and bunkers before rising sharply to the green.

The eleventh hole

La Boulie

La Boulie, headquarters of the Racing Club de France two kilometres from Versailles, was the venue for the first seven Peugeot French Open Championships between 1906 and 1912, with the lowest winning score being Arnaud Massy's 284 in 1911. When Severiano Ballesteros won there in 1986 he shot 269. Brian Barnes, Nick Faldo, Peter Oosterhuis, Kel Nagle, Dave Thomas, Byron Nelson, Bobby Locke, Walter Hagen, James Braid and J.H. Taylor are other celebrated players who have taken the title over the heavily wooded course.

Provided you avoid the out of bounds to the right, the opening hole, a 375-metre par-four, presents no particular problem. Nor does the par-four second, when once again a big green awaits the second shot. The 156-metre third, however, is more difficult than it appears, with a huge, horseshoe-shaped sand-trap guarding the front and three putts a common occurrence.

Woods biting in on the left and a steep drop to the right discourage all-out attempts to get up in two at the 485-metre fourth, while the fifth is a classy par-four. Avoid driving left at all costs, with a big bunker waiting, and aim to fade your ball on to the plateau on the right.

The par-four sixth is a left-hand dog-leg around the trees, with a delicate second shot in demand to a narrow target, while the short seventh, with trouble left, right and beyond and a long front bunker to clear, demands accurate club selection, especially in the wind.

At the par-five eighth you must not drive too far left or the trees will prevent you from attacking the two-tier green, but that is the side to favour. On the short par-four ninth, however, aim for the right half of the fairway, but don't overshoot in two or you could find water.

There is a long carry to the par-three tenth through the trees, and four bunkers to avoid, but the 467-metre eleventh is the easiest par-five on the course.

Very long hitters might try for the green at the 323-metre twelfth, despite its ring of bunkers. Pitch and putt birdie attempts are preferable. At the short thirteenth you must fly the five front bunkers, while at the par-four fourteenth leapfrogging three fairway bunkers and another short left is the priority.

Out of bounds at two o'clock and five sand-traps ranged around the front of the green demand precision at the 175-metre fifteenth, and accuracy with drive and second shot along the narrow par-four sixteenth hole is vital.

Your drive must be perfect to stay on the fairway at the par-five seventeenth, and if you stray to the left with your approach you could finish unplayable.

The home hole, a 426-metre par-five, offers the chance of a last gasp birdie – even of an eagle. But beware the out of bounds right and beyond the putting surface.

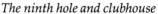

The ninth hole and clubhouse

The par-three downhill tenth hole

The par-three thirteenth hole

The sixteenth hole playing downhill towards the Mediterranean

The fourteenth hole, with the town below

Mont Agel

There can be few more spectacular courses in Europe than the Monte Carlo golf club at Mont Agel, perched high in the mountains above the principality of Monaco, a panoramic view which players can enjoy from the tee at the cliff-edge par-three fourteenth.

Getting to the course in the clouds from your Mediterranean base – an alternative is to stay halfway up in the village of La Turbie, rich in Roman relics – is a 'bendy' business, with the road frequently hugging the edge of the precipice, and a niggling problem during recent Torras Monte Carlo Golf Opens has been swirling low cloud, which can slash visibility to a few metres.

When the sun shines – as it does for most of the year – the steeply undulating layout, on which Prince Rainier indulges his love for the game, is a thrilling test of golfing skill, stamina and patience.

The par-five first tumbles away down the hill, with trees crowding in right and left, then you turn round to play back up the hill to the tree-ringed short second, before once more sending your ball winging down the mountain towards the par-four third.

Next you play a 197-metre par-three from a tee high in the hills to a green with a perilous plunge beyond, then it's a steady climb up the par-four fifth.

The 379-metre sixth requires a blind tee shot to be struck over the hill, keeping right of a marker tree but not straying too far right down towards thick rough and more trees, while you must land in the right half of the fairway at the seventh to get a clear view of the target round a spinney, as you play your short pitch.

At 199 metres, and all uphill carry, the eighth hole, with trees lining the left and a steep fall in the land to the right, is a true test, while the par-four ninth, up from the tee then down to the green with out of bounds beyond and trees and bushes situated left and right, is no walkover.

It is down the hill again, then back up it for the par-four tenth and eleventh, before tackling a pretty par-three from the clubhouse out towards the sea to a target almost surrounded by trees.

The tee shot at the thirteenth is a truly thrilling experience, as you drive out from the hilltop to a fairway narrowed by trees way down below. After drinking in the Monaco panorama you hit to a sloping green guarded by trees and a big drop beyond at the short fourteenth, then bid to pick up a pocketful of birdies on the home straight.

There have been scores in the low sixties galore at Mont Agel – Britain's Robert Lee shot twenty-seven for nine holes *en route* to a sixty-one in 1985 – but the mighty Seve Ballesteros came a cropper when he tried to drive the green at the uphill 267-metre fifteenth in 1988, and you are well advised to try to play it as a left-hand dog-leg.

The par-four sixteenth, long and narrow, is one of the toughest holes on the course, but there is a real birdie chance at the par-five seventeenth, provided you don't get stuck up the bank on the right, and another at the downhill dog-legged eighteenth, where you face a short pitch over a pond.

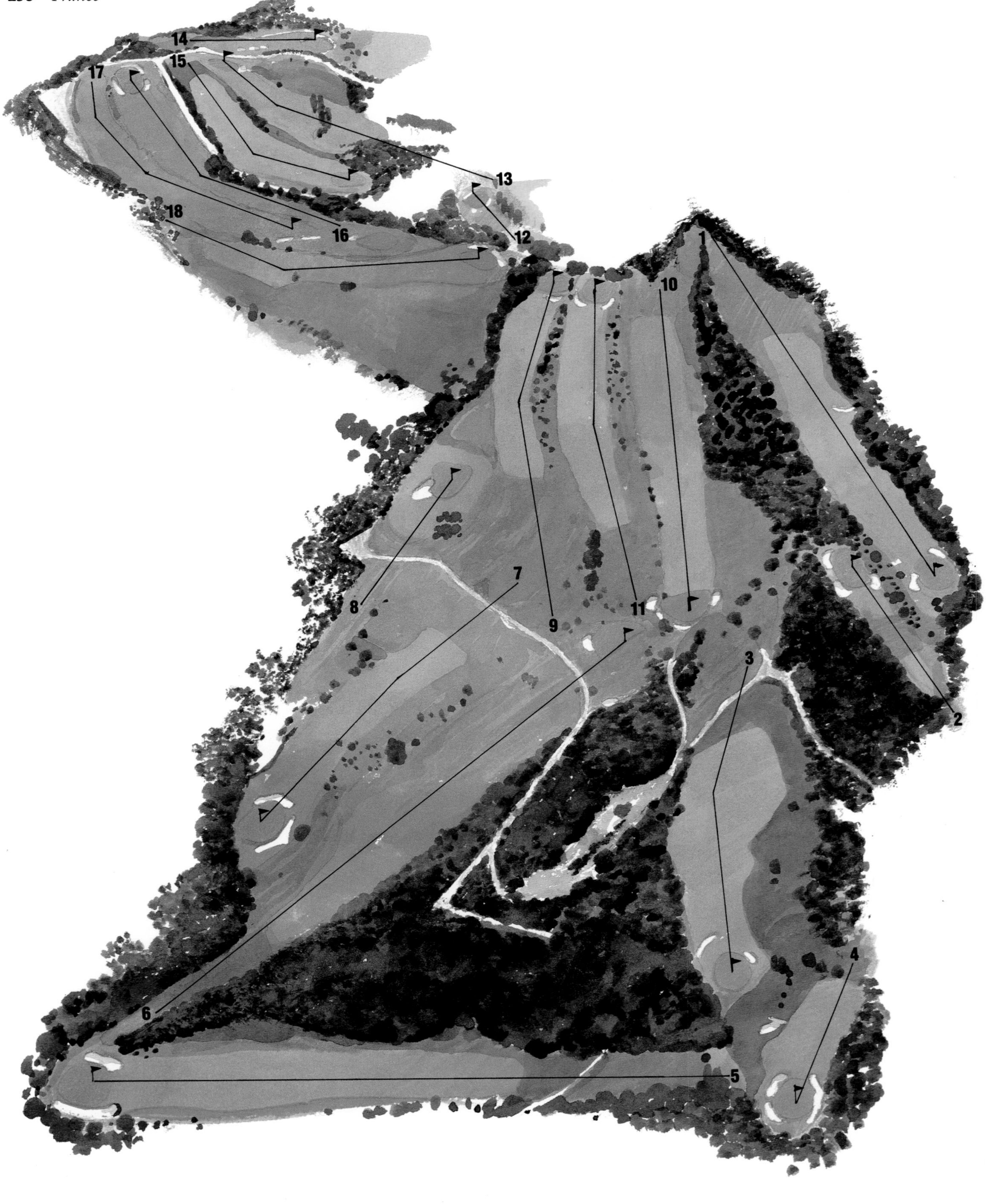
1
2
3
4
5
6
7
8
9
10
11
12
13
14
15
16
17
18

The thirteenth hole

The seventeenth hole, with the clubhouse behind

The eighteenth green and clubhouse

Golf de St Cloud

Henry Cotton, Flory van Donck, Roberto de Vicenzo and the Australians Bruce Devlin and Greg Norman are among the international stars to have carried off the Peugeot French Open title at St Cloud, a short drive from Paris past the great racecourse.

Bernhard Langer won here in 1984 – triumphing over that particular week's putting problem by placing the blade behind the ball and standing square to the hole to check he was lined up properly, before walking round to the putting position without moving anything.

The neat white post-and-rail fencing round the car park and multi-tiered, balconied residential clubhouse are stylish features of one of France's great golf clubs.

A bunker right, towards which the fairway falls, must be avoided at the par-four opening hole, with its tight, tree-ringed target, while at the par-four second there is a ridge across the fairway short of a green with a bunker the length of its left side.

Drive too far right at the par-five third and there are bunkers and rough, and a pushed-out second faces similar problems. A range of sand-traps to the right faces you off the tee at the fourth, with another big bunker facing you if your approach is from the right.

The fifth is a gentle dog-leg left between big trees, with a narrow entrance to the green, while it is downhill all the way to the 145-metre sixth, with a large, jagged sand-trap confronting you below the trees to the right.

It is trees all the way once more up the par-four eighth, with a long, narrow green to aim at, and you must take the aerial route into a green protected by a veritable sea of sand at the 160-metre eighth, before heading along the rolling ninth fairway.

You drive all the way downhill at the picturesque par-five tenth, with all the problems facing you clearly visible, then turn sharp left to tackle the short eleventh with its gaping wrap-around sand-trap 'twixt you and the target.

Keep left of centre from the tee at the undulating par-four twelfth, which plays a slight dog-leg left through the trees, then plunge down to the 185-metre thirteenth, with its big bunker left and three more traps to the right between green and trees.

At 290 metres the fourteenth offers a real birdie chance once on the fairway, but if you are looking for a four at the par-five fifteenth you must keep left off the tee, with trees intruding into the fairway short right.

The 285-metre sixteenth presents a great chance of a three if you can keep your ball on the high ground in the left half of the fairway and avoid a cauldron of trouble down to the right.

Bunkers off to the left will trap a stray second shot at the par-five seventeenth, and the big green at the eighteenth, where Howard Clark three-putted to lose out to José Rivero in 1987, calls for a precise approach.

The seventh tee, with the sixth green behind

The twelfth hole

Le Golf National

It took a very brave decision to look at a completely flat plot of land, some thirty-five kilometres outside Paris, and foresee the first 'National' golf-course complex in France. The French Golf Federation, together with their Chief Executive and Principal Course Designer, Hubert Chesneau, took the decision to go ahead and create a 'stadium'-style golf course, capable of holding the largest of major tournaments, together with a shorter course for general play and even a 9-hole starter course for those players just getting the golfing 'bug'. Four hundred giant tipper trucks per day, for two years, enabled not only a rolling golf course to be designed, but each hole to be separated by huge spectator mounds, giving unrivalled views of the Albatross Course.

The first hole is a slight dog-leg to the right and, having negotiated the bunkers on the right-hand side and the water on the left, an accurate second shot is required to the long, narrow green, cut into the large lake on the left-hand side. The second is played back across the same lake and is all carry to the front edge of the very wide green, which gives ample opportunity to change this hole from a smooth six-iron to a 183-metre plus carry, to a pin position on the back left of the green.

The water on the right-hand side of the 485-metre par-five third hole should be avoided, and longer hitters will consider that the green is within reach with two strokes. However, careful note should be taken of the continuance of the water hazard across the fairway, which must be considered when playing this hole into the wind. A slightly drawn approach shot could come to rest near some of the very few trees that are on the course, and the solitary tree and cavernous bunker provide ample protection for the hole cut on the right-hand side of this green.

The 402-metre, par-four fourth hole climbs gently to a plateau green, and the huge bunker on the left-hand side should be avoided on both this hole and the fifth, which returns in the opposite direction and plays approximately 365 metres in length. The green here has many subtle slopes and is guarded by a large bunker on the left-hand side.

The sixth, being the shortest par-four at 347 metres, is the only hole on the course without a hazard – save for the boundary fence which runs its entire length on the right-hand side. A very small mound, just short of the front edge of the green, together with three tiers drop-

Water hazards dominate the eighteenth and fifteenth greens

At the first green and second hole, water also threatens

ping from front to back, deceives the player as to club selection, and many will find themselves in the rough behind the green.

The tee shot on the par-four seventh hole must be played away from the sharp drop on the right-hand side, and the drop down to the green, with its very narrow entrance guarded by bunkers, gives the impression of being less than its 402 metres. A long iron is required at the par-three eighth hole and, again, deception comes into play, as the tee is some six metres higher than the green.

For those players even attempting to putt for an eagle, at the par-five ninth hole there is an element of danger, with a lake on the left-hand side, to be avoided on the drive before turning slightly right towards the long, narrow green. The lay-up second shot must avoid the bunkers on the left-hand side, and the huge bunker on the right cuts into the three-tier green. Having successfully negotiated the water on the left-hand side, the short iron approach shot to the elevated green could leave you with quite a sloping putt! Then the par-three eleventh hole is played over a lake-filled valley, but at a shade over 174 metres it should not present too many problems for the accomplished player.

At 400-plus metres, dog-leg to the right, with bunkers waiting to catch the tee shot and steep slopes on either side of its elevated green, plus playing into the prevailing wind, it was no surprise that the twelfth hole was statistically the most difficult in the 1991 Peugeot French Open. On paper the thirteenth, at a little over 365 metres, with a slight dog-leg to the right, does not pose too many problems. But consider the lake on the

right-hand side of the fairway, and the huge expanse of water guarding the front and right-hand side of the green, together with an additional water hazard on the back left, and you realize that this hole must be treated with the utmost respect.

Unless downwind, the 512-metre par-five fourteenth hole must be played to what appears to be a very narrow fairway, but it is generous in comparison to the area in which the second shot should be played – two large bunkers and a hollow of rough could make the approach shot to this front-to-back, downward-sloping green extremely difficult. A huge bunker also guards the front and left-hand sides of this green.

You would not be blamed for feeling you were in Florida for three of the last four holes, as huge lakes and island greens abound. Despite being shortened to 357 metres, one 3-ball grouping in the 1991 French Open lost seven balls to the water that guards the tee shot and all but the back left of the fifteenth green.

Accuracy rather than length is, once again, required at the sixteenth, where water must be carried to reach the green and avoided on the right-hand side.

The seventeenth and eighteenth holes run in opposite directions and, with the former rising gradually to the green, and the latter descending gracefully, a score of nine on this par-four/par-five finishing stretch is quite acceptable. Two greenside bunkers are the only hazards on the left-hand side of the seventeenth, in contrast to the eighteenth, where water extends down the entire length of the left fairway and must eventually be traversed to reach the large green. However, bear in mind that there is more water waiting behind the green.

The dog-leg fifth hole

Golf de St Nom la Bretèche

Frank Nobilo's final-round sixty-five in 1991 was enough to edge him a single shot clear in the Lancôme Trophy at St Nom la Bretèche, ahead of David Gilford, James Spence, Open Champion Ian Baker-Finch and Peter Fowler. He succeeded José Maria Olazabal, who had won the title in 1990 in dramatic fashion from Colin Montgomerie, on this parkland course created by Britain's Fred Hawtree in 1959 a short drive from Versailles.

A new composite of the Red course, used for tournaments until 1989, and Blue course was used for the 1989 Lancôme Trophy: holes one to five, seven and fifteen from the Blue and then holes seventeen and eighteen of the Red comprising the outward half, with the Red's regular front nine being used as the back nine. Par for the 6,177-metre (out 3,058, in 3,119) layout was seventy (thirty-five, thirty-five), and Argentinian Eduardo Romero's winning aggregate of 266 was fourteen under. Swede Mats Lanner carded a record sixty-two in round three.

St Nom, with its beautiful old clubhouse and outbuildings, ornamental gardens and ponds and lovely on-course homes, rarely produces a freak champion. It is a stern test.

On the Red course, bunkers situated left must be avoided off the tee at the uphill opening par-four hole, then it's downhill all the way to the second. A pond beyond the second green lies to the right of the par-three third, which measures 173 metres from the championship tees, while the fourth hole is a dog-leg left between the trees.

The fifth, played as an 'easy' par-five until 1988 when it became a par-four 'with muscle' at 427 metres, is a testing left-hand dog-leg, with a long second to an elevated green.

You turn left and play up a steep hill through the trees to the par-four sixth, then right to tackle the first par-five of the round, an even more steeply uphill hole, measuring 465 metres, not normally reachable in two.

Trees left and right spell trouble at the 386-metre eighth, where the last place to be is over the back in the bushes. A spectacular tee shot from the top of the hill down to the green at the 191-metre ninth must not drift right into a pond, or be overhit and bounce on into the lake in front of the clubhouse.

The tenth takes you back up the hill, with trees at the corner of the right-hand dog-leg to be flown or given a wide berth, while the eleventh is a straight-along par-four. A par-five of 498 metres follows, then a 187-metre par-three, where Ronan Rafferty hit a four-iron to three metres in his sixty-three in 1988.

The fourteenth, a downhill 'drive and flick', and the fifteenth are very birdieable holes, but the short sixteenth demands great care and attention. Players with a good score going confidently expect to pick up another birdie at the par-five seventeenth, but it is no soft touch at 465 metres, all uphill, and most fours are single-putt affairs.

Birdie-birdie finishing flourishes – like Rafferty's in 1988 – are common, for the downhill eighteenth measures only 332 metres. But beware the pond left of the putting surface!

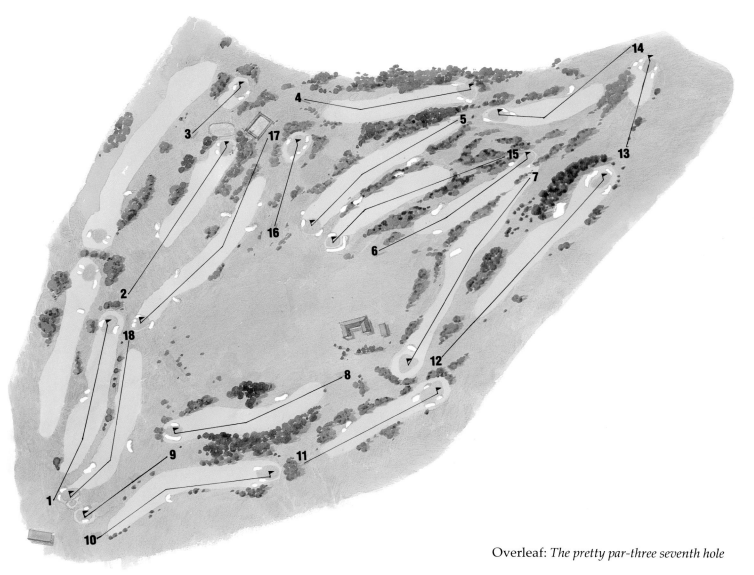

The par-three third hole

The fifth hole

Le Golf de la Grande Motte

The basically flat seaside course of La Grande Motte, near Montpellier in Southern France, became a PGA European Tour stop in 1989, when Ryder Cup international Mark James of Britain won the AGF Open there. In 1990 Brett Ogle took the title with a four-round total of 278. The annual PGA European Tour qualifying school is now hosted jointly by La Grande Motte and Massane.

La Grande Motte is an impressive modern resort complex, with a magnificent marina and de-luxe hotels, apartments and restaurants, within easy reach of the big cities of Marseilles and Nimes. America's Robert Trent Jones designed the course, with its proliferation of lakes, and it is frequently made more testing by the stiff sea breezes.

The course opens up with a relatively easy par-four of 372 metres, but beware two big bunkers left awaiting the offline drive, and water running all the way along the hole on the same side. A 40-metre-long green, with a big bunker and water beyond to the right, presents the chief problem at the 376-metre second, while cross-bunkers 240 metres out challenge the tee shot at the par-five (472-metre) third, and a lay-up second in front of a road and two huge traps could prove prudent with a lake beyond the green.

The 322-metre fourth, flanked by a lake left, is no place for hookers and you must hit over the edge of the water to a three-tier target. At the 123-metre fifth you fly your tee shot over a lake to the green, which can be tricky to read, and you will need to play two solid shots to reach the green at the 425-metre sixth – longest par-four on the course.

With water left and right off the tee as well as in front of the green, the 510-metre seventh is no place for the faint-hearted or reckless. Water in front and to the left, bunkers left and right, and an often tricky wind make the eighth more testing than its 159 metres suggest, while the 393-metre ninth, a dog-leg left, demands a long and accurate tee shot beyond four bunkers on the corner left, with a lake awaiting a sliced drive.

There are birdie chances if you are long and accurate at the 455-metre par-five tenth, but the water is back in play with a vengeance at the 383-metre eleventh, lying short, right, left and beyond the green. To open up a green guarded by water short left and right you must steer your tee shot beyond another lake towards the left side of the fairway at the twelfth, while the green at the 166-metre thirteenth is almost ringed by bunkers.

The 365-metre fourteenth is a dog-leg left, whose green is set between three big bunkers and a lake, while at the 375-metre fifteenth, a gentler left-hand dog-leg, the tight line for the pros is over a nest of sand-traps left.

Don't be short or left at the 138-metre sixteenth or you will surely finish in a watery grave. Water – off the fairway down the right – should not be a factor at the 452-metre seventeenth, but bunkers short left and right, several hidden, wait to swallow up underhit approaches. The 365-metre home hole demands that the tee shot bisect bunkers left and right, but the big test comes in judging the approach to a multi-tiered target.

The eighth hole

The double green, with the fourteenth flagstick on the right and the third hole to the left

The sixteenth hole

HOLLAND

In order to understand and appreciate the distinctive flavour of golf in Holland it is necessary to delve into the history of European club and ball games, if only briefly, during the first part of the millennium. Cross-country games involving the striking of a ball with a club are as old as civilization, and different versions, probably evolved from the sport of the Roman forces of occupation, were played throughout Europe. None precisely resembled golf as we know it, although of course we have no real knowledge of what the Scottish game of golf was like in the earliest days. The distinctive aspect of golf is the combination it requires of physical effort in despatching the ball great distances and delicacy in holing out. By that token there was one game played in the Low Countries which bore a marked similarity to our presumptions about early golf. It was called *colf*, not to be confused, as so many historians have done, with *kolf*, which was quite different and played in a courtyard. The first written reference to *colf* occurs in the year 1360, a hundred years before any written reference in Scotland to golf, or *gowf*. By itself, the written evidence proves nothing except that the Dutch had a much older tradition of literacy than the Scots, but it does provide the first link in a chain of circumstantial evidence about the origins of the sport.

In 1297 a nobleman was murdered at Loenen aan de Vecht and the conspirators responsible for the dastardly crime took refuge in the castle of Kronenburg. The castle was besieged and the conspirators broken on the wheel. In order to celebrate the triumph of justice, a *colf* competition was arranged, with groups of four playing stroke-play, starting outside the court of justice and covering four holes, a total length of 4,500 metres. Each hole ended with a defined target, one of them being the kitchen door of Kronenburg castle, from which the conspirators had emerged. The competition, which was fully recorded in 1360, continued to be played on Boxing Day every year in an unbroken sequence until 1831, when the castle was demolished.

After that first written reference, there followed a wealth of recorded material about *colf*. Citizens were heavily fined for playing it within the city limits and, since they could not produce such large sums on the spot, their clothes were forfeit, to be redeemed when they had paid off the fines. We can imagine the jibes of the crowd as the miscreants left the court in their skivvies. City councils designated open spaces in perpetuity outside the city walls for the specific purpose of *colf*. More pertinently, since there were no castle doors or other suitable targets on these open spaces, the *colf* players used posts as targets at the end of each hole. These posts were elaborately carved and painted and, as such, liable to be stolen if left *in situ*. Here is another vital link in the chain of circumstantial evidence, because it takes no great leap of the imagination to realize that when no competition was in progress, casual players perforce had to play to the holes left in the ground. And there we have the game of golf as we know it.

If we attach a few more historical links – the close trade and military ties between the two countries (which, incidentally and possibly uniquely among European nations, have never been at war with each other), the flourishing export trade from Holland of golf balls to Scotland and the very terminology of golf – then the balance of probability tips strongly in favour of golf having been a Dutch invention which was taken up by the Scots of the east coast and refined into the national sport. Such a sequence of events would not make golf any less a Scottish game, any more than the bagpipes are less Scottish for having been introduced into Scotland by a Crusader returning from the East.

At all events, Dutch golf is deeply influenced by its history and, but for the unexplained fact that the game died out entirely in Holland around the year 1700 for the best part of 200 years, the Dutch would probably press

The eighteenth hole at Noordwijk

their claims to paternity with more vigour. Actually, the game had a perilous existence in Scotland before the arrival of the durable gutta-percha ball in the nineteenth century gave the game its popular impetus. During the feather ball era there were times when the sport was kept alive by no more than 500 well-to-do sportsmen.

What is beyond dispute is that the Dutch have an immensely long heritage of golf, and among Europeans they are the most zealous defenders of the style and manners of the game. They are more Royal and Ancient than the Royal and Ancient itself, and their clubs reflect this tradition. Woe betide the visitor who attempts to enter the dining-room wearing cut-down jeans and T-shirt. In the early days of the Tour some of the brasher young players caused distress by failing to match their appearance and conduct to the expected standards.

As for the courses, they tend to reflect the old-fashioned virtues, albeit to a very high standard. Most people perceive Holland as unremittingly flat and featureless, but such is by no means the case as far as the courses are concerned. Noordwijk, for instance, is positively hilly, because it is built on the mighty ridge which forms part of Holland's essential defence against the invading sea. As such it is a highly sensitive ecological area where the sandy soil must be keyed with a dense covering of trees. The result is a curious hybrid among golf courses, a cross between a forest course and a links, by the sea but not, in the accepted sense, seaside golf. It therefore offers elements of the best of two worlds – the beauty and protection of dense vegetation with the advantage of seaside turf and incomparable, tight lies.

This club, incidentally, was the scene during the Dutch Open of 1976 of one of the more infamous footnotes in the history of the PGA European Tour. Some months earlier a rule had been introduced, and endorsed by all participating bodies, that competitors in European Tour events must be members of recognized professional golfers' associations. The Dutch Federation interpreted this rule as covering all competitors except those for whom they had the gift of special invitations, and they invited three American players who belonged to no PGA. Furore was followed by impasse. The three American players were invited to withdraw and duly declined. The Dutch Federation was invited to withdraw their invitations and also declined. The European Tour players went on strike and the first-round field consisted of a few local players and the three Americans. The commercial sponsor was deeply unhappy at this turn of events and that first round was cancelled. The Americans were persuaded to withdraw from the championship under the curious compromise that they could still play and be paid from a separate prize fund. So faces were saved and the championship was played over three rounds, in conjunction with an unnamed contest over four rounds contested by a field of three.

The clubhouse overlooking the eighteenth green at Hilversum

Another regular site of the Dutch Open is Hilversum, also heavily wooded and on undulating ground. It was here in the 1980 Open that Severiano Ballesteros produced a stretch of golf in the third round which will long live in the memory of those who were privileged to watch it. This was in his cavalier, crash-bang-wallop period when he gloried in his youthful strength and hit the ball as hard as he could, relying on his remarkable powers of recovery to get him out of trouble, in the manner of the young Arnold Palmer. For nine holes he thrilled the gallery with mighty drives, towering recoveries over the trees, superbly controlled shots faded or drawn around obstacles and immaculate putting. It may not have been the golf of the purists but it was sublime, possibly the greatest justification for his tactical aggression he ever produced, and at the end of the round he had a course record sixty-five which set up his ultimate victory.

Holland, of course, had given Ballesteros the first win of his remarkable career four years previously at Kennemer, a superb heathland course by Harry Colt, carefully restored after the war to its former glory by the

removal of seventy-six concrete gun emplacements and two anti-tank walls built by the occupying German forces. When an American player was reproved by a committee member for walking in the clubhouse in spiked shoes, the player replied that from the look of the floor he was not the first golfer to do so. He was gently informed that the club committee had been unable to regulate the behaviour of those who had disfigured the floor, since the marks had been made by German jackboots. In fact, Kennemer had been saved from even worse depradation during the war by a German officer, himself a golfer. Anyway, Ballesteros opened up with a typically swashbuckling course record sixty-five and held on to win.

Utrecht's De Pan is an inland forest course with the sandy subsoil which gives so many Dutch courses their exceptional playing quality. It was here that another brash youngster first made his mark on European golf in 1982. Paul Way, still a teenager and newly turned professional, put in a final round full of dash and adventure which left the experienced veterans trailing in his wake.

There are so many good courses in Holland that most of them would have been worthy of hosting the Open in the days when the championship was a low-key sporting event attracting only a handful of fans. The golf explosion has limited the possible championship sites to clubs which have amenities for car parking, a tented village and all the appurtenances of a major sporting promotion, and there must be a question mark about the future of The Hague as a championship venue. That would be a pity because it is a course of very distinct character, with switchback fairways and matured trees, and it has hosted many championships, including the first one in 1919. It was here that Aubrey Boomer won the title three years in a row from 1924, only to have his winning sequence broken the following year by his brother, Percy. And it was at The Hague that the Natal Indian, Sewsunker Sewgolum, universally known as Papwa, won the championship in 1959, using his distinctive cack-handed grip. How long will it be, one wonders, before another black South African professional follows Sewgolum and Vincent Tshabalala (French Open, 1976) to win a major European golf title?

Hilversum

You reach the Hilversum golf club along a wooded driveway, and trees play a crucial role on this testing par-seventy-two – such a contrast with Holland's famous North Sea links courses.

The second of Severiano Ballesteros's three Dutch Open victories came at Hilversum, and British golfers have always fared well here, Cecil Denny (twice), John Jacobs, Brian Huggett and Brian Barnes being among its winners, and Gordon Brand Junior and Mark Mouland taking the Dutch title on the 6,103-metre course in 1987 and 1988 – Welshman Mouland with a brilliant closing sixty-five.

You must avoid the trees to the right as the fairway narrows at driving distance at the par-five opening hole to set up the approach to a well-guarded green, and an iron off the tee is recommended at the short par-four second to land the ball on a plateau, from where you need a precise short iron approach to a green tucked in the trees.

With out of bounds and sundry lesser troubles to the right, you must be left off the tee at the par-four third hole to get a clear view of the open target, while the only real problem at the eminently birdieable par-five fourth, as long as you are not suffering big slice or hook problems, is a patch of rough short situated left of the green.

It is all carry to the hole they call 'the pancake', the 114-metre fifth, with big bunkers ranged around the front of the green and trees beyond. The tee shot at the 417-metre sixth must favour the right half of the

The fourth hole

The par-three fifth

fairway, as the hole dog-legs gently to the left into a wooded glade, but dead centre is the target with the tee shot at the 385-metre seventh, rated one of the toughest holes on the course. There is a big bunker twenty-seven metres short of target, with rough right and sand left.

You must carry rough and a pathway from the eighth tee and try to land your ball in the right half of the fairway, avoiding a sizeable bunker, and the same applies at the ninth, where trees jut in from the left.

The 204-metre tenth is the longest par-three on the course, and the tee shot should be kept left away from tall trees and sand, while at the eleventh the fairway is generous, but beware out of bounds to the right and bunkers on both sides of the green.

The twelfth, flanking the third, is a narrowing par-five, dog-legging slightly left, so aim for the right half of the fairway, then take care to dodge the wide bunker fronting the green.

A wickedly sloping green presents problems at the 132-metre thirteenth, while overshooting the green is the danger at the fourteenth back towards the clubhouse.

Bunkers front, left and right, trees everywhere and a tough recovery if you overhit make the 144-metre fifteenth a tester, and you face blind seconds at the sixteenth and seventeenth.

Then you have to tackle the magnificent par-five last hole, which dog-legs right around the trees towards a well-guarded target.

The sixteenth hole

Kennemer Golf and Country Club

When the Dutch Open returned after six years to the Kennemer links in 1989 spectators witnessed the longest sudden-death play-off in PGA European Tour history – a nine hole affair in which Spain's José Maria Olazabal finally saw off Northern Ireland's Ronan Rafferty after Roger Chapman, who also figured in a three-way tie, went out at the first.

Severiano Ballesteros's first PGA European Tour victory came on the course near Zandvoort, half an hour's drive from Amsterdam, which Harry Colt laid out in the 1920s.

For the 1989 Open three nines were used to produce the championship eighteen. The Van Hengel or 'A' course comprised the front nine; holes ten, eleven and twelve were the first three holes on the Pennink or 'B' course; and the last six were holes thirteen to eighteen from the Colt or 'C' course.

The opening hole is a testing 403-metre par-four, gently bending right to left with a big bunker left of the green, while the second is a long par-five of 518 metres, this time with a bunker short right of the putting surface.

You turn back towards the clubhouse to play the par-three third, an all carry hole of 139 metres, and the fourth – reversing direction once more – is a straight-forward medium-length par-four with a greenside bunker to the right. The fifth is a fairly severe right-hand dog-leg, so position off the tee is of paramount importance, and the same applies to the shorter par-four sixth, another right-hand dog-leg with a much narrower driving area between trees to the right and a bunker left.

Yet another dog-leg to the right is the par-five seventh, similar in length at 519 metres to the second but decidedly narrower, while the eighth is a par-three of 203 metres, with two bunkers on the left and woods beyond the green. The ninth, back to the clubhouse, requires an accurate tee shot to an angled fairway with trees left and right.

Bunkers left and right must be bisected from the tee at the par-four tenth, and two more traps guard the entrance to the green, which has trees to the right. The eleventh is another all carry par-three of 151 metres, the twelfth a demanding 479 metres par-five dog-legging to the left, with trees short left of the putting surface.

The par-four thirteenth is in the opposite direction. The fairway is wide and welcoming but the green is protected by two bunkers and there are more trees beyond. Bunkers left and right also guard the green at the par-four fourteenth, and there are two sand-traps to carry from the tee at the par-three fifteenth, and two more to fly with your approach at the 431-metre sixteenth.

The seventeenth is the second nine's third par-three – 154 metres and all carry to a target protected by three front bunkers – and the last a 364-metre par-four, with bunkers on the right to avoid off the tee and three more lying in wait left of the green.

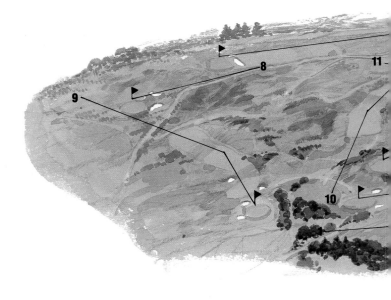

The fifth hole

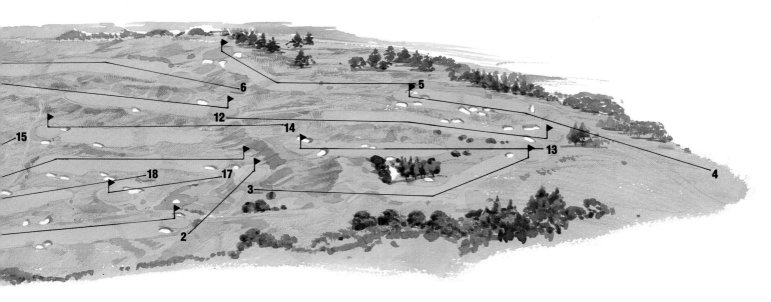

Overleaf: *The first hole*

Noordwijk

In 1991 Payne Stewart took the Dutch Open title by a margin of nine shots, one better than Severiano Ballesteros achieved the last time the tournament was played at Noordwijk in 1986. Two remarkable things had happened when the Dutch Open was played on the North Sea links of Noordwijk then – one good, one bad. The former was the aforementioned victory of Severiano Ballesteros by the same runaway eight strokes' margin by which he won the very first of his professional titles ten years before at nearby Kennemer. His victory made him Europe's first winner of more than £1 million in prize money.

The unhappy happening was the gouging of deep holes in the third and eleventh greens by anti-apartheid demonstrators, which forced PGA European Tour officials to take them out of play for one round. Thus Ballesteros's score of 271 was for seventy holes only.

Noordwijk's opening hole, played from an elevated tee, is a slight dog-leg left of 358 metres, the second an enormous 550-metre par-five, with a water hazard in the rough on the right to catch the wayward tee shot and heavy rough behind the green.

The wind can be a major factor at the 151-metre third, with plenty of trouble to the left, including out of bounds. It can make up to six clubs' difference. Don't be scared off by the tree on the right. There is plenty of room there to receive your tee shot on the par-four fourth, but you must aim left at the par-four fifth, which dog-legs

The thirteenth and fourteenth holes

right through dense woods to a sloping green, with bunkers right and trees all around. The bottle-neck entrance to the green at the 177-metre sixth is only ten metres wide and, as well as tree trouble, there is a big bunker on the right, while the seventh is a 349-metre dog-leg, with a 190-metre carry over the woods if you take the short-cut and a raised sloping green.

It is back out into the open to play the 357-metre eighth, another left-hand dog-leg, and the par-five ninth, where the ideal landing zone for the drive is on the right side. Not a bunker in sight at the 411-metre tenth and only one left of the green at the par-five eleventh, where the line off the tee is over a small tree. Beware trees right of the green.

At the 1986 Dutch Open Amsterdam's Diamond Foundation offered a one-carat blue-white diamond for a hole-in-one at the 140-metre twelfth, where trees and wind are twin menaces.

Aim the tee shot at the right half of the fairway at the par-four thirteenth and par-five fourteenth, where out of bounds left is very definitely in play. Then aim out over the dunes on the right side of the fairway at the right-hand dog-leg fifteenth.

Keep left off the tee at the next, while at the 178-metre seventeenth the shallow green is the big problem. The eighteenth presents a genuine birdie chance at 351 metres, as long as you miss the bunker on the right off the tee.

The ninth hole

The thirteenth hole

The eighth hole, with the clubhouse in the distance

GERMANY

No one who takes an interest in the development of golf can doubt that Germany is destined to become one of the powerhouses of the game, or overestimate Bernhard Langer's influence on his countrymen in popularizing the sport. Severiano Ballesteros used to complain that he was not appreciated in his own country, but from the time Langer began to make a name for himself in professional golf he won the recognition of a national hero. To cap even his outstanding performances in winning championships, including the US Masters in 1985, he and partner Torsten Giedeon won the World Cup for Germany in 1990 at Grand Cypress in Orlando. Germany could hardly have had a better sporting ambassador to personify the national spirit. The Germans see themselves, and would like the world to share this view, as serious-minded, hard-working, shrewd and dependable members of the community of nations, and these are the very adjectives which all who know him would apply to Langer.

His story is a twentieth-century version of John Bunyan's *Pilgrim's Progress*, a lengthy catalogue of pitting himself against the most daunting obstacles and prevailing against them without ever wavering in his faith in his own destiny. Although he did not realize it at the time, Langer was following in the long tradition of champions who began their careers as boys from poor backgrounds who helped to eke out the family finances by caddying for the well-to-do members at the local golf course. At least the likes of Harry Vardon, Ben Hogan, Gene Sarazen and Lee Trevino were raised in communities where golf was an established, if privileged, element of life. In Bavaria during Langer's schooldays only the tiniest minority of the population had even heard of the game. So he had to overcome the opposition of his family, his teachers and his friends before he could even set his foot on the lowest rung of the golfing ladder as a boy caddie. And having overcome that obstacle, he discovered that the real difficulties were only just beginning. The progress of this golfing pilgrim seemed slow and arduous to him at the time, although in retrospect it was positively meteoric. He was sustained by the help and encouragement of loyal supporters in the shape of golf professional Heinz Fehring and Jan Brugelmann, who was to become President of the German Golf Federation. It must be doubtful whether even Langer's iron will could have sustained him through his struggles if fate had not directed him to such wise counsellors. As it was, he came close to breaking point when he fell prey to the most dreaded golfing affliction – the twitch, or yips. By sheer perseverance he overcame that disability, although it was to return to torment him further, and he made himself into such a good putter that in 1985 he won his place alongside the greatest champions in golf by claiming the US Masters title. Small wonder that the German people were inspired to hail his triumphs and encouraged to try this alien game for themselves.

The explosive expansion of golf in Germany will doubtless bring many of the new clubs on to the tournament scene, but it was the old established courses which filled Germany's television screens as the stage for Langer's epic performances. Incomparable among these is the Club zur Vahr near Bremen, created by Bernard von Limburger, one of the greatest and least acknowledged of European golf course architects. The setting gave the course a head start, for it is built in a mighty forest, providing the golfer with the most precious bonus the game can offer: the feeling of isolation and remoteness from the everyday world. The recreative value of golf lies in getting away from it all, and at Bremen you play eighteen holes without catching sight of human habitation or, if you pick your moment, of another human. For peace and tranquillity in beautiful natural surroundings Bremen is supreme, with only the occasional glimpse of a wild boar, if you are lucky, to disturb your idle reveries.

The eighteenth hole at Frankfurt

Tournament professionals, of course, are not much given to lyrical reflections on their surroundings. Their interest lies in the playing quality of the course and the condition of the greens, and at Bremen they face a challenge to match the best of the world's inland courses. Every hole demands the shaping of a shot to find the optimum position, and several offer tactical alternatives to suit the strengths of different players. One hole is a classic of design, a par-five which tempts the big hitter to take a short-cut out with a heroic second shot across water, to be rewarded with a birdie or an eagle or severely punished if he falters.

Von Limburger was also responsible for the delightfully named Stuttgarter Solitude Club, guarantee enough of the playing qualities of the course. It must be admitted that the land with which he had to work recalled the architectural dictum that the most important part of a golf course is below the surface or, as one designer put it, 'The secret is to put in as many drains as you can and then, if there is any money left in your budget, to put in more drains.' This club lies in a rich agricultural area of what farmers call 'strong' land where grass crops turn into lush pastures, which are fine for cows but not ideal for golfers. Having said that, it must be acknowledged that the club presented the course in fine fettle for the 1982 German Open, and again since 1987 for the Mercedes German Masters. As a tournament site it has the great advantage of a closing hole rich in potential for dramatic climaxes, as in the Open when

Bill Longmuir found the green with two mighty shots and holed out for the eagle which tied his score with Langer's. So the crowd, which had been agog to hail the hero, had the exquisite agony of waiting to see whether the anticipated triumph might be dashed in the lottery of the play-off. In the event, Longmuir drove into the woods and Langer cruised to victory with a steady par. Langer repeated the feat in 1991, when he holed a three-metre birdie putt to force a play-off with Rodger Davis and then, as before, a regulation par was enough when Davis missed the fairway.

Frankfurt is a classic park course by Colt and Morison, heavily wooded and possessing a quality which is difficult to analyse or define, but which can perhaps best be summed up by the word 'charm'. It makes you wish all those tournament professionals would go away so that you could take your clubs and go out and play, for you feel that here, at last, is a course where your latent talent will achieve its finest flowering. That beguiling attraction is, of course, an illusion, because Frankfurt deals harshly with romantics, requiring hard, pragmatic appraisal and precise stroke-making to yield a satisfactory mathematical sequence on the score card.

One of the more memorable dramas enacted at Frankfurt was during the German Open of 1979, when Tony Jacklin finally came in from the wilderness of five years without a victory. During that lean spell he had become a martyr to his putter and in his despair had considered giving up tournament golf. Using a putter

Bernhard Langer putting on the ninth hole at Stuttgart during the German Masters

Langer plays his second shot to the eighteenth on the way to winning the 1989 German Masters at Stuttgart

borrowed from Ben Crenshaw, doubtless hoping that the club would retain some residual magic from the hands of that master of the greens, Jacklin found his salvation. He said that this victory gave him more satisfaction than winning the Open championship a decade earlier.

Hamburg, yet another von Limburger course, has regularly hosted the German Open, for the very good reason that this rather short woodland course is a demanding test which can be guaranteed to bring the best golfers to the fore. And so it proved in 1981, with the most exciting German Open in recent memory. The championship carried a strong emotional charge because Langer's star was clearly in the ascendant. He had just finished as runner-up in the Open championship, and all of Germany felt that after seventy years surely he must be the saviour who would become the first German golfer to win the national title. The papers were full of Langer and his responsibility to uphold the honour of German golf by ending the long reign of foreign domination. He could not move without being mobbed by well-wishers. Seldom can a golfer have carried a heavier burden of expectancy into a tournament, and many a strong man would have succumbed to such intolerable pressure. It was a critical moment in

Langer's career and he knew it. All golfers want to win. They try their hardest to win and, having given of their best, should feel no disgrace if they do not do so, which is the case most weeks of the year for everyone. Not for Langer on this occasion. This week he had to win.

The effect of this daunting challenge was that Langer had to play a different golf course from the others. National fervour narrowed the fairways for him and shrank the holes to egg-cups. He then faced the further threat of a rampaging Tony Jacklin, back to the form which had beaten the world's best on both sides of the Atlantic. Langer's confidence was not at a crest because he had been pipped into second place five times that season and, as golfers well know, the bridesmaid syndrome can be a most persistent condition, witness Nick Faldo's eight second places in 1988.

In the final round Jacklin had an eagle and three birdies before the turn, putting him right on Langer's heels, and then moved into the lead when Langer dropped a stroke to par at the twelfth. Langer weathered the crisis and reasserted himself like a champion as Jacklin's challenge ran out of steam. Langer was to go on to greater victories, but when the time comes to review his career that week in Hamburg will surely qualify for the Churchillian accolade as his finest hour.

The par-four eighteenth hole

Golf Club Hubbelrath

This delightful course is situated in a lovely area of rolling countryside some thirteen kilometres to the east of Düsseldorf. It is laid out on a wooded hill and was designed by one of Germany's most famous architects, Bernard von Limburger. It was originally opened in 1964 and has since played host to many prestigious events, including the German Open on no less than five occasions (1973, 1977, 1986, 1990 and 1991).

The comfortable clubhouse is built on the hill, with views of many parts of the course. From there, the 379-metre first hole plays down into a valley, which leaves a tricky, if not too demanding, second shot to a relatively generous green. The second is a dog-leg right, but with the fairway sloping right to left, the premium is on hitting the fairway. The 328-metre third hole is a delightful par-four and is followed by a short but equally attractive par-three, with bunkers right and left. The 288-metre fifth hole is a temptation for the longer hitters, but a bunker guards the front entrance to the green.

The dog-leg, par-five sixth hole sweeps up over a large hill and can be reached in two only by the very longest of players. The 191-metre seventh hole is one of the toughest on the course, with a lake to be carried and a narrow avenue of trees to be played through.

The par-five eighth hole (which, like many on the course, is a dog-leg) is played to a plateau green, and anything short will run back into the valley. The relatively short ninth hole is played uphill and back to the clubhouse.

The tee shot at the tenth should be played to the top of a rise in the fairway and may only require an iron. From there it is a short iron to a shelf green. The 202-metre eleventh hole is the second long par-three, but is compensated for by a large green.

A well-positioned drive, using the contours of the fairway, will make the par-five twelfth hole easily reachable in two. A blind tee shot at the 353-metre thirteenth is followed by a relatively short, but difficult, shot to a small green. Another demanding tee shot is required at the 185-metre par-three fourteenth hole, and the delightful par-four fifteenth reaches the highest point at the far end of the course.

A fade is needed from the sixteenth tee to find the right position and avoid the out of bounds on the left, while the monster 523-metre seventeenth hole, which is mostly uphill, requires three very good shots to reach the raised green.

The eighteenth is arguably the toughest par-four on the course, with the tree line being very tight, both right and left, for the tee shot. The green falls sharply from back left to front right, demanding a very accurate second shot to be placed below the hole to make the first putt easier.

The tenth hole

The first hole

Frankfurt

Frankfurt Golf Club, conveniently sited close to the city centre and the international airport, is a heavily wooded course which first staged the German Open in 1938, when Henry Cotton won. Flory van Donck won there and so did Jean Garaialde, Graham Marsh, Tony Jacklin and 1989 British Open pacemaker Wayne Grady of Australia.

When Zimbabwe's Simon Hobday took the title there in 1976, the 'patron' of the *Bierkeller* he frequented throughout the week presented him with a barrel of his best lager, while fellow Zimbabwean Mark McNulty's winning score in 1987 – 259, twenty-five below par – established a Tour record. With two eminently reachable par-fives on the back nine the true par for the pros is sixty-nine.

Trees right and left make the par-four first seem narrower than it is. You must drive left to miss a bunker, then avoid another short left of the green and, though the trees are sparser and there is a long carry from the tee, the pattern is similar at the second.

The third is a long par-four, with trouble to the right off the tee and four bunkers guarding the green, and the fourth a 155-metre par-three with bunkers short right and left to confuse your judgment. A long carry, with trees right and a bunker in the landing area, confronts you at the par-five fifth, and another bunker lies in mid-fairway short of a green with woods beyond.

The sixth is a short dog-leg left with a bunker to drive over and another set in the front left of the green, the seventh a long par-three with two sand-traps to catch the faded tee shot and more woods over the back.

You must steer right from the tee at the par-four eighth – not as far right as the two bunkers in the corner of the left-hand dog-leg – then hit uphill to a green with two protective front bunkers, while the ninth demands a drive between a sand-trap left and the trees right, and an approach over a ridge and a bunker.

The drive at the short par-four tenth is from a raised tee, with a big bunker right to be avoided before facing a short pitch to the green. The eleventh is an uphill par-three of 160 metres and the twelfth a downhill par-four, half of whose length is carry, with a strategically sited bunker within driving range.

At the par-four thirteenth the bunkers to miss from the tee lie one behind the other to the left, while veer too far right to miss the fairway trap at the par-four fourteenth and you face rough or even tree trouble, and a difficult shot to a target guarded by two bunkers short centre.

The fifteenth, at 445 metres, offers a birdie chance as long as you are left of centre off the tee. Anything short or left at the par-three sixteenth ends in sand, but there is another glorious birdie chance at the 435-metre seventeenth, as long as you hit straight and true over four central sand-traps down the narrowing hole.

The fairway at the eighteenth is generously wide with an uphill second to a green protected by a long south-east corner sand-trap.

Early morning sun breaking on to the course on the second hole

The eighteenth hole

The eighteenth hole

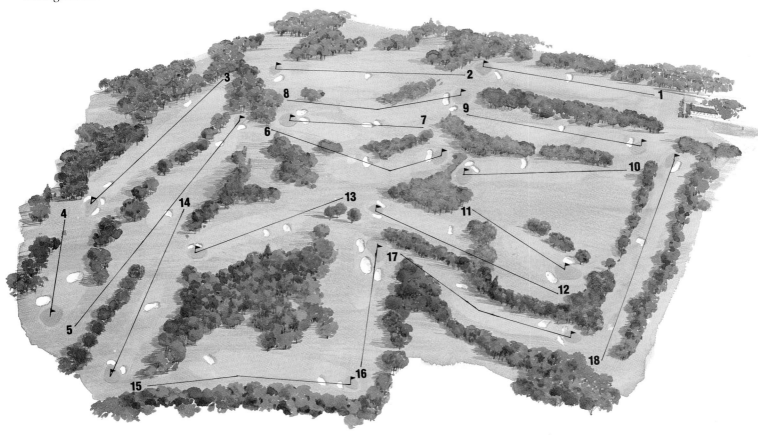

The thirteenth hole

Hamburg

Bernhard Langer brought the house down by becoming the first home winner of the German Open in the event's seventy-year history at the Hamburg golf club at Falkenstein in 1981. A third-round sixty-four containing eight birdies spreadeagled the field, but the Bavarian was made to fight all the way by Tony Jacklin, who fired a final day sixty-seven to end only one stroke adrift on this tightly wooded layout.

The opening hole is a 305-metre par-four, which dog-legs to the left between two bunkers, while the second is a 520-metre par-five with a premium on keeping your tee shot out to the right.

Don't be short left at the par-three third or you will end up in the sand, but off the tee at the par-five fourth the place to land your drive is left of a big bunker at the corner of the right-hand dog-leg.

The par-four fifth is a right-hand dog-leg, too. Hug the trees on the right too tightly and you could be in trouble. Yet another right-hand dog-leg follows at the 390-metre sixth, with a bunker left set to trap the loose tee shot. You then drive over a longish carry at the seventh and must avoid a big bunker set in the fairway, centre left, then two more short of the green slightly to the right.

The 170-metre eighth is all carry, with bunkers left and right and trees beyond, while at the par-four ninth,

back towards the clubhouse, the correct line off the tee is to the left of a big fairway trap, with sand and trees again a major factor as you shoot for the target.

At 180 metres the tenth is another all carry par-three with bunkers left and right, then it's left along the road at the par-four eleventh and twelfth, the latter having an expanse of rough stretching across the fairway two-thirds of the way home and an enormous greenside bunker on the left.

The 355-metre thirteenth could well prove unlucky if you stray left off the tee into the woods, or too far right into a strategically placed bunker at the corner of the left-hand dog-leg.

There is a goodly carry through the trees as you turn round to play back up the par-four fourteenth, with a bunker guarding the left half of the fairway, and again you must fly your tee shot all the way home at the short fifteenth, taking care to dodge two traps on the left.

The sixteenth is a dog-leg left with most of the trouble on the left as you play to the green, and the par-five seventeenth is a similar shape, presenting similar problems only more so, with a big bunker left, close to which you must drive, and a lengthy expanse of no-man's-land then between you and the green.

No traps face you off the tee at the eighteenth but there are bunkers front, left and right of the green.

The tenth hole

The second hole

Stuttgart

The quality of the Stuttgart golf club, quaintly named 'Solitude', was underlined when it produced champions of true class in Sandy Lyle, José Maria Olazabal, Bernhard Langer and Sam Torrance in the first five German Masters. It is a wooded course offering plenty of birdie opportunities, and one of its features is its undulating greens, which are extremely quick.

The opening hole, a 420-metre par-four, is a long uphill toil with a large tricky green, while the second, a 510-metre par-five, plunges away downhill from the tee, with bunkers and trees on the left, where you must try to drive to open the way for a birdie attempt, with the green heavily bunkered to the right.

A bunker at four o'clock forces you left at the par-three third, but don't overdo it and end in the bushes. Trees left and right are the worry at the 320-metre fourth, a gentle dog-leg left. The even shorter par-four fifth hole bends the other way but the problems are similar.

Big sand-traps just off the fairway right in the narrow landing area lie in wait for the errant tee shot at the sixth, where the direct route to the green is over another big bunker left of the snaking fairway short of the target. The seventh, with three bunkers to the right facing the drive, is a gruelling uphill haul to an elevated green.

Ireland's Des Smyth, joint runner-up to Olazabal in the 1988 Masters event, holed-in-one with a seven-iron

The twelfth hole

at the 125-metre eighth, where you hit down along the ridge to a well-bunkered target in the trees, while compatriot Eamonn Darcy holed out with a pitching wedge from ninety-five yards for a spectacular eagle two at the downhill par-four ninth in an opening sixty-six. Seve Ballesteros, however, tangled with a deep bunker at the eighth during the 1989 tournament and took seven strokes.

The 190-metre tenth is an exhilarating downhill par-three, with trouble below and beyond the green and a bunker right, while a bunker left and trees right await an offline tee shot at the uphill eleventh, with its 'wicked' green.

It is back downhill for the twelfth with the approach played over a pond, then uphill again at the par-four thirteenth before tackling another 510-metre par-five, which offers a birdie opportunity if you avoid sand and tree trouble off the tee. A big bunker to the right and a pond over the back must be missed at the par-three fifteenth, and you must be left of centre off the tee at the sixteenth to have a clear sight of the target.

Two bunkers short right will claim the pushed approach at the long par-four seventeenth, and the drive must be straight to avoid trees left and right. At the 505-metre eighteenth the out of bounds to the right on the practice ground can suck in your second shot.

ELASTIC EUROPE

Sports administrators are not normally required to wrestle with metaphysical concepts, but at the European Tour headquarters the growing popularity of tournament golf presented the staff with a challenge to the time-space continuum. In short, they had to reverse the continental drift which occurred many millennia ago and restore to the European land mass selected parts of Asia and Africa – no mean feat. How, one wondered, would they set about rearranging geography to incorporate Morocco, Tunisia and the United Arab Emirates into Europe and, from 1992, Thailand?

'Very easily,' said a spokesman for the European Tour. 'By involving Morocco, to take one example, we do not imply an act of annexation or any redrawing of the map. Morocco becomes a part of the European Tour simply because it becomes a destination of the European Tour Membership, and we recognize that it remains firmly located on the African continent.'

The story of the United Arab Emirates and the European golf connection is rather less than plausible, for all that it is true. The Minister of Defence, Sheikh Mohammed bin Rashid al Maktoum, is known throughout the Western world as a leading owner and breeder of thoroughbred racehorses. In the Middle East he is esteemed as an equally dominant figure in camel racing. He also owns a desalinization plant on the Arabian Gulf which some years ago had a serious problem of over-production. He sought the counsel of his advisers and one of them came up with the idea of creating a golf course. The following dialogue may not be entirely verbatim but it conveys the gist of what was said, as well as providing an insight into the mind of potentates who can take a bold decision without having to consult their accountants.

'What is a golf?' enquired the Sheikh.

Anxious to dispel any notion that a golf might be a racing animal capable of absorbing a surplus million gallons of water a day, the adviser replied, 'You may recall the background view from the winners' enclosure at Newcastle, in the open space beyond the rails, your Excellency. Curious figures may be seen in the distance armed with iron implements and engaged in what might appear to be the killing of snakes, or possibly digging for truffles. In fact, they were playing the game of golf, an extremely popular sport and a powerful tourist attraction.'

The mention of sport engaged the Sheikh's immediate attention. The government of Dubai has a policy of encouraging sport and has provided splendid amenities for many sports in pursuit of its aim of becoming the sporting capital of the Middle East. Since water costs £8 a gallon in Dubai, some twelve times the cost of petrol, the only golf course, Dubai country club, has sand greens and barren fairways – £8,000,000 a day for irrigation being somewhat beyond the pockets of its members, even in such a thriving community.

'Build a golf course,' commanded Sheikh Maktoum without further ado, 'and while you are at it, build me another palace in a secluded corner of this course so that I may entertain my friends there.'

And so it was done. The American golf course architect Karl Litten was engaged, and the first problem he encountered was an exceptionally high water table, and brackish salt water a few inches below the surface. He excavated ornamental lakes and used the spoil to raise the playing areas with undulating fairways. The lakes were stocked with 4,000 Japanese koi carp which quickly multiplied fivefold. Litten planted thousands of mature palm and casuarina trees and many flowering shrubs. The clubhouse, a fantasia of marble based on the theme of a Bedouin encampment, duly arose, as did a splendid royal palace. As the sprinklers dispensed the bounty of the desalinization plant's surplus, the course was transformed into an oasis of vivid green, doubly so to eyes grown accustomed to the drab desert hues on the drive from the city.

The fourteenth green at the Emirates

The starter and caddie-master in front of the magnificent clubhouse at the Emirates

More than a hundred species of migrating birds quickly adjusted their flight schedules to take in a stop-over at the new Emirates golf club, to be followed early in 1989 by a rather larger number of migrating tournament professionals. Doubtless, in due course, an even larger migration of golfing pilgrims to the only grass golf course between Caesarea and India will ensue. As a tournament test it is tough, measuring 6,490 metres, and a rare beauty.

Morocco has long flirted with professional golf in the shape of the annual pro-am for the Trophée Hassan, a highly prized bejewelled dagger. The event is as much a social occasion as a sporting competition, involving splendid banquets fit for a King – necessarily so, since golf in Morocco is under the aegis of the golfing King Hassan II. In the early 1970s there was an unfortunate incident when the golfers came under fire and were held in great discomfort for several hours during an attempted *coup d'état*, but this was soon forgotten and golfers awaited their invitations with keen anticipation. This was due partly to the lure of a week of luxurious living, but more to the challenge of the red course at the royal club of Dar es Salaam at Rabat, one of Robert Trent Jones's more distinguished creations.

The course is built on flowing land with sandy soil of impeccable golfing pedigree thickly grown with cork oaks and conifers, olive and citrus trees. To these promising raw materials Trent Jones added ornate lakes with flamingos and decorative water fowl, as well as his distinctive Welsh wizardry, which is designed to frustrate the golfer who plays on auto-pilot. He presents the golfer with a generously wide fairway, but the unthinking player who bangs one down the middle is liable to find his shot to the green balked by a mound, or a subtle curve of the fairway or an obtruding stand of trees, presenting him with a difficult bending shot if he is to find the target. The man is an illusionist who provides a target area for the drive no bigger than a tennis court in some cases. It is fairly presented for those who pause to recognize it and, of course, it moves according to the siting of the flagstick. So Trent Jones courses have to be played backwards in the mind before a club is selected, which is why they are so popular with the good players and reduce unthinking golfers to despair.

As Tunisia became an increasingly popular destination for goose-pimpled refugees from the rigours of the north European summer, it became evident that some concessions must be made to the peculiar tastes of holidaymakers. To the classical recipe of sun, sand and sea must be added such spices as Watneys Red Barrel to accompany the couscous, high-rise hotels with HP Sauce on every dining-room table, emporia selling gim-crack souvenirs and remedies for turbulent stomachs, and two-day-old *Daily Mirrors*. The days when Sir Winston Churchill needed only an easel and a box of paints to complement the indigenous delights of Tunisia had long since passed and the sophisticated modern vacationer needed an environment in which he could imagine that he had not left home. For this illusion to be fully realized it was necessary, of course, to provide golf. So arose El Kantoui (and a number of other potential venues) and, in order to spread the word that Tunisia could sustain civilized life as we know it, the Tunisian Open, a worthy championship venue and one surely destined to return to the Tour calendar.

Golf del Sur and Amarilla might have been included in the chapter on Spanish golf, but since Tenerife is way out in the Atlantic Ocean under the lee of Africa's left shoulder, it is not associated geographically in the minds of most people with the Iberian peninsula. This new addition to the European Tour represents a considerable culture shock to golfers conditioned by the courses of the temperate zones, where in the natural order of things fairways are bounded by swathes of semi-rough with thick rough beyond, or possibly trees. It represents a further dimension to the variety of courses which European Tour members have to tackle and a novel challenge to the newcomer.

When developers acquire difficult sites the stock reaction is to send for Pepe Gancedo, an architect with a reputation for making silk purses out of sows' ears. Tenerife, which was created by a recent volcano, was a real wart-hog of a site, a moonscape of lava rocks. The conventional way of tackling this problem would have been to pulverize the rocks, give the ground a good covering of topsoil and then irrigate it liberally. This procedure was not available to Gancedo because of the acute shortage of water, so he was forced into the compromise of creating green target areas snaking through the lava. Hit a wayward drive at Golf del Sur, or fail to make the carry off the tee, and the ball finishes unplayable in what amounts to a rockery. So what do you do then? The answer has been provided by a considerable exercise of the imagination, namely by designating these waste areas of lava as lateral water hazards. Those of a literal turn of mind may find it curious that anyone could describe some of the most

arid material on earth as water, but golfers are well accustomed to turning logic on its head. After all, they frequently have to deem a moving ball to be stationary, to accept the definition of a stroke as starting with a forward movement when it clearly starts with a backward motion, to accept that a ball sitting there in plain view is 'lost', to talk of an object constructed exclusively of steel as a wood, to find a parched and deeply cracked area surrounded by water hazard posts, and to blithely ignore a referee's decision which is legally designated as final. They delight in being well below par, which in the real world means to be chronically sick.

So at Golf del Sur the recourse for the player who misses a fairway is to retrieve his ball from the parched rocks, drop sideways on to the grass under penalty, enter into the spirit of the deception by drying his hands and play on, sugaring the pill of his disappointment by absorbing the views of the blue ocean and the sunlight making patterns on the mountains.

Having established that Europe is a state of mind and is not bordered by white out-of-bounds posts, the Tour's sphere of operations is now limited only by such mundane considerations as the price of airline tickets. Egypt, with its long tradition of golf and great golfers – Mohammed Moussa and Hassan Hassanein being outstanding examples – must come into the reckoning before long. It is possible, with a little effort, to imagine that one day sanity will return to earth and that the Tour will be able to organize a segment of its schedule with a swing along the north coast of Africa and into Asia Minor, with stops at Caesarea in Israel and in Lebanon, where golf once flourished.

The Soviet Union's tentative flirtation with golf might well, in the spirit of *glasnost*, flourish into a full-blown love affair. Eastern Europe is an area of vast potential, with Greece and Yugoslavia likely to lead the way into the brotherhood of competitive professional golf. Sweden has been the lusty pioneer of Scandinavian tournament involvement, but Denmark, Norway and Finland are increasingly succumbing to the golf epidemic.

Without doubt the major problem for the European Tour in the future will be to find enough tournament weeks during the short north European summer to accommodate the demands of all its constituents. The day is fast approaching when the Tour will be a year-long succession of major tournaments. Europe may be flexible but, alas, there can never by any elasticity in the calendar.

Emirates

The spectacular Emirates golf club, the first championship course in the Arabian Gulf and host to the Desert Classic, is no mirage – it is a lush green oasis in a sea of sand: a veritable miracle in the desert.

American architect Karl Litten has fashioned a jewel of a course, on to which up to 750,000 gallons of desalinated water from the Gulf are pumped daily.

Course and clubhouse – an arrestingly artistic cluster of concrete and marble Bedouin 'tents' – cost $10 million to build and were opened in March 1988 by the late General Zia of Pakistan. A second course is planned.

Emirates, with its perfect climate and superb practice facilities, is an ideal early venue and Britain's Mark James took full advantage of this in 1989 to launch his return to Europe's Ryder Cup side by winning with an eleven below par 277 total, after a play-off against Australian Peter O'Malley. Eamonn Darcy succeeded James as champion in 1990, but the Gulf War caused the event to be postponed in 1991.

The first hole is an uphill dog-leg left of 398 metres, the second a much shorter par-four, where you play to an island fairway over the sand, then pitch over more sand to a green, bunkered to the right. The third is a long, narrow, uphill par-five of 484 metres with bunkers

The fourth hole, with the desert behind

short left of the target, and the fourth a 168-metre par-three from an elevated tee, with a lake along the right.

You hit from the fifth tee to another fairway island in the sand, then head on to an island green ringed by trees, while the sixth, coming back, dog-legs to the right in the landing area, and the 168-metre seventh is all carry over a lake brimming with fish.

There is a long carry from the tee at the par-four eighth, whose green is ringed by bunkers, then it is downhill at the tough 423-metre ninth, with an approach over the edge of the lake, left, to a huge green shared with the eighteenth.

There is another island landing area at the tenth, a 502-metre par-five, followed by an all carry tee shot to the 154-metre eleventh, while a nest of bunkers to the right must be avoided at the left-hand dog-leg twelfth.

The thirteenth is another left-hand dog-leg, this time a par-five of 494 metres, and so is the fourteenth, with the fifteenth another all carry par-three. The sixteenth, at 358 metres, and dog-legged seventeenth, at 321 metres, offer real birdie opportunities, provided the tee shot is correctly placed. So does the 500-metre last, a sharp left-hand dog-leg requiring a lay-up second, then an accurate pitch across the lake to a big target.

The par-three fourth hole

The second hole

The ninth and eighteenth greens, with the sun setting over the magnificent clubhouse

The ninth hole

The second green

Golf del Sur

In 1989 the PGA European Tour got under way at the then unprecedentedly early date of 23 February with the arrival of the first Tenerife Open on the spectacular new layout of Golf del Sur, and in José Maria Olazabal it certainly produced a home winner of true class.

Fittingly, the sun shone from start to finish as the pros tackled the new course, which has bunkers filled with black volcanic ash instead of sand. During the Open some were deemed 'water' hazards by PGA European Tour Tournament Director John Paramor, and the pros were permitted to lift and drop under penalty of one stroke.

The opening hole is a gentle dog-leg to the right with a second shot to a high, semi-blind green embraced by a horseshoe-shaped bunker, the second an island par-three of 188 metres entirely surrounded by 'sand'. There is out of bounds to the left as you drive up the par-four third hole with a *baranca*, or rubble-strewn gulley, to the right, and there is water to the right as you attack the green.

A ditch and a bunker wait to thwart attempts to drive the green at the 260-metre fourth, while at the par-five fifth, a dog-leg left, you must drive short of a cross-fairway gulley and steer clear of the out of bounds to the right.

The green at the 141-metre sixth is described as 'deep and noble with no complications', while that at the 270-metre seventh is 'small but with a strong fall', and a bunker and a *baranca* will inhibit attempts to carry the dog-leg left.

At the 314-metre eighth the dog-leg is in the opposite direction, and once more players have to decide, depending on conditions, whether to try and fly the 'basalt rush' across the neck. Out of bounds hugging the left side of the 530-metre ninth and bunkers all along the right are a double worry, while a blind second shot, bunkers all the way up the left and trouble short and beyond the green leave golfers with plenty to think about at the par-five tenth.

The par-three eleventh is one of the most spectacular holes on the course, with the tee set hard against a drop into a deep ravine and an enormous bunker left of the green, and the twelfth is one of the most difficult, with trouble left and right all the way to a narrow green.

Drive too far right at the 300-metre thirteenth and you must fly a rocky ravine to a high green, and if you cut your tee shot at the par-five fourteenth you could find bunker or *baranca* trouble prior to approaching a tricky two-tier green.

The fairway tends to kick your tee shot off to the right at the fifteenth, which also has a two level greens, and at the sixteenth you must avoid four bunkers from the tee, before firing to the green beyond and to the right of the water. You then fire across the lake to the par-three seventeenth, and hope to finish on a high note at the birdieable 360-metre home hole.

The eighth hole in the tournament

The seventeenth hole

Overleaf: *The twelfth hole*

Royal Dar es Salaam

Morocco's golf-playing monarch, Hassan II, was a prime mover behind the staging of the Moroccan Open at Royal Dar es Salaam in 1987, when Britain's Howard Clark held off the challenge of his close friend and Ryder Cup colleague Mark James to take the title after a superb third-round sixty-six.

The King has his own course in the palace grounds, but he frequently plays on the course he engaged America's Robert Trent Jones to construct close to Rabat. Scooped out of the forest of Zaers, it is a sports complex without parallel in Africa, comprising three golf courses as well as equestrian and tennis facilities.

First hole on the par-seventy-three, 6,800-metre Red Course is a 366-metre par-four, which dog-legs left be-

tween two bunkers some 200 metres from the tee and has even more sand either side of the green.

The second is a long par-three at 212 metres, with bunkers guarding the entrance, and the third a long par-four with a narrow driving area between bunkers and trees 225 metres out, and a sideways-on, heavily bunkered green.

Bunkers left and right again narrow the landing area for the tee shot at the par-four fourth, while the 517-metre fifth is a huge par-five, dog-legging left round the trees, and the sixth a narrow par-four with a tricky approach to a sloping green.

You dog-leg to the right around a big sand-trap at the seventh, then fly a big clover-leaf bunker in front of the

The tenth hole

green, while trees left and right make the 532-metre eighth a monster of a par-five.

The 172-metre ninth is a much talked-about par-three, spectacularly played across a lake to a small island green, and you hit across the water from the tee at the par-five tenth, eminently birdieable at 440 metres if you drive clear of a big left-side bunker.

A long iron to a shallow green, defended by five bunkers, is demanded at the eleventh, a tight dog-leg right, while you drive over a huge lake, then play down its right-hand bank at the 481-metre twelfth.

An iron off the tee is recommended at the 351-metre thirteenth to fall short of three big sand-traps at the corner of this left-hand dog-leg through the trees, and at the par-three fourteenth you must fly three big bunkers before tackling a testing green, which slopes front to back and right to left.

Once again a big bunker bites in from the right in the driving area and a long iron might be wiser at the short par-four fifteenth. There are bunkers left and right in driving range at the left-hand dog-leg sixteenth and more sand to clear as you hit to an elevated green, with dense woods beyond.

With a lake to the left and beyond the green and a bunker right, the long short seventeenth is a testing hole, and the eighteenth is a long, narrow 505-metre par-five, dog-legging left uphill through the trees towards a narrow target.

The twelfth hole

The thirteenth hole

The eighteenth hole

SAFARI CIRCUIT

The Safari Circuit, as the African tournaments were commonly known, is not an integral part of the European Tour, although it has now been assimilated into the ever-growing Challenge Tour. However, it is an important element in the Tour's operations, both from the players' point of view and as an evangelical exercise in stimulating professional golf in Africa. For the players it represents an immensely valuable opportunity to sharpen their games under competitive conditions in preparation for the European season, and to finance their campaigning for the rest of the year in many cases. For the countries involved in the circuit it represents a major addition to their sporting calendars and gives the local professionals a chance to measure their progress against the strongest international opposition. International goodwill through sport is a phrase much used to justify overseas tours, more in pious hope than in the consummation in the case of some sports, but in the case of the Safari Circuit it is well justified. It is a very friendly tour since in several places the visiting players are accommodated in the homes of host club members and firm friendships are established. This leads to an atmosphere of informality, which breaks down the usual barrier between the remote figures walking the fairways and the spectators segregated behind the ropes. And nothing adds to the excitement of a sporting event more than personal friendship with the participants.

In Nigeria the flagship event is the Nigerian Open, played at the Ikoyi Club in Lagos where the players enjoy – and enjoy really is the word – the novelty of putting on oiled-sand 'greens', or browns as they are called locally. Because of the nature of these surfaces, the convention is to have a caddie drag a heavy sack along the line of your putt to smooth the irregularities of pitch marks and footprints. The nature of the browns, concrete saucers filled with the oil-sand mixture, means that the surfaces are level and every putt is consequently straightforward. There is an opportunity, therefore, for exceptional putting rounds, but it does not necessarily follow that the score for the round will be exceptional. The challenge of Ikoyi is to hit those browns, tiny targets by the standards of normal turf greens. Peter Tupling created a world record total for seventy-two holes at Ikoyi with a score of 255 (par 288) in 1981, which represented shot-making of extraordinary accuracy to complement his sure putting. During the championship's pro-am, David Jagger had the rare distinction of breaking sixty, with a score of fifty-nine. In addition to the Open itself, the players make forays up-country to play pro-ams and bring first-class golf to expatriate and Nigerian golfers on the big sporting occasion of their year.

Zambia is probably the most golf-conscious nation of central Africa, thanks to the enthusiasm of President Kenneth Kaunda, undoubtedly the most successful captain of any golf team anywhere in the world at any time during the history of the game. During the professionals' visit the President habitually hosts a match on his private course at State House, Lusaka, a beautiful layout which does double duty as a nature reserve. Herds of antelope normally take priority on the course, although they have come to accept that fairways must occasionally be vacated to permit golfers to play through their grazing grounds. The State House team has never been beaten, owing to a special local rule which the President, as the unchallenged authority in his own domain, has promulgated. It proclaims that the handicaps of his State House team will not be assessed until after the match, when adjustments will be made to guarantee a victory for the home side.

The course at Lusaka for the Zambian Open is a beauty, the lush tropical vegetation being supplemented by termites nests', extraordinary feats of engineering which tower three metres high and which require a special local rule to provide the relief of a free drop. This is a necessary precaution, because it was in Zambia that Jack Newton was assailed by an army of these aggressive insect warriors, of the variety known to South Africans as *bal bijters*. In his frenzy at the stinging assault of the invaders, Newton threw off all his clothes while his wife, Jackie, mounted a spirited counter-attack, flapping at the creatures with his golf towel. Newton's caddie, who knew the damage which the insects could inflict, fled to safety well clear of the battleground.

Time no longer permits an extended stay in Zambia with tournaments up-country in the copper belt, which is a pity because the players are deprived of the opportunity to play some exceptional courses. Copper mining is a water-intensive industry and waste water has been used to remarkable effect on what might be termed the jungle courses of northern Zambia. N'changa in particular, with its local rule permitting a free drop from hippo footprints, is one of the unknown gems of the game – and, in the opinion of the late Bobby Locke, one of the world's greatest courses. With its extravagance of flowering trees and shrubs it is certainly a rare delight.

Muthaiga, home of the Kenya Open, is a no-nonsense course presenting plenty of elbow room, very necessary when the fairways are firm and the ball runs great distances. It is flattish (most welcome in a climate which makes hill-climbing an ordeal) with its fairways bordered by great trees (again welcome, for their shade if not for their obstructive properties). Its honour roll of champions, including Severiano Ballesteros, Eamonn Darcy, José-Maria Canizares and Ian Woosnam, testifies to its calibre as an examination in identifying the great players.

Yamoussoukro, deep in the heartland of the Ivory Coast, is perhaps the most unlikely venue for championship golf in the world. The country's President was born at Yamoussoukro and was determined to honour this tiny jungle settlement by creating a great metropolis. This was to be another Brasilia, a major city built from scratch in the wilderness. The skeleton of the ambitious plan, a grid of noble avenues, was created, complete with bridges over the river in which gigantic crocodiles provided a novel tourist attraction. For a few pence you can purchase a live chicken and an attendant will feed it to the croc of your choice. An army of Italian craftsmen was imported to build a mighty marble presidential palace, and the architect of the Pan Am terminal at Kennedy Airport was commissioned to exercise his fertile imagination in creating a wondrous domed clubhouse for the golf club. Apart from the adjacent hotel, that was just about the extent of Yamoussoukro when the Safari Circuit made its first excursion into the jungle. If you can imagine the Champs-Élysées bordered by the makeshift market stalls of street traders, interrupted by the occasional modern building, you will have some idea of the formative stages of Yamoussoukro. Thanks to the President's enlightened sense of priorities the hotel, the course and the clubhouse, all that are needed for a tournament if you can afford to disregard its function as a spectator sport, were in a splendid state of readiness for the introduction of championship golf to the Ivory Coast in 1981. The inaugural championship was conducted virtually in private, although one of the handful of spectators, it should be recorded, was American President Richard Nixon.

Professional golfers are not political animals. They conduct their lives by a simple litmus test of looking at a tournament's prize fund, the likely strength of the field, the cost of travel and accommodation, the amount of time it will occupy and the alternative possibilities of gainful employment. They then assess the chances of coming out ahead of the game and plan their itineraries accordingly.

Once upon a time their calculations persuaded many of them that they could make a profit during the winter months by playing the circuit in South Africa and returning home via Rhodesia. One day some of those who were headed for Salisbury were somewhat disconcerted by the instruction to fasten their seat belts because the plane was about to land at Harare. Diversions are an occupational hazard for pro golfers, frequently involving missing the practice round or, worse, the chance of picking up some pocket money in the pro-am. The golfers on this occasion were even more disconcerted on entering the immigration hall to be arrested and bundled on to the next flight out of Zimbabwe, on the grounds that their passports contained stamps which proved conclusively that they had consorted with the devil. Word spread on the locker-room grapevine that something odd was happening in Africa and that in future you could either play here, here and here – or there, there and there – but not both. Actually a few enterprising souls continued to play here and there by the expedient of asking the authorities not to stamp their passports because they wanted to keep the pages clear for working out their stroke averages, collecting Arnold Palmer's autograph and suchlike. But only journalists, by definition politically naive and morally bankrupt, were able to cover both tours.

One link remains, however. The Rhodesian Open at Royal Salisbury, once the highlight of the South African circuit, is now the Zimbabwe Open at Royal Harare and the highlight of the Safari Circuit. *Plus ça change*, as they say on the practice ground when hours toiled to eliminate a slice induce an uncontrollable hook. At least the magnificence of the championship course and the warmth of the welcome have survived the transition.

And the improved political situation in South Africa has seen the country return to international competition, finishing runner-up in the 1991 Dunhill Cup.

THE FUTURE

The 1960s were turbulent and traumatic times for the two major professional golfers' associations. With the growth of television, tournament golf was emerging as an important spectator sport, and in America the players chafed under the domination of its organization by the club professionals. The players wanted to run their own show and broke away to form their own division of the PGA. These events were precisely mirrored in Britain some years later. The players automatically turned to John Jacobs to direct the new division of tournament specialists because, with his background as a successful player and his solid grounding in business administration, he was the obvious choice. They chose better than they knew, because Jacobs not only turned out to be an efficient chief executive in the pragmatic area of administration but also possessed the gifts of a visionary. He had, so to speak, both feet firmly on the ground and at the same time his head in the clouds. It must also be said that he was a big enough man to delegate responsibilities to his assistant, Ken Schofield, who had thus served a valuable apprenticeship by the time he succeeded Jacobs as chief executive. Jacobs recognized, greatly to the apprehension of many players conditioned to regard all foreigners with suspicion and mistrust, that the future of tournament golf lay not just in the British Isles but must share the dream of a Europe united in economic co-operation. So was born the European Tournament Players' Division of the PGA.

For a decade or more the main thrust of this fledgling organization was to attract sponsorship, no easy task on a continent where golf was a mystery to all but a tiny minority, and to improve standards of play, pay, practice and amenities. The vast gulf between standards in America and Europe was forbidding and the administrators had only one ace in their hands, the star attraction of Tony Jacklin who abandoned his American career to help popularize golf as a spectator sport. To compensate for his inevitable loss of earnings from the rich American circuit, Jacklin was permitted to seek financial inducements to play on the new European circuit. Thus the concept of appearance money was officially sanctioned, with acrimonious consequences as new stars such as Severiano Ballesteros became international headliners. For once there may be some justification in that mixed metaphor suggesting the bridging of a gulf with a playing card, because such was more or less the situation in what might be termed the cap-in-hand era of the European Tour. As Ballesteros, Bernhard Langer, Sandy Lyle and Nick Faldo made their marks on the international scene, and golf blossomed into a major sporting attraction, so the PGA European Tour found itself in a buyers' market, able to be selective in accepting the most attractive sponsorship offers and with the scope to rationalize the geographical progress of the Tour by following the sun and minimizing travel.

Success brought its own problems, notably a shortage of golf clubs with the space and amenities to cater for a major sporting promotion. The Royal and Ancient Golf Club of St Andrews faced the same problem, and the roster of Open championship clubs had to be trimmed in the face of the intractable dilemma of fitting a quart into a pint pot. The Augusta National Golf Club also had to come to terms with the growing popularity of its Masters tournament, over the years making revisions to the course by providing vantage points for the galleries in the form of spectator mounds. This concept of stadium courses was taken up by the PGA Tour of America with its programme of Players' courses. In partnership with commercial developers, the American Tour created a series of purpose-built tournament courses, the first of which, at Sawgrass, Florida, became the permanent home of the Tour's flagship event, the Players' Championship. Inevitably the PGA European Tour had to start thinking along similar lines. In 1988 an agreement was signed between the PGA European Tour, the Co-operative Wholesale Society and Alfred McAlpine.

At this time the agriculture industry was contracting in the shade of growing mountains of surplus produce and the Co-op, as one of Britain's largest landowners, was seeking alternative uses for spare farmland. The Tour needed land for purpose-built tournament courses. And McAlpine needed land for house-building. These three strands of mutual advantage were drawn together in an ambitious agreement to create golf developments in strategic parts of England and one in Scotland.

Each development would include a major tournament course, specifically designed for the convenient viewing of the game by large crowds of spectators and by the television cameras, a second course for club members and fee-paying visitors, and an extensive housing development. It is an economic fact of life that houses associated with golf courses command a higher price than similar houses elsewhere, and so this premium would make the construction of the courses virtually self-financing. The agreement was that PGA European Tour Properties would administer the golfing elements of these developments, thereby inheriting a valuable source of income and tournament sites able to accommodate the most ambitious of golf promotions. The ten-year development plan also included country club amenities such as swimming, tennis and squash at each site.

This ambitious project, involving an investment of some £250 million, was a considerable act of faith in the future of tournament and social golf. That confidence sprang largely from the Tour's progress over the previous decade: a tenfold increase in the prize money; ten victories in the major championships by PGA European Tour stalwarts; failure by the narrowest possible margin to win the Ryder Cup at the PGA of America headquarters in Florida in 1983, followed by a comprehensive victory in 1985 at The Belfry and a successful defence at Muirfield Village in 1987; and a new world rankings system whose top ten places were dominated by PGA European Tour players. Such a prospectus had impressed the hard-headed investment counsellors of big business.

The first of the PGA European Tour courses, Weston Hall in South Cheshire, close to Crewe, involved an investment of around £50 million, and the former Ryder Cup player David Thomas was contracted to design the championship course. His plan called for a course of some 7,200 yards with water in play on twelve of the holes and sufficient spectator mounding to accommodate 25,000 people. Neil Coles, another former stalwart of the Ryder Cup team and latterly, as Chairman of the PGA European Tour Board of Directors, an influential figure in the development of the Tour, designed the secondary course, also par seventy-two and measuring some 6,900 yards. For the second ETC Coles would design the championship course and Thomas would have responsibility for the secondary course.

None of this meant that the Tour was turning its back on the traditional centres of tournament golf or that new private developments would be excluded from consideration for major golf events. Far from it. And while the concept of ETCs on the Continent was a valid possibility for the future, it was clear that the spate of private building throughout Europe would produce many courses of championship calibre. For example, Tony Jacklin made no secret of tournament ambitions for his development at San Roque, near Gibraltar, and three Jack Nicklaus courses – St Mellion in Cornwall, the second course at Crans-sur-Sierre in Switzerland, and Gut Altentann in Salzburg – were all realistic contenders for major competitive golf. The French National Golf Course near Paris, and the Italian Federation Golf Course at Le Querce, Rome, are prime examples of what can be done.

The PGA European Tour started with high hopes. At that time the problem was to find good players and tournaments, and somewhere to play. With the formation of a Seniors Tour in 1990, added to the ever-expanding Challenge or 'Satellite' Tour, there are in fact now three Tours in Europe. Courses will be needed for a Tour comprising the most international group of players in the world, and by the end of the decade purpose-built spectator courses designed and operated by the PGA European Tour should be a reality.

INDEX